# ¡JUSTICIA!

## The New Mexico Landgrant Movement 1956-1968

*Emancipation Begins with the Liberation of the Spirit*

FEDERICO ANTONIO READE

English-language edition ISBN: 9-798-6349-7586-3
English-language hardback ISBN: 9-798-8373-1613-5
Spanish-language edition ISBN: 9-798-6945-0483-6
Spanish-language hardback ISBN: 9-798-8373-1576-3

Cover key art by Dave Briggs



Although the following narrative is based on actual events, the author has changed the names and taken a degree of creative license to create a coherent story. Some names and details have been changed. Any resemblance to actual persons, living or dead, or events in the story are coincidental.

# PRAISE FOR *¡JUSTICIA!*

"Dr. Reade through personal knowledge, interviews, and a profound understanding of the Aliancista movement and history of the 1960s has provided new insights—and yet another chapter—on the social strife and struggles of northern New Mexico's Hispano-Hablantes. Added to his running narrative are elements of the intimacy and religious faith of La Hermandad, or Penitente Brotherhood, to which most of the Aliancistas belonged."

—Anselmo F. Arellano, author
*Los Pobladores Nuevo Mexicano y Su Poesía 1889 -1950*

"Federico Reade's docu-Novela is an important addition to the saga of the New Mexico landgrant movement. Using fictionalized characters based on the real-life principals of the movement, he retells the saga of a people and events that made headlines in the 1960s around the world, launching the largest manhunt in recent U.S. history. His inclusion of the corridos from the period underscores the significance of a struggle that has continued from ancient times to the present."

Jesús Salvador Treviño, writer, producer, director, *Juan Seguin*

"Federico Reade provides a wide-ranging tale of the valiant struggle of Nuevomexicanos for their civil rights. His account is based on many interviews of the principals involved in the Alianza Federal de Pueblos Libres, which fought to recover communal lands that were stolen from Spanish/Mexican landgrants. He also infuses the saga with his intimate knowledge and participation in the Chicano Movement, and a practicing Hermano.

Reade's book offers a much-needed corrective to the official story of these events. Language is central to culture and identity. As a colonized population, Chicanos have had to deal with the confluence of multiple languages. English has been imposed on us by the dominant Anglo-American culture, while the Spanish of our ancestors has been marginalized. As a result, we have had feelings of insecurity with our handling of these languages. Our Indo-Hispano-accented English is somehow not good enough and we feel the pain of losing our Spanish. In his writing, Federico Reade fearlessly embraces our multiple language heritage and values our code-switching. He opens a language door that leads to our emancipation and empowerment."

Dr. Ricardo Griego, author
*The Spanish Language of New Mexico: A Cultural History*

"Historical accounts, religious exegesis (a critical explanation), and thick descriptions of communal cultural practices form the bedrock upon which native son Federico Reade erects a passionate fictionalized account of a community revolt which erupted in Northern New Mexico in the sixties. Blending past tense narrative description and present tense cinematic sketches, this docu-novel brings to life the struggles of Nuevomexicano Aliancistas to reclaim the communal landgrants that, across more than a century were illegally appropriated by Americano newcomers supported by biased government agencies and corrupt government officials and lawmen

"A central thread that runs throughout the narrative is the history of the Hermandad, Los Penitentes. Elaborate descriptions of their spiritual beliefs and practices and their ensuing historical oppression by the Catholic Church shore up Reade's treatment of land loss, class exploitation and racialized discrimination which spurred the Alianza to action. That to be Hermanos is to be an Aliancista, and to be an Aliancista is to be an Hermano is pivotal to developing the narrative and Reade's resolve to rewrite Nuevomexicano history from the bottom up. The limpieza de los Hermanos return to the cleansing water of physical reward and empowerment to continue their struggle for cultural survival. A must-read for aficionados of New Mexico history and culture.

"Interspersed corridos enrich the narrative and bear testimony to the creative and spiritual juices that nourished the physical and psychological struggles of the Aliancistas involved in this epic moment of Nuevomexicano history. A must read for aficionados of New Mexico history and culture."

Erlinda Gonzales-Berry, Language and Cultural Studies Professor

*In loving memory of my children, Federico Antonio III, Felicia Alma*
*My mother, Priscilla, and brother, David*
*And to my father, Federico, Sr., and sister, Patricia*
*Without their support, this project would have never been possible*

# CONTENTS

# PREFACE

THIS *DOCU-NOVELA ECOS la voz del pueblo*; a story of people who rebelled against the marginalization they experienced from an emerging colonial capitalists' frontier. This story is about the most significant social protest movement in the North American Southwest. It began with the 19th century annexation of the "American" Southwest and culminated in the 1960s. These multigenerational, battle-hardened, landgrant activists persistently objected to the largest "legal" chicanery land grab to date and is disputed to this day. Although people will argue that Native Americans were the victims of this land grab, I argue that we, the acculturated North American Natives and "Mexicano" Nativos de Las Américas too, are victims of conquest, for they are one and the same.

I chose to tell this story in the first person, taking creative license by collapsing narratives from various principal players and creating characters that would allow the story to flow. My first interviews were in the spring of 1980. They began with interviews of *corridistas*, men who documented the *Alianza* movement using the ballad tradition. This led me to the surviving *Aliancistas*. It took a lot to gain their trust, for an unspoken prerequisite was the ability to speak Spanish. At the time, my proficiency in that language was poor due to an educational system that did not allow children to develop their bilingual skills.

That was during the last vestiges of Jim Crow laws, worsened by a form of ethnogenocide of indigenous people. What followed was a journey of gaining an education from illiteracy to literacy and an emancipatory one. In the words of Eric Fromm, I had to break those shackles of illusion. I then had to gain the confidence of these landgrant activists. My persistence in wanting to know their stories and our spending some time together so they could get to know me eventually led to their acceptance, and these honorable people shared their most intimate insights and their understanding of their story with me. I have done my absolute best to give voice to these people while maintaining all the academic rigor I could muster to preserve a truthful voice for this complex history.

I have strived to articulate the worldview and the emerging Nuevomexicano ideology of these landgrant activists. These people are the product of a rugged frontier and a colonial political structure based on race and ethnic identity that began with initial European contact. This story shows how class interest was manipulated in favor of los americanos.

This New Mexico history shows us how Nuevomexicanos came to define who they are and who they have become, resulting in the realization of an ethnic, national consciousness of their very own. They first reacted with prolonged vigilantism beginning in the 19th century. Legal chicanery and manipulation fomented these people coming to object to these land thefts, and it cumulated in the late 1950s and 1960s after decades of waiting for their landgrant cases to be heard in the "Americas Court" systems. During this time, Nuevomexicanos found their cases systematically being lost. They reacted by mobilizing, demanding that their grievances be heard.

This history has been shrouded by smoking mirrors of deception and competing ideologies. Because of these events, land barons accumulated unfathomable fortunes at the expense of Nativo Nuevomexicanos. Historically, the New Mexico colonial experience was unlike that of other regions of North America. Arizona was considered to be part of New Mexico until 1912, when the United States Congress divided the New Mexico territories into two states, Arizona and New Mexico. They were both annexed to the Union on the same day within hours, and New Mexico "officially" became the 47th state.

# INTRODUCTION

THE TIME HAS COME for historical narratives to be told from multiple perspectives. This is the only way to objectively view our history and understand our present reality. The absence of history told from the losing side is commonplace; history is told from the "winners"' point of view. Telling history in this way is misleading and only serves to promote further exploitation—for without the perspective of the contesting groups, states, nations, and ethnic communities are misled and needlessly exploited. The fact that those who participate in the making of history are left out results in stunting the collective consciousness of humanity, for without a balanced view we are denied a well-rounded narrative that would provide a paradigm to understand how civilizations function.

Because the Spanish language was a defining prerequisite to participate in the inner circles of the landgrant movement, I wrote much of the Spanish text to bring to light the attempted ethnocultural "cleansing" Nuevomexicanos were experiencing at this time. I also wanted to show the varying degrees of acculturation between classes. This is why the reader will note that those New Mexicans who didn't speak Spanish are those who were further along in the process of acculturation, compromising their ethnic identity; those who spoke their heritage language were predominantly the poor and marginalized who felt the heavy hand of discrimination.

I wish to make a point that it wasn't only Black Americans who experienced the iron boot of an emerging apartheid in the United States of North America. One must consider that over three hundred Mexicanos were lynched from 1914 to 1915 in Texas alone, not to mention the lynchings that occurred in California, Arizona, and New Mexico, all while nomadic Native Americans were murdered in mass and rounded up into the glorified concentration camps, we have been conditioned to call reservations. This prolonged smoldering ethnogenocide played out politically and in our educational systems. This depreciates their ethnic identity while relegating their ability for economic progress on the basis of class, race-ethnicity, religion, and language. The color bar is forever present in all these categories and engaged in an unlimited variation of intersections. These paradigms offer a way to understand our history and honor the words these people shared with me, seeing them through a micro and macro lens to understand the building of an empire and human dynamics. This methodology offers a framework from which to understand the various social, political, and economic intersections that make us who we are today. This sociohistory recognizes a frontier community in transition, unwilling to give in to the overwhelming sociopolitical odds, stubbornly determined to maintain their sacred right to both self-determination and preservation.

In this text, I have used Spanish to emphasize that it was the language of empowerment for the disenfranchised. It served to reclaim their cultural identity and pride. I have translated their words into English for those who do not know or know little Spanish and to encourage readers, particularly of Hispanohablante descent, to both learn their heritage language and history in el voz del pueblo.

Furthermore, for non-Hispanic heritage speakers, I wish to encourage you to learn Spanish as a second language. You will see that I did not translate everything. That is deliberate, I want to communicate that Nuevomexicanos were in transition. This transition is characterized by code-switching between two worlds as a natural expression. By using their heritage language in mainstream society, they empowered themselves in the midst of a world in which they were no longer equal partners.

As for my literary style, it reflects my interdisciplinary professional background. My creative endeavors started in the realm of cinema graphic storytelling and ethnographic filmmaking. Now that I am treading the field of literary creation, I want my work to reflect part of my former creative journey. Therefore, my style is deliberately embellished with screenwriting hues. I see this process as a metaphor for my own in-betweenness, navigating the dual waters of languages, cultures, and traditions. As a Chicano, my literary style reflects my people's complexity, and the cinema graphic style that I first used to tell my people's story follows the musical meanders of the corrido, whose notes and lyrics are scattered throughout the story. As I invite readers to witness the unfolding of this narrative, it is also my hope that my style will invite them to literally walk in the shoes of the Hermanos and Aliancistas, who were all given the stellar role of their lifetime during the unfolding of the real events depicted.

As participants in the last vestiges of a segregated society arranged by class, race-ethnicity, language, religion, gender and color, those ethnic communities in power lent little value to those disempowered communities. Intercultural mixing expresses itself in the language reflected when code-switching. The process of melding one's language with another culture is an attempt to maintain the heritage language while building self-identity and esteem in a dominant-subordinate relationship. I have therefore chosen to tell the story of those people who have lost their heritage language and to tell their history as it unfolded.

Although I recognize this may limit some of my reading audience, I felt it important to keep the flow and authenticity of the story true to la voz del pueblo and, by doing so, to show how language is critical in the maintenance of a Nuevomexicano worldview. I have also taken liberties to deviate from conventional rules, like putting the words "anglo" and "american" or Nativo Nuevomexicano respectively in lower and upper case to emphasize status and the point of view that I am attempting to communicate in the text. I felt it essential to code-switch throughout the story because that is how this history unfolded. This was a time of accelerated ethnocultural transition and a frontier bonanza of land-mineral-timber-and later uranium-seizure. The first step after military control of a region is to appropriate its natural resources. The next step is to take psychological control by demeaning all that empowers the subordinate group and all that they hold dear. This begins with subordinating their spiritual worldview, dismantling their indigenous one, and imposing the spiritual worldview of those in power as superior, a characteristic of Manifest Destiny.

This story is meant to empower those who read it, especially Spanish-heritage speakers. This is a history told from the bottom up. As civilizations evolve, the disenfranchised communities adapt and create a language that borrows from the language of those in power while maintaining elements of their heritage language. These subtle differences in grammar rules between languages play on the sociopolitical relationships of who controls the modes of production and accumulation of wealth. In spite of the fact that the Spanish language is the second most spoken language in the world, followed by Chinese, we must recognize that the language of power and money, at the moment, is English. Likewise, I chose not to italicize the Spanish because it would distinguish the languages, making English the dominant language of the narrative and, therefore, one superior to the other. I wish to convey the message that they are on equal footing as one gets further into the text.

When I choose the spelling "American" I make a statement that "American" is an all-inclusive term to identify a people of the Western Hemisphere. By writing it in this way I draw attention to how anglo-american arrogance has appropriated ownership of this continental identifier. The United States of America is not exclusive to the white Protestant people of the United States of "North" America, for *las* américas pertenecen al pueblo. The United States of Mexico, also lies in the Americas, as do Canada, and "Central and South America," which is to say that the predominant language of the American continent is the first colonial language, Spanish. Why then, I may ask, is this country so adamant about not embracing a second language or culture that has so contributed to making us who we are today? We mustn't forget that had it not been for the economic assistance of the Spanish Empire the United States would have never defeated the British empire during the American Revolution of 1776. Yet still today white, racial, and ethnic supremacy dominates the political landscape throughout the continent. In other words, one finds many of those supremacist attitudes even in the Spanish-speaking world.

Furthermore, I have chosen to capitalize Nativo Nuevomexicano for political emphasis to impress upon the reader the power in naming oneself. Spanish convention dictates that it be written in lowercase. Again, I emphasize in the context of this narrative that if I were to stay true to this convention, I would belittle the story of activists and also send a subconscious message to the reader about the sociopolitical status of an indigenous people, i.e., that Nuevomexicanos are lesser than "americanos."

I also challenge the subtle bias and power built into language by making the conventional spelling of land grant(s) as one word, landgrant(s). Making it a compound word empowers the idea of community landgrants. Keeping it separate is to think of "land" and "grant" as separate ideas, while as far as landgrant activists are concerned, they constitute an all-encompassing concept. Community landgrants for Nativo Nuevomexicanos are not two separate concepts but a single concept, and to treat them as separate entities diminishes the spirit of communal property. La Merced, the word used in New Mexico to describe communal property, or el ejido in the Spanish-speaking world, are other terms used to express the same idea in this text. In addition, I chose to change the names of the characters because of the degree of creative license that I took to make the story flow, occasionally deviating or collapsing several characters to create new ones. I did adhere to maintaining historical accuracy while embellishing the story, allowing it to flow cohesively.

The better part of my adult life has been devoted to producing this document, and I feel fortunate to bring these voices to life in the form of the docu-novela. Throughout this journey of self-discovery and storytelling, I have endeavored to provide the reader with an understanding of what it is to be Nuevomexicano. However, my approach to telling this historical epic may be considered somewhat nontraditional.

This community has entrusted me to tell their story, which took place during an age of optimism. Like the moment the sun rests on the horizon, como un crepúsculo de una nueva era (the dawn of a new age), this story began with a collision of continents giving birth to una Raza Cósmica. Even though initial colonization may have occurred without incident, unsettling conflict is certain when competing for resources, ideologies, or conceptual worldviews. This is what led to the Pueblo Revolt of 1680. Even by then, there had been nearly a hundred and fifty years of miscegenation between local tribes and predominantly Mexican Natives and some European blood people. This lent itself to a common language, religion, and varying degrees of acculturation that controlled their capacity for social mobility. All of which contributed to dissatisfaction with a colonially imposed caste system sowing the seeds of revolt. After americano occupation, Nuevomexicanos, more often than not, were treated as immigrants in their native land. This is a grave misrepresentation of who Nuevomexicanos and many Spanish-speaking peoples throughout North America really are. Yet they have thrived, contributing to making this nation.

This work has been a journey of discovery, a search to understand our history. This story originates in the present and seeks to understand the evolutionary processes of people persistent in confronting their dispossession and sociopolitical disenfranchisement. They came to a conscious awakening, demanding equal access to education and an education that promotes critical thinking skills to empower their heritage community. As the optimist that I am, I believe that the United States of North America has come a long way, and life has become better for many. However, time and history have left Nuevomexicanos at a disadvantage due to years of subjugated history that has shaped unhealthy and inaccurate worldviews. Nonetheless, ideologies are fluid and forever evolving. They are organic, in constant change, like the seasons with their life cycles of creation. Our job, then, is to shape a vision for ourselves and humanity in which we all contribute to making a better world and the life we all desire.

# CHAPTER ONE

## MORADA

UN FUNERAL EN 1968. La Patrona de la Muerte, Doña Sebastiana, waits in her carreta (A funeral in 1968. The Patron Saint of the dead, Doña Sebastiana, waits in her two-wheel cart).

The Hermanos are finishing the rosario—trementina (piñón incense), filling the air, candles, and lanterns fluttering—a Kiva fireplace holds crackling embers. Mourning women, las Carmelitas, a religious prayer group, crying and wailing for the deceased. It is said that the wailing guides the deceased through the darkness of their entombed journey from the afterlife to Heaven, where San Pedro guards the gates. The women's heads are covered with tápalos (shawls) and completely covered in black. The younger women are sitting with their families and are dressed in contemporary 1960s clothing, wearing a mixture of colorfully patterned scarves over their heads. The Hermanos de la Cofradía de Nuestro Jesús Nazareno (the Brother of the Fraternity of Jesus the Nazarene) kneel. The men that partake in the cofradía are merely referred to as Hermanos. They pray over a body wrapped and sewn up in a Pendleton blanket, lying on a ladder made of latillas (small aspen or piñón tree branches or poles, three-inch diameter) sitting on two workmen's sawhorses. In the native way, the body is buried with a ladder so that the deceased can take it with them to climb out of their grave into the afterworld.

Indio Gerónimo is on his knees with other Hermanos. They sing una despedida, an alabado (religious song) traditionally performed by the Hermanos to send off their deceased brother to his transition. Other Hermanos are preparing to carry the body out and load it on Doña Sebastiana's carreta.

| | |
|---|---|
| *Ay Dios, Hermano, te has ido* | Oh my God Brother you have departed |
| *Hoy has hecho tu separación* | Today, you have made your separation |
| *Jesucristo te acompaña* | Jesus Christ accompanies you |
| *Y te da tu Salvación* | And he gives you salvation |

The Hermanos walk backward not to turn their backs to the altar. Other Hermanos follow their brethren, y los particulares (ordinary people) follow them. The somber alabado melts into the twilight as they load the body onto la carreta. Doña Sebastiana proudly sits on her two-wheel carriage, holding the reins. They tie the body down. Hermanos on both sides of the horse take a rein near the bridle, and, in procession, they walk to el Campo Santo, where three large crosses in silhouette sit high atop a hill. The sun is setting. The clouds are dark, rolling in a brilliant blue, orange, and violet sky. The earth rumbles. Lightning cracks across the sky, striking the horizon. Libertado rests his hand on Indio Gerónimo's shoulder and tells his uncle-brother, "Está libre. Hermano, al fin está libre de los dolores y las injusticias de esta vida." (He is free, my brother. He is finally free from the pain and injustice of this life.) He contemplates the stories his tío would tell him of his communities' history.

Indio drifts in thought as he joins his brethren in singing the Gregorian alabado they all know so well. It comes as natural as having a conversation. It bids goodbye to the fallen Hermano as the body is symbolically escorted to his last resting place...

| | |
|---|---|
| *Ay Dios para siempre Adiós* | Oh God Forever Farewell |
| *Gloriosamente te suben a los cielos* | Gloriously they raise you to the heavens |
| *Hasta aquí te acompañamos* | Up to here we accompany you |
| *Ay, Dios por siglos eternos* | Oh, God for eternal centuries |

His life unfolds as they finish the alabado and the Hermanos cover the grave. A fading memoria (memory) sung in a melodic tone, a lone Hermano sings the reverent memoria to his beloved brother from a distance. The song lingers in the thick summer evening air. The person singing the memoria is nowhere to be seen. Only his voice is heard. The downhearted homenaje (homage) melts into a light breeze as la memoria drifts heavily through the canyon, becoming one with the warm summer river as it meanders into the abyss. The Hermanos lay their brethren to rest en su última morada (in his final resting place).

### 1953 Northern New Mexico

Indio Gerónimo's mother, Calixtra, has the reins in hand. The wagon winds down a road. There are few men present. Young boys and girls are playing and helping in the fields. Elders and women are working the fields y limpiando las acequias (and cleaning the irrigation ditches). Indio Gerónimo sits beside his mother, Calixtra, with his sisters in tow - they cross the river towards the village.

Country store and gas station. A woman clerk in her mid-forties, "¿Cómo estás, Calixtra?"

Calixtra is in her thirties, thin, pretty, and morena (tanned). She has strong Indian features, "I miss my Viejo (literally means 'old'; in this context: [romantic] partner), it's so lonely."

Woman clerk, fair skin, "Yes, I know, I miss my viejo también. I pray he comes home safely."

"Yes, mine, too." Calixtra sighs. "I am always praying."

The woman clerk, "Aquí tienes correo, parece que viene de tu esposo." (Here you have mail; it looks like it's from your husband.) She takes the letter, opens it, and asks the clerk to read it for her.

The clerk clears her throat. "Muy querida Calixtra: Aquí estoy en la montaña cerca de la frontera de Korea del Norte. El terreno es muy parecido a mi tierra Nuevomexicana, los inviernos son bien fríos y los veranos calientes. Aunque a veces está tan lindo con flores, no tan bellas como tú, mi querida, me hace pensar en ti y cuanto deseo tenerte en mis brazos, mi corazón. ¿Cómo están todos? ¿Mis hijos? Espero que estén con buena salud, creo que mi hijo ya está cortando la pastura, ¿verdad?, tan buen muchacho nos prestó Dios, ¿verdad mujer mía? Espero que no estén batallando tanto para mantener el rancho y espero que las muchachas estén con buena salud deles un abrazo fuerte de parte de su papa...oh mi querida, como extraño tus respiros. Tu querido esposo." (My dear beloved Calixtra, here I am in the mountains near the border of North Korea. The geography is a lot like my New Mexican land, the winters are really cold and the summers hot. Though sometimes is real pretty with flowers not as beautiful as you, my love, it makes me think of you and how I yearn to have you in my arms, my love. How is everybody? My children? I hope that they are in good health, I believe my son is now cutting the pasture, right? Such a good kid that God lend us, right my love. I hope you are not struggling a lot to manage the ranch I'm sure the girls are doing fine give them a strong loving hug from daddy...oh my love, how I miss your breath. Your loving husband)

Calixtra sighs, "Le ruego a mi Dios que me lo devuelva sano" (I pray to God that returns he to me in good health.)

She pays, takes the change, puts it in a small coin purse, and puts it between her breasts along with the letter. Then she picks up her box of groceries and leaves the store, her children trailing behind. She gets on the wagon and heads up the mountain for home. Indio sitting beside her - his mind's eye fades into the sun's blinding light. His sisters sit in the back of the wagon.

### La Borregera

Indio and his cousin, Libertado, are in the high country, tending sheep and goats on a mountain vega (a meadow) covered in a beautiful mosaic of wildflowers, lavender, and green pasture. Aspen and then Ponderosas lead up into the forest high country. Young Libertado and Indio are wrestling, tumbling and horsing around.

Indio is six years old. His uncle-brother, Libertado, is a few years older. The boys are rough-housing. Libertado lobs a dry clod of sheep dung, hitting Indio on the back. He falls forward from its weight and stumbles but keeps his footing. Indio gives chase to Libertado, diving and tripping him with his hands. They are tumbling wrestling.

Indio is trying to get away and picks up a chicharra (beetle) from the grass and put it into Libertado's mouth. Indio is laughing, and Libertado spits and gags.

"Caa...cabrón", Libertado stutters, as he runs after Indio. "Meee...meme...me la vas a pagar," shouts Libertado.

Indio Gerónimo, "¿Por qué te fastidias, hermano? Todo lo que quería hacer era ayudarte a dejar de tartamudear." (Why are you so angry brother, all I wanted to do was to help you get rid of stuttering).

He laughs and runs from his cousin.

"¡Caaabrón! ¡Sanamabiche! Me, me...me la vas a pagar," (Shit! Son-Of-A-Bitch! You are going to pay for that!) Libertado goes after him, not noticing the two Forest Rangers on horseback high on a hill in silhouette looking down on them. They ride towards the boys. As they get to them, one ranger yells out, "You boys get that livestock out of here, and pronto!"

The boys are startled. They turn blinded by the sun as the two horsemen ride towards them.

Indio Gerónimo, in a frightened stutter and strong Spanish accent, "We...wee we always use this vega and my grandpa yu, yu, yu uses this vega, too."

"Yea, yea, yea, ésta es La Merced." (Yeah, this is the community landgrant), "that we and everybody from La Merced uses," exclaims Libertado in surprising clarity.

"You damn Mezcans! I told you to get those sheep off these pastures. It's federal land now!"

The rangers start moving towards them. They take their lariats' that hang from the pommels of their saddles. In an easy gallop, they toss the ropes, lassoing the boys as they run away. The rangers drag them across the pasture amused with their antics. The boys manage to get loose and run down the side of a canyon. They hide under a rock out cropping...un peñasco.

The rangers look at each other. "Eeyaah—let's take the sheep down to the station corrals," says ranger White.

They move the flock down the mountain towards the road. The boys run in the opposite direction and make their way back home. On arriving, they tell their mothers what happened. Tranquilina is raising Libertado as her own son because Tranquilina and Calixtra's mother died giving birth to him. Libertado es un cambio de vida de cariño, ( a loving change of life baby). The women calm their sons down. Calixtra looks at her sister's coal-black eyes and tells her, "Vamos por las borregas." (Let's go get the sheep).

They get in the wagon, and the boys follow on horseback, dogs in tow. On their arrival, Indio's mother, Calixtra, opens the Forest Service corral gate and begins to herd the sheep out, instructing the boys to get them home. His tía Tranquilina helps. The rangers come out of the station cabin.

"Now, what do you think you are doing, you goddamn squaw? You'd better get them their sheep back into the corral, or you are going to be in lot of trouble," says the rinche (ranger)White.

Calixtra, "You—no, you can't take our sheep. It-it-it's, all we have, me los voy a llevar." (I am taking them back.)

Ranger White, "You think so, do you? Well, we will just see about that."

Ranger Evans attempts to redirect the flock. The dogs are working the flock. He pulls Indio off his horse and backhands him. One of the dogs attacks the ranger. The ranger shoots the dogs. "You dumb Mezcan, what do you think you're doing?"

Libertado comes at them on horseback and attempts to separate the rinche Evans and Indio. The horse rears up, throws Libertado, and stomps him. Rinche White manhandles Calixtra. She attempts to run off, but the ranger slaps her and she falls to the ground. Calixtra yells out to her sister, Tranquilina.

"¡Váyanse!" (Go away!), she yells.

Libertado, wounded from the fall, does his best to help with the flock while his mother, Tranquilina, fails to notice how hurt her son is. Indio takes a rock and hits Rinche Evans on the head, knocking him to the ground before he can get his hands on his mother. Calixtra yells at

Indio to get the sheep out. She pulls a bowie knife from her hip and swings it, cutting the ranger on the arm.

"Oh, that's the way we're going to play it, is it?" The rinche punches her and she falls. Rinche White picks up the knife. Indio jumps him from behind and the rinche grabs him by the head flipping him over. Indio scrambles to get up; the rinche picks up the knife and cuts Indio on the cheek and kicks him to a pulp until he doesn't move. He punches Calixtra again as she attempts to stop the rinche from beating her son. She falls; he grabs her by the hair and drags her into the cabin.

Tranquilina helps Indio up and puts him in the wagon while Libertado continues to move the flock down the road, holding his shoulder Indio is bleeding profusely from the cheek. Inside the Forest Service cabin, Calixtra kicks the rinche, doing everything she can to escape. Rinche Evans is still lying on the ground outside.

Rinche White, "You're going to pay, squaw!" He ties a rope around her hands and throws it over a viga. He stretches her up onto her toes. He slides the back of his hand across her cheek down her chin and neck to her cleavage and cups her breast. He walks behind her and tears her dress. Then he walks over and takes a whip hanging on the wall, snapping it, positioning himself behind her, snapping it again across her back, slashing her. Calixtra screams—she bites her teeth; she is afraid that her son will come for her. After striking her with the whip, he steps around and tears the dress from her body, admiring her perfection, her radiant brown skin and black hair that glimmers midnight blue in the light shining through the window. He looks into her coal-black eye—he sees his reflection in her eyes. He runs the back of his hand across her face again and over her breast... Ranger Evans walks in, takes a rifle hanging on the wall, stops and admires the woman. He goes back outside.

Rinche White whispers to her, "You're a fine specimen, you don't even smell half bad for being a squaw."

Indio attempts to run back, but he's too hurt and his tía Tranquilina holds him up and walks him to the wagon. Blood is everywhere. He yells in pain holding his ribs as the wagon makes its way down towards their ranch. The sheep are scattered, but they run in the direction of their home. Libertado is doing his best to keep the flock together, everyone is noticeably hurt and upset.

Tía Tranquilina tells him, "She will be alright, m'ijo (my son). Let's get the sheep home."

Rinche White yells, "Shut up. If those boys come back, I will kill them."

Rinche Evans fires a shot as they turn on the road behind a bluff. The flock runs along the road, bleating "baa - baaa." The rinche is too hurt to pursue them; he stands with the cabin behind him, rifle in hand, takes aim, and fires again. The gun jams, and he tries to get the bullet out of the chamber, but to no avail. Libertado is leading the sheep, his mother in the wagon, and Indio lying in the back moaning as they turn on a bow in the road out of sight of the rinche.

Not far from the ranch, Indio is grief-stricken about leaving his mother. He rolls out of the wagon as they arrive home. Tía Tranquilina stops the wagon and helps him up. "Voy por mi mamá," he takes the reins tied to the wagon and mounts the horse to go for his mother. His tía Tranquilina tries to convince him not to go. Indio, in a hypnotic out of body state, trots off back down the road on horseback with a rag tied over his head across his bleeding cheek. Libertado holds his mother as Indio gallops off. The dogs guide the sheep into their corral.

Tranquilina takes her battered son Libertado inside to care for him. Indio meets his mother on the road. She is bludgeoned, her torn dress barely covering her naked body. He takes off his shirt and wraps it around her. He helps her onto the saddle and walks the horse home holding the blood-soaked rag to his check.

Tranquilina takes a needle and sews Indio's cheek. Calixtra is in the bedroom bathing, Libertado lies in bed with his ribs wrapped, his face bruised and disfigured.

## ZARFARANO (ZARA) 1937

Migrant worker Zara (short for his namesake Zarfarano) is a young boy poking the ground with a stick. His father scolds him, telling him to get to work. They are picking potatoes.

"¡Zara, apacíguate, estate quieto!" (Behave, stay still.)

"Mamá, tengo sed. ¿Puedo ir por agua?" (Mother, I am thirsty, can I go for water?) asks Zara poking the potatoes with his stick.

"No, quédate quieto," (No, stay still).

"Ándale, malcriado, trabaja, no andes picando las papas con ese palito," his father snaps in a stern voice. (Hurry you bad boy and get to work. Don't be poking the potatoes with that stick).

Zara, "Papá, estoy cansado—hace tanto calor, tengo sed Papá." (Father, I am tired, and it is so hot. I'm thirsty, Father).

"Ya, ya otra hora y acabamos pepenando para hoy, hurry. Antes que baje el sol." (Okay, okay, another hour and we are done picking today. Andale before the sun sets.)

It's 6:00 pm and the workers are coming in from the fields to their camp. People collect water from a central water faucet, the women prepare dinner, the men wash up, and the children play. People are happy that the day is over.

The women share the woodstove preparing meals while the men build a campfire preparing to fry rabbit meat. As people eat and settle down, instruments begin to play. José María composes a corrido of their lives working the migrant trail. Some are already packing to move on to the next camp. They will be getting paid in the morning.

The adults call to the youngsters to get ready for bed. Four to six people to a mattress cover the floor in a one-room shack 20x20. Little Zara is awake. Young Mari-Lupita is asleep. Her father turns and puts his arm around her and cuddles up to her in a spoon position. She awakes and looks at her brother lying on the floor. The blankets ruffle, Mari-Lupita squints in pain and a tear runs down her cheek...

"Ya, ya m'ijita," whispers her father.

### Alfonso Sánchez Story, Mid 1930s

The sun is setting on the llano (desert plain). A small adobe home. A summer breeze. A windmill fluttering in the wind. A young boy pulls on his mother's apron in despair. "Mamá - ¿dónde está mi Papá?" His mother, in her thirties, answers in a trembling and frail voice, "No sé, no sé m'ijo". His baby sister is crying, standing in a cast iron crib, reaching out to be picked up. An older sister takes her out of the crib and cuddles her. The mother is in distress in the kitchen warming water and mixing atole, a blue corn meal—she has seven children and her husband left in search of work and has not returned. Two daughters gather around her. One holds her by the waist, and the other by the leg. She puts her arm around one and rests her hand on the head of the other reassuring them that everything will be alright, explaining to them that she will be leaving early to go talk to la Miss Smiley in Los Lunas, asking her for more work and delivering the clothing she and her daughters have washed and ironed. Alfonso and his brother Salomón decide that they will go to the García's and ask for work making terrones (sod blocks). He is building a house for the ricos, the Lunas.

The family goes to bed. Alfonso and his brother talk about their plans for the morning. Their younger siblings are whimpering and sobbing themselves to sleep with hunger. Their mother is lying in bed praying. Una vela (a candle) flickers under the image of Jesucristo en la columna, bloodied, his thin and battered body mangled, torn flesh exposing nerves and bone.

Roman soldiers witness the beating of Jesucristo. One soldier stands before the crowd bloody from the whipping of Jesus, handing a disciplina (a short whip made of cactus) to an assistant, next to him with a towel, and a washbasin to clean his bloody face and arms. Alfonso's mother hasn't had anything to eat for quite some time. Her husband was due to come home several days ago but has yet to arrive with provisions. Her son, Alfonso Sánchez, and the others listen to their mother pray while they are all in bed. The dispirited rhythm of her prayers calms them, easing their hunger and fear until slowly and gently they all fall into a peaceful slumber.

## SANTA FÉ PLAZA 1940S

Robert Oppenheimer, John Von Neumann, and General Leslie Groves and their wives pull up in a 1940 Buick Sedan to the front of La Fonda Hotel in Santa Fé, New Mexico. They enter the hotel. In the center of the hotel is an open-spaced patio used as a dining room in the summer. To the left is the receptionist and the bar just beyond in another open room. Cowboy fiddle music comes from the bar. In the dining area, a Spanish guitar serenades the diners. They sit at a table with their wives. Frank has arranged for a general contractor and architect to meet them for dinner. Frank is leasing a ranch in Pecos and uses his local contacts to help with the building of the Los Alamos Laboratories. They see their guests and wave at them to get their attention. They settle down and order while greeting one another with the niceties of handshakes and introductions. The women comment on their impressions of New Mexico.

"Oh my, the menu has so much Spanish in it, you'd think we were in Mexico," says Von Neumann's wife Marietta.

Robert Oppenheimer's soon-to-be wife Kitty exclaims, "Oh dear, but we are!"

Isn't this exciting?" responds Grace, General Groves' wife.

"Oh no, we're not in Mexico. We are in New Mexico," says Marietta.

"Did you see those Indians under the portal of the Governor's Palace?" says Grace.

"Please, Grace. Can't you see that they are all around us? Even the housekeepers speak Spanish," remarks Kitty.

"I even heard them speaking Indian," remarks Grace.

"You mean Tewa. I think those women were talking Tewa, at least that's what I was told by the receptionist," responds Jackie, Frank Oppenheimer wife.

"Yes, have you seen the beautiful blue and green stone jewelry?" asks Kitty.

Looking at the menu, "What are these *sopfalapillas*?" asks Grace.

"You have to have some, they're delightful! Pillowed fried bread," Jackie explains.

General Groves, Robert and Frank Oppenheimer are talking.

Robert asks, "So tell me about the location; it's a basin of a volcano. It sounds like an ideal location."

General Groves, "Yes, I believe we have the perfect location. Let me introduce you to the contractor."

The contractor, "Hello. I'm Tomas Reynolds, and this is my architect, Zane Toombs. We have been up to the location and have made preliminary drawings and plans so you can see what we are thinking as far as the layout and geography."

Robert Oppenheimer says, "Yes, we need to get started as soon as possible."

"Other scientists are preparing back east as we speak," says General Groves.

Frank is listening and observing his surroundings. The next day, military vehicles escort them all to the location. As they make their way up the ancient volcano, they pass a Genízaro village, Guachupangue, a village of Mestizo, pueblo, and Criollo people who speak Spanish and Tewa and are Catholics. Children playing on the dusty road stop for a moment to allow the military jeep and the Buick Sedan to drive past. Bernardo, who would later become sheriff, later known as Benny Naranjo, makes eye contact with General Groves. Bernardo's buddy throws the ball at his friend, hitting him in the face.

Bernardo's friend says, "Vamos, te toca a ti. Let's go!" He picks the ball up and throws it back, missing him. They both go off running between the houses, laughing and cursing at each other.

"Whose land is this?" Frank Oppenheimer asks.

"Oh, the natives use the area as summer pastures. It's part of what the locals call a community landgrant and the area we are looking at is land held in common so, the Forest Service has been passing legislation to take control of the area," General Groves responds.

Some time passes, the military knocks on doors in the village and surrounding ranches delivering eviction notices from the commons. If no one answers, government officials tack an eviction notice on the door, ending an era of indigenous control of the Los Alamos Basin. People are conflicted on how to react, some are angered being denied access to summer pasture yet empathetic to support the war... time passes...

## School House Scene 1950s

A one-room schoolhouse. Coming in late Libertado disrupts the classroom. He is restless and fidgety. He is lost and doesn't have a clue what the teacher is talking about.

The schoolteacher glares at him as he takes his seat smelling of manure.

"Tuve que darles agua y pastura a los animales," (I had to feed the animals and give them water) Libertado tells his friends.

Later that afternoon, Libertado's mother comes to the schoolhouse. She explains to la Maestra Jaramillo that she needs Libertado. She takes him away, sending her son up the Canjilón Mountain to find and bring down the cattle before it gets too late while she goes off in the opposite direction, searching for cattle. The sun is setting.

Libertado is tired. He unsaddles the horse and goes inside the house.

Indio Gerónimo comes home from school. His mother is in bed with a cold. He stokes the fire, gathers wood from outside for the evening, opens a can of pork and beans—He warms them over the wooden stove.

# CHAPTER TWO

## THE LAND GRAB

IT'S 1951. BILL MUNDY is a thin man of medium height, the son of a dust bowler whose father landed in Las Cruces, New Mexico, in the late 1930s and bought a farm some years later. Both father and son are at the Doña Ana Cattle Auction when they hear about a property for sale in Río Arriba County, New Mexico ... cheap. Mundy had just mustered out of the military and recently married. He is looking to get out on his own and has the GI Bill available to him to acquire property.

Mundy calls the owner of the property Karl Brusselbach, Jr., the nephew of TD Burns, a land grabber from the mid-nineteenth century is selling. Mundy meets Brusselbach in Santa Fé. Brusselbach and Mundy drive up to Tierra Amarilla (TA). They ride much of the 11,000-acre ranch on horseback, high on the ridge of Los Brazos, a sort of mini-Rock of Gibraltar. They gaze over the Chama Valley. Mundy is taken aback by the mountain landscape. He ponders as he gapes at the Chama Valley, a stunning property beyond his wildest dreams. On the ride back he notices a jacal, a Mexicano style log cabin with the posts buried in a trench and plastered with mud. He notices roads on the property. Obviously, people are using the land. He sees flocks of sheep, herds of cattle, wood being harvested, and pastures of alfalfa under irrigation.

Brusselbach clears his throat and tells the history of how he came to "own the property."

"My great grandfather, Thomas D. Burns, on my mother's side arrived here in the late 1850's. He was from Wisconsin, and as the story tells, at 16 years, old he followed the Colorado gold rush. Well, he failed miserably as a miner, so he wandered into Tierra Amarilla (TA), New Mexico in 1866, where a Capote Ute promptly stole Burns' mule. A year passed and the U.S. Government built a frontier outpost near TA. My grandfather Burns became their quartermaster. Soon thereafter, he married a local girl and opened a mercantile, first in Tierra Amarilla and then in Los Ojos, another community a few miles from there. As a merchant my grandfather would allow the locals to take merchandise on credit. He quickly amassed a fortune and within two years grandfather boasted $200,000 in commercial wealth."

"Yee-haa...he was a pretty-sharp cookie! Those guys made quite an alliance, great Grandpa Burns and his partner Thomas Catron. They sure did. Catron also arrived about the same time from Texas, and within ten years he owned millions of acres in New Mexico. He and grandfather formed a partnership."

"Great Grandpa Burns' flock numbered in the tens of thousands. He controlled the sheep and timber industry in Río Arriba County while Catron focused on clearing title and investing in mining, oil, timber, and the railroad. Catron had been a Confederate soldier, and after the war he made his way to New Mexico, learned Spanish, and got a license to practice law. By the 1870s, less than ten years after arriving, he and my grandfather had control of the entire 600,000 acres of the Tierra Amarilla landgrant, not to mention ownership in other landgrants. Grandpa Burns got ownership of just about all of the

San Joaquín de Río Chama Landgrant just south of here from the Mexicans by calling in debts that the locals had accumulated from his store, leaving them little choice but to sell their land to Grandpa to pay off their debt. Grandpa Burns in turn would lease the land to Catron. In this way, they would establish a chain of title. At that time, the sheep industry dominated the region. By the 1890s, Catron claimed three and a half million acres of New Mexico. Grandpa Burns laid claim to thousands of acres and much of the Piedra Lumbre Grant. In the winter of 1933, the sheep industry went bust. There had been a series of extremely harsh winters. The cold decimated the sheep industry, and we never recovered our former glory. That's when we started to sell. This ranch is all we have left in the area."

"Disgruntled locals have been fussing, claiming that the land belongs to the landgrant, which cannot be bought or sold. Back in the 1860s, however, Catron had gotten the Tierra Amarilla Landgrant patented as a private landgrant, not a community landgrant, which was what the locals were claiming. Just think, those stupid Mexicans have the audacity to think they own this land. At any rate when all was said and done, the court's decision was made. This freed up the entire 600,000 acres for people like you and me to develop. Hell, those locals ain't capable of developing this land like us Americans can."

## LOS HEREDEROS, 1933

Elders sit around a campfire drinking whiskey, rolling tobacco, passing the punche (mountain tobacco) over to the man next to them, discussing what it means that they have lost the trial and have been forced away from their traditional pastures and access to water. The property in question had been in use since the dawn of time for these people who were now acculturated and seen as Mexicans. They are asking themselves who gave the gringos permission to fence off La Merced.

It is 1933, early in the morning before sunrise, a sizable group of mounted horsemen ride into Tierra Amarilla - José María II, a boy in his teens is among them. They ride up to the Tierra Amarilla courthouse door. An elder dismount. He goes up to the front door and nails a proclamation on the door.

Another elder, on horseback, turns and announces to the men, "Están robando La Merced, y es de nosotros, es nuestra responsabilidad proteger nuestros terrenos, de cualquier manera, que podamos, con o sin la ayuda de la ley." (The landgrant is being stolen and it is ours, it's our responsibility to protect our property in whatever way necessary, with or without the help of the law.) José María puts on a glove, dips his hand in some black gruel, and leaves a handprint on the door. They ride off into the dark of night.

Una banda de La Mano Negra (a band of men known as the black hand) is combing the countryside, tearing down fences and destroying property the gringos' encroachers were claiming. They ride to Placita Blanca, taking sympathizers from their homes, beating them and warning them that collaboration with outsiders will not be tolerated.

Medardo Abeyta, a small man, is constructing a legal argument to get the encroachers off La Merced. He spends every waking moment researching and telling the Herederos of the illegal shenanigans and of how americanos have and are usurping the land from them. The people of Tierra Amarilla incorporate La Merced as stipulated in the original Mexican title, a community landgrant. They sent emissaries to Washington, D.C. with documents in hand to prove ownership of La Merced de Tierra.

Early in 1938, the consejo (council) hires an attorney and files a series of petitions to intervene in the HND Land & Cattle Company's quiet title on behalf of Los Herederos for the Los Brazos track of land. The consejo attorney bases his argument on Mexican-Spanish law which prohibited anyone but the original colonists from acquiring land from the grant. The claim was that the landgrant was equivalent to church ownership for perpetuity, or manos muertos, to those original families that settled La Merced. The judge, however, rejects the argument and dismisses the attorney's cross complaint, allowing the quiet title of HND Land Company. Even though the individual hijuelas (Spanish land titles) included all of La Merced, according to the judge Los Mercederos failed to prove color of title to those common lands. The judge later changed his position and contradicted himself when he allowed the original 1836 Mexican hijuelas as valid and saying that they were never meant to be for exclusive use to Mercederos, thereby upholding Thomas Catron's position that land held in common was a fabrication by the Mexicans to inflate their holdings. Yet the hijuelas Catron acquired included all of La Merced and were bought fair and square.

The Herederos (Mercederos or heirs) argued in accordance with Spanish Mexican custom, La Corporación de Abiquiú Merced de Tierra Amarilla had been occupied and in continual use since 1836.

José María Martínez el primero (José María Martínez the first), acted as the signatory, the equivalent of a corporate chairman of the board responsible for the administration of La Merced or recognized throughout the Spanish speaking world as hujuela. His job as representative was to administer for the greater good of all landgrant heirs. Those private properties in use and with improvements by individual heirs could be sold, but only to other heirs, and the commons were to be held collectively for the wellbeing of all those landgrant heirs.

## KARL BRUSSELBACH INHERITS TD BURNS PROPERTY

"Yep, according to the history of how the family got the property Grandpa Karl married Emma Burns' daughter to TD Burns, and they were the executors of great grandpa TD Burn's estate. They rented the land to Herculano Herrera sight unseen. Herculano means Hercules you know, yeah, those Mexicans has some funny names, don't they? Anyway, upon arriving in TA, Herculano comes from somewhere around Española, and when he got to the land, he found the pasture in use. He talked with the rancher using the property and he said that he had permission from the Landgrant Counsel and that the land was part of the landgrant. I took them to court and the Mexicans testified that they had always used the property. But according to Catron, who was still alive and had written the title, had bought the land, but there was a family that was using it. He didn't bother evicting them. It was just too much bother. And went ahead and filed his title.

Well, things got a bit messy, and the Mexicans back in the early 1930s that incorporated the landgrant. Grandpa Burns had already passed away, but Catron testified in court in 1937, and the court ruled that the corporation was illegal. Well, five years ago I was taken to court again, and during the whole process the land granters tried to revive the Landgrant corporation. Let me tell you what, boy, I put a stop to that and got the area ranchers to sign a petition and we filed a counter lawsuit. We just couldn't allow that because it would challenge all of our properties, casting in doubt all of our titles. Anyway, the judge ruled in our favor, ejected the lawsuit against me and the land granters were ordered off the property. Boy oh boy, you should have been there. The judge gave them a scolding telling them they could never use the property again, but as you can see, they're stubborn and I'm tired of dealing with this mess I'll give you a deal, that is if you are ready to mess with these dumb Mexicans. I've had enough of it."

Bill Mundy and Karl Brusselbach are driving back to Santa Fe.

"Well Karl, in spite of this complicated history I am going to take my chance to acquire my dream of a lifetime and go for it, I want the ranch. Let's go ahead and draw up the paperwork," Mundy tells Brusselbach.

They pull up to La Fonda Hotel. They shake hands in the lobby. "Okay, we'll see you in a couple of hours for dinner. Our wives should be getting ready now," says Karl, and they go to their rooms.

## MUNDY BUYS THE RANCH 1951

In 1951, third generation José María Martínez III—un hombre de la sierra (a man of the mountains) like his grandfather, stoic, a working rancher, sturdy, but reserved, found himself spokesperson of La Corporación de Abiquiú Merced de Tierra Amarilla. He along with the council continued with what Abeyta had started, filing lawsuits and informing heirs of the land grab. Kenneth Heron, the Spill bothers, the Unser's, and the Chama Land and Cattle Company all participated in the land grab in the immediate area well into the 1950s. The entirety of Northern New Mexico was under siege. Landgrants throughout were faced with similar methods of double-dealing.

At the same time the civil rights movement was gaining momentum with an expanding class, race, and ethnic consciousness setting in motion social change on an unprecedented scale never before experienced not only in the United States but abroad as well. The people of Tierra Amarilla were realizing their inability to win favor from the legal system. The decades of fighting in court made them realize the extent of legal bias favoring americanos. José María, respected and influential with other traditional factions of landgrant heirs, bridged traditional forms of objecting to their usurpation from their land base with the tactics of the Civil Rights Movement. By the end of the Second World War both the legal system and the government had completed establishing mechanisms of racial-ethnic control. The landgrant movement had yet to coalesce. Each landgrant had its own particular story of dispossession, and the heirs realized the consistent theme of land loss.

Given the series of legal defeats and unheeded seizure of landgrants, the Herederos realized that United States courts were not there to protect Nativos, but to protect the interests of americanos. They found themselves at a loss as to what to do next. Vigilantism and lawsuits were proving hopeless

Bill Mundy filed an ejectment suit against the Herederos to get them off "the land." It wasn't until 1958 that the court ruled on the Martínez vs Mundy case in favor of Mundy. The Payne Land and Cattle Company followed suit claiming another large section of land. Legal mechanisms were ruling on case after case in favor of the americanos. The United States economy was on the move towards growth like never before, and banks were making money easily available to americanos. Racial and ethnic lines were being drawn making the age of affluence available to whites only. The better jobs and bank loans reflected the gerrymandering throughout the country affecting all levels of society.

Mundy meets with an attorney from the Catron Law Firm in Santa Fé. The attorney assures Mundy that he will get him title insurance, enabling him to acquire a VA Loan to make the purchase. Mundy signs the real estate papers, taking possession of the 11,000 acres of El Rancho de Los Brazos. He immediately sets out to build a house and mend fencing.

Despite the obvious question of who owns the property, Mundy signs the real estate papers taking possession Del Rancho de Los Brazos. He immediately sets out to build a house and mend fences. No sooner do the fences go up than they are torn down. His home gets burned down while under construction and again when it is completed. The locals continue to use pasture that Mundy believes his. One afternoon he comes upon vaqueros from the landgrant and confronts them with two Mexican ranch hands and an anglo foreman he brought from Las Cruces, NM.

"Hello, neighbor," says Mundy in a brash manner.

José María continues stoking the campfire with branding irons. Another vaquero helps. He stands up and turns to Mundy, pauses, looks him over, and turns. He walks over to his horse and gets a small coffee pot from his saddlebags. Other vaqueros are nearby separating the calves for branding acutely aware of what is happening. The Mexicanos that came with Mundy are uneasy, recognizing that they have gotten themselves into a situation that will put them at odds with fellow Mexicanos and their employer.

Mundy, "I said good afternoon ... Ah, ah ... amigo. I just come down to ask whether or not you know anything about those cattle on my pasture over this hill." Silence ... "I thought I saw you working those cattle. Didn't you see that fence and no trespassing sign down by the river, señor?"

José María, without looking at him, says in Spanish, "Esos terrenos pertenecen a La Merced, no pueden ser tuyos." (That land belongs to the landgrant, it cannot belong to you.)

Mundy responds, "No, I bought that land. I got title. I got title insurance. I can prove it."

"No me interesa qué es lo que tengas, estos terrenos son de La Merced y no son para vender, que no entiendes, o...quieres que te lo diga en inglés." (It does not matter what you say that you have, these lands are the landgrant, and they are not for sale. Don't you understand, or do I have to tell you in English?)

Mundy looks dumbfounded, not sure what he said or how to answer. "Well ... well, we ... we will see about that. I will call the Sheriff and take you to court. I have title to this property - Do you understand!"

"Nos pescaste dormidos, pendejo. Compraste ese terreno bajo pretenso falso. Estábamos alegando con el Brusselbach, ya te lo dije, y si quieres, te llevamos a la corte también. No tengo más que decirte, por qué no te vas." (You caught us asleep, stupid—you bought that land under false pretenses. We were arguing this in court with Brusselbach. I will not tell you again, and if you like we will take you to court too! I have nothing else to tell you, why don't you go now.)

José María puts the pot of coffee on the fire and turns and takes the branding irons, getting them ready for use. Mundy is unsure if he fully comprehends what happened. He takes a moment...he turns around, "You GODDAM Mescan!"

We'll see, we'll just see who will end up with the land after I talk to the judge, we'll see...and talk to me in English, we're in America!"

"¡No! Estamos en las américas que es un continente que incluye México, Colombia, y todo Latinoamérica. Estos son territorios ocupados por los Estados Unidos, este es Nuevo México y el idioma español está protegido en nuestra constitución, y por esa razón, tú tienes que hablar nuestro idioma materno. Váyase de aquí o te voy a hacer alguna cosa de la que voy a tener que arrepentirme." (No! We are in the Americas, which is a continent, and it includes Mexico, Colombia, and all of Latin America. These are territories occupied by the United States and the Spanish language is protected in our Constitution. And because of this reason you have to speak our mother tongue. Leave us, or I am going to do something that I will have to repent.)

Mundy, on horseback, pulls the reins, grumbles under his breath, turns his horse and leaves, "You God-damn Mescan, we'll see who wins this fight." He rides off followed by his ranch hands

The other vaqueros have stopped what they were doing. Some of them have picked up their weapons; others are holding hot branding irons and glaring at the anglo rancher as he rides south towards home.

## MARTÍNEZ-VS-MUNDY 1951-1958

The Herederos file a lawsuit to eject Mundy from 11,000 acres of land. The judge moves the case from Tierra Amarilla to Santa Fé. He believes it is impossible to find an impartial jury in Rio Arriba County, so he divides the case in two, allowing a jury trial as requested by the Herederos, but after the Mundy ejection lawsuit was heard. This action suddenly made the Herederos defendants in their own lawsuit. This would determine whether La Merced was a private or a community landgrant. The judge flipped the position in the case and agreed with the lower court that property ownership could only be proven by metes and bounds. This ruling rejected the notion of common property rights and/or traditional land use and emphasized that the hijuelas (titles) did not include the Merced, that is the land held in common, and deemed the landgrant to be a private landgrant, thereby allowing it to be sold to the private sector. The judge argued that the hijuelas were only meant for the Herederos' homes, and their villages. The commons were therefore, made available for private sale, and the 600,000 acres of the Merced became free of title and available for settlement by americanos. The position of Los Nativos was that La Merced was a reserve for those original indigenous families who had settled the region for multiple generations; furthermore, they held a European form of title, a colonial legal contract held by Nuevomexicanos, and occupied for traditional use.

Los Herederos also petitioned the county to hold an election to revive La Corporación de Abiquiú Merced de Tierra Amarilla. The judge allowed the election, stipulating that it would not be official until the court ruled on the outcome of the Mundy ejection lawsuit. This of course leaves Los Herederos at a disadvantage because the Mundy ejection lawsuit takes precedence over the Herederos claim to La Merced. Moreover, the courts' ruling made the Herederos claim invalid on the grounds of not only the original intent of the hijuelas but also because the Herederos did not ever have La Merced properly surveyed.

During the trial, the judge not only continued to encourage the prosecution to develop their argument of metes and bounds but allowed the defense to focus on the pattern of land use to prove a break in the title. Mundy's attorney's focus was on the chain of title, which allowed it to be used as evidence of proof of transference. When José María and the others were questioned about their land use they explained that it depended on the condition of the land and the needs of the community, while the defendant, Mundy, kept to the argument of metes and bounds and coordinates on a map. The Court made a deliberate choice to look at all landgrants as property surveyed. At the same time, the only proof the plaintiffs (the Herederos) had was historical occupation of the land. The Herederos constructed an unquestionable argument of continual use of La Merced with physical proof as well as numerous affidavits. But the Court held that ownership was only able to be determined after the land was surveyed. The boundaries of the Herederos' hijuelas were determined by pragmatic coordinates, rendering the claim of eminent domain null and void. Thus, the court ruling favored the defendants, making Bill Mundy the sole owner of 11,000 acres of La Merced.

The judge stated that 70 years had passed since the landgrant had operated privately. There had not been a landgrant corporation before 1937 when Medardo Abeyta and the consejo were first formed. Since the corporation had been nonexistent before 1937, this would have constituted a break in title. The Court, then, allowed for the use of the hijuelas as evidence that the landgrant had always been used as a private grant, thus making the lands held in common available for sale. The twenty-five anglo ranchers filed suit against La Corporación de Abiquiú Merced de Tierra Amarilla, and Mundy's quiet title lawsuit was upheld. This decision cleared the title for Mundy and laid to rest the question of a community versus private landgrant for La Merced de Tierra Amarilla.

The Court not only ruled in Mundy's favor, but the judge addressed the Herederos, scolding them as though they were children—warning them that if anyone was found interfering with Mundy or his development of property or vandalizing any other property, they would be punished to the fullest extent of the law.

Following Mundy's victory, he took his family to Las Cruces to celebrate. While away, their newly constructed home was burned to the ground for the third time, 40 miles of fence were cut down, and haystacks were set ablaze—not only on his property but on other encroachers' properties as well. No one was ever convicted of the arson. This act did little to sway Mundy. He purchased another 12,000 acres, cleared more land for cultivation and put up even more fencing, bringing more cattle from his father's ranch in Hatch, New Mexico and Mexican families as ranch hands.

Later that year, the Payne Land & Cattle Company filed quiet title to an additional 12,000 acres of La Merced de Tierra Amarilla, just below Cerro de Los Brazos. Bernardo Rivera and other Herederos worked 7,000 acres of said property. The Payne Cattle company invoked Catron's 1883 quiet title and contacted him. Catron acknowledged that the Herederos claimed ownership of said property. Despite this evidence, the Court awarded The Payne Land and Cattle Company a warranty deed. The locals were furious with the decision—again buildings were set ablaze, fences cut, cattle shot, ranchers and businesses threatened, and vehicles and farm implements vandalized. La Mano Negra retaliated ferociously—private properties were set ablaze, and anglo-americans left, abandoning their properties.

## Blowback

The Mercederos are in a debriefing meeting on the court case they just lost. They have run out of alternatives. Exasperated, they realize that the so-called unbiased legal system has systematically failed to support indigenous people's human rights. Even with a European title, they cannot keep their homeland. A campfire just outside a community meeting house holds a large cast iron pot of posole. Another holds menudo, and in a smaller pot, there is red chile con carne. The women inside are making tortillas, cooking them on a wooden stove. They wrap them in a linen dish cloth set in a bandeja, a deep round steel porcelain covered tray used as a washbasin as well. Martín and Libertado come in holding the pot of posole with a six-foot latilla, a piñón branch without the bark five inches in diameter. They set it on the table. Indio Gerónimo follows with the chile con carne.

Gregorita calls out, "Ya está la comida." Tranquelina and Calixtra are helping in the kitchen. The Herederos form a line and are served. They take their seats. They are agitated. They cannot allow the injustice to go unanswered. People are finishing eating.

Gregorita stands in front of the dining hall:

"Les quiero cantar un corrido que compuso mi cuñado. Me parece que expresa bien cómo nos sentimos con lo que nos pasó en la corte, bien frustrados, pero tengo confianza que La Merced se nos va a retornar y finalmente, de todos modos, vamos a ser victoriosos." (I want to sing a corrido composed by my brother-in-law. I think it expresses well how we feel about what happened in court. We feel frustrated, but I am confident that in the end we will be victorious and we will finally get our landgrant back.)

She clears her throat and begins to sing without musical accompaniment.

**La Negra Cortina**

1.
*Voy a cantar unos versos*
*Y abrir la negra cortina*
*Si quieren saber lo que guardo*
*Es la liberación nuestro terreno*

1.
I'm going to sing some verses
And open the black curtain
If you want to know what I maintain
It's the liberation of our land

2.
*Esta visión es derecha y justa*
*Luchamos por nuestro pueblo*
*Toda la gente decía*
*Que tengan fé y sigan luchando*

2.
This vision is true and just
The struggle for our people
All the people would say
To have faith and keep fighting

3.
*Trabajamos por el pobre*
*Desde el grande hasta el chico*
*Para quitarles lo que es nuestro*
*Hacemos temblar a los ricos*

3.
We work for the poor
From the oldest to the youngest
To take from them what is ours
We make the rich tremble

4.
*Y si todos me permiten*

*De hablarles con la verdad*
*Trabajen con el consejo*

*Porque traemos la realidad*

4.
And if all of you will permit
me
To speak the truth
Work with the landgrant
counsel
Because we speak the truth

5.
*Yo les digo por igual*
*Robarle al pobre no vale*

*Y la mentira se esconde*
*Hasta que la verdad sale*

5.
I tell you the same
To steal from the poor is
shameful
And the lies hide
Until the truth comes out

6.
*Ya que ahora vino la realidad*

*Mandada por providencia*
*Trabajen con el consejo*

*Porque traemos la evidencia*

6.
Now that the truth has come
out
Sent by providence
Work with the landgrant
counsel
Because we have the evidence

7.
*Toditas nuestras Mercedes*
*Ya se las llevan los lobos*

*Y a nosotros nos dejaron*
*Bebiendo leche de polvo*

7.
All of our landgrants
Are being carried away by
wolves
And they left us all
Drinking powdered milk

8.
*Nomás se hace justicia*
*Con todos esos malvados*
*Yo les aseguro a ustedes*
*Que correrán como venados*

8.
When justice is done
With all those wicked people
I assure you all
That they will run like deer

| | |
|---|---|
| 9. | 9. |
| *Lo que haga este presidente* | What this president does |
| *Pronto lo vamos a ver* | We will soon see |
| *Y si no hace justicía* | And if he does not serve justice |
| *Su nombre no es LBJ* | His name is not LBJ |
| 10. | 10. |
| *Cuando compuse estos versos* | When I composed these verses |
| *Me vino de corazón* | They came from the heart |
| *Pensando en esos malvados* | Thinking about those wicked ones |
| *Que nos jugaron traición* | That played us with treachery |
| 11. | 11. |
| *Les hablo con la verdad* | I speak the truth to you |
| *Que caiga donde caiga* | I don't care where it falls |
| *Porque traigo la verdad* | Because I bring the truth |
| *Porque Diosito es nuestra corte* | Because God is our court |

## ABRIR LA NEGRA CORTINA

A Southerner-owned lumber company is awarded a lease from the U.S. Forest Service to harvest hundreds of thousands of acres of the forest in Northern New Mexico and Southern Colorado. They build a sawmill near Chama, a short distance north of Tierra Amarilla, hiring few locals, bringing in their employees from Georgia. The lumber company puts up a gate denying access to traditional pastures. Nicolás López of Plazita Blanca is headed up to his summer pasture, his trailer loaded with cattle. He is making his way around the back of Los Brazos when he finds a locked gate cutting him off from entering. He and his nephew, Sebastiano Archuleta, get out and inspect the gate.

Nicolás turns and says, "Vete a la troca y agarra la cadena."

They wrap the chain around the gate post, put the hook in front of the truck and yank the post out. They continue up through the canyon and release the cattle on the east slope of La Bandeja ("The Wash Bowl"). They drive back down the mountain to the Victory Bar in Tierra Amarilla where they find other Herederos, and Nicolás tells them what he found on the east pasture. They sound the alert, and by the end of the day a consejo meeting is being held.

José María proposes, "Ahora tenemos que reunirnos y ponernos de pie en contra de la ocupación de La Merced; he consultado con varios de ustedes y me parece que mañana estamos de acuerdo con llevar vacas a la Bandeja. Vamos a hacer campo, de modo que traigan provisiones por algunos días. Si hay alguien en contra ahora es el tiempo de decir algo." (It is time for us to unite and stand up for the occupation of the landgrant. I have been talking with many of you, and it looks like we agree to go take cattle up the Bowl tomorrow. We will make camp, so bring provisions for a few days. If there is anyone that is not in agreement, now is the time to speak up.)

He looks around. "Bueno, parece que estamos de acuerdo. Hacemos la entrada a las doce del mediodía. Bueno, nos vemos." (Well, it seems we all agree. We will get started at noon. See you then.)

The meeting is adjourned. Some mill around and talk. Still others leave to get prepared. José María, Indio, y Libertado leave together. They get ready, hitch up the trailer, and back it up to the corral. Then they go into the house to have supper and Indio Gerónimo takes out the rifles and cleans them. José María goes into the bedroom and comes out with three boxes of bullets. Libertado is outside his house putting his rifle in his truck.

The next morning, on the drive up the dirt road, they see that the gate is reset, and sawmill workers are armed to the teeth, ready for a fight. Deputy Sheriff Dan Rivera and his partner, Undersheriff

Jaramillo, are speeding down the highway. Siren's screech, lights flash. They reach the turnoff onto a county road, arriving just behind the Herederos. The sheriff hits his breaks hard, kicking up a cloud of dust. They get out of the patrol car and hurry towards the standoff. Sheriff Jaramillo stands a short distance away from the ruckus. "Okay, men what's going on?" He turns to the Herederos, "¿Qué está pasando? ¿José María, qué piensas hacer? Más vale que no hagas lo que estoy pensando, no te quiero llevar a la cárcel por una matanza, hablaré con ellos a ver si podemos resolver la situación." (What's going on? ... José María, what do you think you're doing? You better not do what it looks like, I do not want to take you to jail for killing, let me talk with them and see if we can resolve this situation.)

He goes over to the americano sawmill workers. "Okay, what's the problema?"

"I'll tell you what's going on, those damn Mesicans think they own the mountain. We have a federal contract to harvest lumber from this mountain, and we have orders from our boss not to allow anyone up here. And hell will freeze over before we allow these damn people on our land."

"Look mister, those vaqueros have been running cattle on those pastures up there long before you boys ever showed up. Now, we don't want a blood bath to ensue, and I'm telling you that is what is going to happen. Have you looked up on that ridge to your left?" The americanos look into the sun. It is blinding, but a rough silhouette of armed men can be seen. Sheriff Rivera calmly tells the americanos to lay their rifles down and allow the rancheros through. Tensions ease, and the spokesman orders one of the men to open the gate. José María and the others get into their trucks.

Pedro, Libertado, and Indio stand guard on the ridge with Sebastiano and Libertado, rifles in hand. Several hours later the three of them make it into camp at the edge of a mountain. Cattle are eating from the vega (pasture), on the campfire beans and chile are warming. "¿Eh, al fin llegaron los muchachos? ¿Tienen hambre?" Nicolás asks (Hey, the boys finally got here. Are you hungry?)

"Ya, ¿cómo que si tenemos hambre? No hemos comido en todo el día," Sebastiano answers. (Yeah, what do you mean are we hungry? We haven't had anything to eat all day.)

They dismount, unsaddle their horses, and let them water and pasture with the cattle while they serve themselves a plate of chile with elk meat, papas, and beans.

"¿Tío Nicolás, has oído la historia de los compadres que fueron para California de Nuevo México? Consiguieron buen trabajo, y al día de pago iban a la cantina a cambiar los cheques, comer y echarse su traguito, ¿verdad? ¿Bueno, había esta vez que uno de los compadres estaba muy calladito y los compadres le preguntaron, ¿qué es lo que tienes, porqué estás tan calladito? (Uncle Nicolás, have you heard the story of the brothers that went to California from New Mexico? And they got good jobs and on pay day they would go to the bar to cash their checks, eat, and have a few drinks, right? Okay, there was this time that one of the brothers was really quiet and the brothers asked what was wrong, why was he so quiet?)

And he answers them, "Extraño mucho mi país." (I really miss my homeland.)

One of his compadres answers, "Ay no, compa, ¿cómo puedes decir eso? Mira el clima, siempre está bonito, fresco. Allá en Nuevo México está frío y puro trabajar partiendo leña, componiendo cercos, batallando con el ganado en el monte. Y aquí en Califas las muchachas, ay que bellas son. Compa, ¿qué tienes? No, no, compa, te apuesto todo el cheque que la vida está tan mejor aquí que en Nuevo México," (¿Oh no compa, how can you say that? Look at the climate, it's always nice here, fresh, and over there it's cold and nothing but work cutting wood, fixing fences, struggling with the animals in the mountains. And here in California, the women are beautiful. No, no, brother, I will bet you all my check that life is better here than in Nuevo Mexico.) They put the money on the table.

The brother who was sad took a piece of tortilla, tore two pieces, scooped up the food and put it in his mouth. He did the same again. He turned and told them, "Miren, está tan buena la vida en nuestro país que usamos una fresca tortilla como cuchara con cada boquita de comida." (Look how much better life back home is, we use a fresh tortilla for a spoon for every mouth of food.)

He gathered the money on the table and went back home to New Mexico. Y así me lo dijeron a mí.

Everyone in the camp laughs. "Sí es cierto que tenemos buena vida aquí en la sierra," answers Nicolás. (Everybody in the camp laughed, yes that's right we have a good life here in the mountains.)

A few weeks later, the Chama sawmill is burned down. Infuriated owners have their goons go into the local bar looking for those responsible for the arson. This only escalates into a fight. The americanos are run out of town.

## ZARA ARRIVES IN TIERRA AMARILLA

Cecilia Porfín of Mesa Poleo, Southwest of Tierra Amarilla, gets to know Zara in a San Antonio Pentecostal Bible school, and shortly thereafter, she meets her soon-to-be-husband, Uvaldo Velasques, from Youngsville, formerly known as Coyote, a village not far from where she grew up. Uvaldo and Zara talk about the landgrants. Later, Zara comes to New Mexico with a Pentecostal mentor to preach. This is when he learns more about the landgrants.

Zara leaves but returns just after the court case between La Merced de Tierra Amarilla and the Mundy lawsuits. Zara continues to do his own research and talks to anyone who knows anything about landgrants. Zara's ability to politicize Biblical rhetoric strikes at the very heart of the Penitental heartland in Northern New Mexico. The silent undercurrent of racial-ethnic subjectivity between Anglos and Mexicanos has reached an all-time high, threatening to erupt at any given moment. Nativos come to a greater collective consciousness of understanding the extent of how race and ethnic relations have affected their lives. With the national civil rights movement gaining momentum, landgrant activists begin to better understand the power of collective action. As in other social justice movements, landgrant activists learn about collective action to redress injustice. They also come to understand court bias and how it has resulted in their dispossession. Zara continues to learn all he can about the landgrant issue, developing an argument of equality and citizenship. As Zara is doing research, he discovers the law of Las Indias and how it addresses citizenship and human rights for the indigenous peoples of the New World. He connects the loss of the landgrants to the Treaty of Guadalupe-Hidalgo and how the treaty sanctioned indigenous rights to citizenship—to los hijos de alguien (children of somebody) - indigenous Native Indians and genízaro-mestizo people of racial-ethnic mixed heritage—thereby lending credence to their right to the land and full citizenship.

Once again, Herederos de La Merced sends an emissary to Washington, D.C. where they meet with Robert Kennedy. They explain the history of land loss to him, but they neither communicate it well nor does Kennedy fathom the enormity of what they are talking about. The thought of land lost on such a large scale was too much for him to comprehend, so he never responded to their request for an inquiry.

Zara convinces the Aliancistas that they need to go to Mexico City to plead with the president to assist them with the retrieval of the landgrants. The inner circle of Herederos stays behind to organize as they had in the 1930s. They generate a mailing list of land encroachers and send them notice to vacate La Merced. Raymond Spill, another land grabber, raises the United States flag on his property, visible just off the highway. This gesture mocks the locals. He quietly amasses a ranch of 686,000 acres from La Merced de Tierra Amarilla y La Merced San Joaquin del Rio Chama and the Pierda Lumbre Grant. It's not long before he, too, finds dead cattle and fencing torn down.

# CHAPTER THREE

## La Sangre de Cristo

ZARA'S BROTHERS, PORFIRIO and Narciso, and their close comrade-in-arms, Feliciano Martínez, go to San Luis, Colorado, after hearing about the beating of local Mexicano vaqueros by the ranch hands of James T. Taylor. In the late 1950s, Taylor had quite titled 77,524 acres of the Sangre de Cristo Landgrant, which lies in Colorado and New Mexico. The property in question is known as "La Sierra" by the locals, who sued to regain the mountain took fifty years to hear the case. In spite of the obvious fact that the inhabitants had been working the land since the early 19th century, the Herederos found themselves displaced. Taylor took possession of the property, bringing in his own people to manage it. He began to harvest lumber in response to the post-war housing boom across the nation. Furthermore, with his Southern upbringing came a boastfulness of antebellum superiority. His workers' attitudes reflected his values. He immediately set out to fence the entire mountain. Putting up no trespassing signs, he began to impound local cattle that would wander onto La Sierra before he had completed the fencing. Taylor dealt with the trespassers heavy-handedly, severely beating locals if found on the property.

On Thanksgiving Day in 1962, Tomás Real and two other vaqueros rode into La Sierra in search of strayed cattle. The vaqueros were having lunch when they were found and accosted by Taylor's ranch hands who accused them of vandalizing a bulldozer. One man stayed on his horse pointing a rifle at the baffled vaqueros while the others dismounted and beat the men with their rifle butts. They made the Herederos walk several miles to the ranch house. Taylor gave them another beating and had them thrown into the bed of his pick-up truck. Then he drove them to the courthouse, which housed the Sheriff's office and jail. He tossed them onto the courthouse steps and demanded the Sheriff arrest them for trespassing. Instead, the Mexicano Deputy Sheriff took them to the doctor, and by the next day, an angry crowd had formed, demanding that the men responsible be charged for the beating. That evening, a town hall meeting was called. The Mayor and Sheriff are present and did their best to appease the natives. The angry crowd continues to demand justice. Zara and his entourage enter the meeting in progress. Zara delivers a blistering condemnation of anglo treatment towards the local population. This intensifies an already heated crowd. They begin to condemn Taylor's racist southern attitude, and these indigenous Spanish-speaking people of the United States Southwest demand justice. They demand that the police and anglo mayor take the men responsible for the beatings and put them in jail. Anglo authorities are apologetic, assuring the Mexicanos that justice will be served and that the men responsible will answer for their behavior. On this trip the Mexicanos begin to talk about forming an organization to include all the landgrant, calling it La Alianza Federal de Mercedes.

In February 1963, the Alianza Federal de Mercedes was formally organized. Their first meeting was held at Davis Hall on North 4th Street and Alameda, a ranching community north of Albuquerque. The Alianza was symbolically incorporated on February 2, the same day El Tratado de Guadalupe Hidalgo was signed in 1848. Zara filed their Articles of Incorporation eight months later, in October 1963. Shortly thereafter, during the New Mexico legislative session of 1964, a memorial bill to address the landgrant issue is introduced. As they had done in the 1930s, on October 20, 1964, the Consejo de la Corporación de Abiquiú Merced de Tierra Amarilla and the Alianza mailed eviction notices to anglo ranchers living on the Tierra Amarilla (TA) and San Joaquín de Río Chama landgrants. They also filed a lawsuit against the Payne Land and Cattle Company. At the same time, federal and local governments instituted a policy that affected the livelihood of the landgrant community. Landgrant heirs could no longer gather firewood to warm their homes and cook, nor could they access pasture for their livestock. Yet, they are seeing outsiders invading their homeland, becoming millionaires, harvesting lumber on land that belonged to them, and getting grazing permits to bring in large herds of cattle.

Federal and local governments formed policies to manage the commons by establishing the Taylor Grazing Act of 1934 (unrelated to James Taylor who purchased La Sierra). By the 1950's, the Forest Service, Game and Fish Department, Bureau of Land Management, and the National Forest Service had displaced the Herederos from their land. In turn, these agencies began leasing public land to companies and individuals who were from other parts of the country. This not only included timber companies but also companies that specialized in the extraction of oil and other minerals from the land. The grazing permits were sold to outsiders who then subleased them to locals at inflated prices.

By the 1950s, a clear pattern had been established. Indigenous communities had been relegated to subordinate status and now could not participate with the anglos equally in this new boom economy. Court biased judges were systematically ruling in favor of anglo land encroachers, giving them quiet title to the Merced. Companies like Duke City and Baldridge Lumber got special concessions to harvest lumber. The companies contracted local workers and also brought in outside workers as fulltime employees. Small local mills were put out of business. The local economy was negatively affected. Unrest persisted as the Nativos lost control of natural resources and could not attain social mobility equally to americanos. Tensions continued escalating in the countryside and urban centers as people struggled for self-determination. At the same time, in reaction to a racially ordered society, a large segment of Native New Mexicans who called themselves Hispanics attempted to accommodate and assimilate into anglo culture. In other words, to become more "American."

## ALFONSO SÁNCHEZ DEFENDS CIVIL RIGHTS 1958

Alfonso Sánchez has just graduated from the University of New Mexico Law School and is looking forward to starting his practice. Although he never completely comprehends the extent of the sociopolitical dynamics of the era, Alfonso is not unscathed by the civil rights movement. He finds opportunities as a lawyer and begins his practice by taking cases involving social justice issues.

Alfonso Sánchez attends an American GI-Forum meeting chaired by Vicente Jiménez, who worked for the Bureau of Business and Research at the University of New Mexico. Jiménez goes through the agenda while other veterans discuss the purchase of bosque land near

Old Town in Albuquerque. They are looking at plans to construct a building for the organization. He files a lawsuit on behalf of the American GI-Forum against the City of Albuquerque for discriminatory practices for failing to promote Mexican-Americans to management positions. Sánchez also prepares a complaint on behalf of the GI Forum addressing sanitation and clean water needs in the Mexicano barrios of Albuquerque.

When the meeting ends, Jiménez, announces Sánchez's graduation from law school and tells the group that he has been offered a position to work as an assistant in the State District Attorney's office in Northwestern New Mexico. Everyone congratulates him. He announces that he will remain as the GI Forum legal advisor. As Sánchez settles into his new part-time job he begins to understand the degree of unrest that exists in Northern New Mexico. Anglo encroachment on land is intense. Native communities are fighting with all means necessary to keep control of their Merced. The ongoing problems of the landgrants and continual problems with vandalism in Río Arriba County are at an all-time high. Many of the landgrant cases filed years earlier are coming to be heard.

The Tierra Amarilla Courthouse proudly stands out as the most prominent edifice of anglo presence in the Chama Valley. The United States flag proudly flaps in the wind from the top of the building. Remnants of a once-bustling western town, Tierra Amarilla is today little more than a ghost town. Horse railings still line the road in town. Abandoned mercantile stores; a 1930s-style theater, still open, shows Mexican films from the golden era of Mexican cinema; cantinas sporadically line the street with Mexican music and local rancheros talk and playing dominos. Benjamín Naranjo, the Sheriff of the County, is talking to his Deputy Sheriff, Dan Rivera in his office on the first floor of the courthouse. Judge Scarborough is presiding over a court case on the second floor. Alfonso is standing next to his clients, José Rivera, Estacio Archuleta, José María Martínez, Nicolás López, and Manuel and Cruz Aguilar are all standing before the judge. The courtroom is filled to capacity.

Then La Merced attorney addresses the Court, "Judge, my clients' families have a European title of a community landgrant deeded to approximately 600 families of predominantly Native but acculturated in Spanish provenance who have been running cattle and sheep in these mountains for the past hundred and fifty years. The United States of America issued a patent to the Herederos, many of whom had Ute, Navajo, Apache, Pueblo, and Hispanic ancestry and heritage. The people of Tierra Amarilla and surrounding communities are being forced off their homeland, being denied grazing permits. Your honor, they are not even able to gather firewood on land that has been in continual use by them. Yes, Judge, on behalf of my clients I submit evidence that the land was granted as a community landgrant and has been in continual use by the heirs of the Tierra Amarilla Landgrant since before 1836, and that Bernardo Rivera has been paying taxes on 7,700 acres of what the Arlington Land & Cattle Company claim of 11,000 acres of said land."

The judge pauses and looks around the courtroom filled with Mexican Americans, people whose survival he knows depends on his decision. He picks up his gavel and announces, "Ladies and gentlemen of the court, this is a matter for the federal government. Therefore, I am going to rule in favor of the Arlington Land & Cattle Company. It will be up to the plaintiffs to appeal my decision."

Bam! He slams the gavel. "This court is adjourned."

The Herederos are both shocked and angered with the outcome.

That evening the members of the landgrant council are sitting around a campfire discussing the outcome of their case. Gregorita

Aguilar stands up and announces a corrido she wants to sing that her brother-in-law Manuel composed. She sips some water, pauses, clears her throat, and announces the title of the corrido:

**Les Viene por Herencia**

1.
*Voy a cantar estos versos*
*Y a darles un por menor*
*Que estas tristes leyes*
*Son pura traición*

1.
I'm going to sing these verses
And give you a short account
That these sad laws
Are pure treachery

2.
*La Merced de Tierra Amarilla*
*Está al norte del estado*
*Y las leyes están muy malas*
*Nos tienen crucificados*

2.
The landgrant of Tierra Amarilla
It's in the north of the state
And the laws are very bad
They have us crucified

3.
*Estoy en favor de la ley*
*Pero que hagan su deber*
*Que juez y abogado*
*Se acaban de vender*

3.
I'm in favor of the law
But they should do their duty
That judges and lawyers
Stop selling themselves out

4.
*Hispanohablantes Mexicanos*
*Los tengo de corazón*
*El que trabaja para el diablo*
*No tiene compasión*

4.
Spanish-speaking Mexicans
I have you in my heart
The one who works for the devil
Has no compassion

5.
*A ustedes les pertenece*
*Les viene por herencia*
*Y las leyes se venden*
*Por una triste licencia*

5.
It belongs to you
It comes to you by inheritance
And the laws are for sale
For a sad license

| | |
|---|---|
| 6. | 6. |
| *Cuiden bien su casa* | Take good care of your homes |
| *Cuiden del enemigo* | Beware of the enemy |
| *Que estas tristes leyes* | Because these sad laws |
| *Protegen al capitalismo* | Protect capitalism |
| 7. | 7. |
| *Dios ponga todos sus medios* | May God make all his resources available |
| *Con una justa razón* | With justifiable reason |
| *Y a nosotros nos bendiga* | And my he bless use |
| *Nos hace su bendición* | May he give us his blessing |
| 8. | 8. |
| *Ya con esto me despido* | With this I take my leave |
| *Tengo mucho que decir* | I have a lot to say |
| *A ver cuando les puedo decir* | We see when I can tell you |
| *Cuiden bien su porvenir* | Take care of your future |

The corrido states that they are no fools and that they understand the legal system is not representative of the people but exists for the wealthy. The implication is to be aware of what is happening to their homeland and to be loyal to their ethnic heritage. Family and community members applaud her performance. People talk and reflect on the history they made. Although they are discontented with the outcome, they discuss what to do next.

Señora López, "Esos gringos hacen papeles para ellos mismos, sirven nomás para ellos, y para nosotros, que nos pertenece La Merced, los que tenemos patente del gobierno federal no sirve...no es justo eso, no es justo - este país está hecho por una bola de desgraciados." (Those anglos make documents for themselves, they are only good for them, and for us, who the landgrant belongs to, who have a claim from the federal government, is worthless...this is not justice - this country is made up of a bunch of disgraceful people.)

José María, "Así como dice el corrido - el que trabaja por el Diablo no tiene compasión, las leyes se venden por una triste licencia protegiendo el capitalismo." (As the ballad says, the work of the devil doesn't have compassion; the laws are for sale for a sad license that is only for protection of capitalism.)

Miguel Aguilar, "Entonces, ¿qué vamos hacer? ¡Ya no tenemos con qué más que la justicia de Dios espíritu (Then what are we to do? We have no other recourse except for the justice of God.)

### Libertado y Martín Van por Leña

Libertado's home is high up against Canjilón Mountain, just below a ridge overlooking the village. He starts up his truck, and walks back into the house. His young wife is in the kitchen pouring them both a cup of coffee.

Libertado, "Eeeeh, está frío, pero 'orita cuando sale el sol se va poner bonito el día. ¿No miras que claro está el cielo? Voy ir a cañones, me estaba diciendo Tobías que había mucha leña seca." (Eheeh, it's getting cold but once the sun is out the day will be nice. Just look at how clear the sky is. I will be going to Cañones, Tobías was saying that there was a lot of dry wood.) He gives his wife a kiss. "Debería de estar en casa para las cinco de la tarde," he tells her. (I should be at home by five this afternoon.)

Libertado finishes his coffee and leaves the house. The axe is on the porch. He takes it and puts it in the back of the truck, and gets in and drives down towards the village to pick up Martín.

Martín is putting on his boots. His mother is in the kitchen stirring beans and warming tortillas over a wood stove. He looks over to his bed, admiring his young bride, her long black hair radiating a midnight blue as it cascades over her shoulders and down her lower back across her hips. Her body glows as the kerosene lamp flickers in the bedroom. When he hears the truck in the distance, Martín looks around for his flannel work shirt and walks into the kitchen.

Martín says, "Buenos días, mamá."

Martín's mother replies, "Apúrate, ya viene Libertado. Aquí tienes un lonchecito, ten cuidado con estos jarritos de café, allí tienes para ti y Libertado - los miro en la tarde." (Hurry up. Libertado is coming. Here you have a lunch, be careful there are jars with coffee and you have enough for Libertado as well - I will see you this evening.)

Martín answers, "Bien, bien mamá, nos miramos en la tarde."

He takes a small five-pound bag of flour to carry his lunch and leaves.

Libertado le dice, "Tráete herramientas, por si acaso se nos pincha una llanta o algo." (Bring tools in case we get a flat tire.)

Martín hands the lunch to Libertado through the window of the truck and goes to his 1967 Super Sport. He gets the tire jack and estrella (the star) lug wrench, throws them in the back of the truck, and gets in. They head toward the canyon, passing la Morada.

## INDIO GERÓNIMO GOES ON THE MIGRANT TRAIL

It's sunrise. In the kitchen a woman in her late sixties stokes the fire in a wood stove where beans are warming. She makes fresh flour tortillas while hydrating green chiles on the stove along with elk jerky.

"Levántese m'ijo, ya es tiempo, te van a estar esperando y quiero que comas algo antes de que te vayas." (Get up, son, it's time, and they will be waiting for you and I want you to have something to eat before you go.)

Indio Gerónimo turns over in bed, looking around the room. It's going to be some time before he sees it again. He drifts in and out of consciousness, lying in his bed and seeing his life unfold in a surrealistic dream state. Hard work lies before him in the beet fields of Colorado. Then he and his fellow workers will go to southeastern New Mexico to pick cotton, chile, and onions, making their way to the Rio Grande valley. The comfort of his bed will be unknown to him for the next few months. He struggles to lift his heavy torso from bed. The warm velas dimly light his mother's room illuminating her bedroom altar. The smell of tortillas y chile and the scent of cedro (cedar) burning from the stove makes his stomach quiver with hunger. As he approaches the kitchen, he smells the coffee as it percolates, the aromas making him salivate as he nips his tongue, taking a sip of water from a pail.

His mother, Calixtra, says, "Aquí tienes unos burritos." (Here you have some burritos).

Indio sips his coffee while sitting at the kitchen table.

"Bueno, vamos a empezar en Colorado cosechando betabeles y acabar la pisca en Las Cruces con la cebolla. Cuando regrese voy a tener con que arreglar el tractor, mamá." (Okay, we are going to start in Colorado picking beets and finish in Las Cruces picking onions. By then we should have enough to fix the tractor, mother.)

He stands up, puts on his coat, and takes a pillowcase filled with his belongings. It's still dark out. The porch lights glimmer in the distance. Indio walks towards his tío José María. A pretty young girl, Fátima, the sister of his closest friend, joins them. Her father was an Indian captive and her is mother from Española. Indio Gerónimo perks up. He hadn't realized that she would be joining them. They load a few more supplies onto the truck. Fátima struggles to throw her bedding onto the truck, Indio Gerónimo helps her. Everyone gets in their vehicles and drives down the twisting, turning road as they make their way out of Canjilón across the creek up to the main road. The twists and turns on the road cause Fátima to slide on the seat against Indio. He looks at her and smiles as they pass La Morada.

## LA MORADA

The Morada is a sacred place of prayer for the religious fraternity popularly known as Los Penitentes. Their official name is La Cofradía de Nuestro Jesús Nazareno. They were first recognized in the late 18th century by Bishop Zubiría, and they addressed themselves as Hermanos de Nuestra Cofradía de Jesús de Nazareno, i.e., Hermanos, the popular term is "Penetentes."

Los Penitentes is an Hermandad, a brotherhood that dedicates itself to the caring of the downtrodden. Hermanos pray and meditate during Lent. It's a time for spiritual renewal. These men are recognized as the bearers of New Mexico tradition because they evolved independently of institutional religion. They developed as a distinctive grass-roots form of spirituality, and their distinctive mannerisms and expressions have resulted in a worldview that has come to be recognized as Nuevomexicano. A people who believes in the message of Jesus and through their firm faith, these frontier people shaped their own brand of Christianity with little to no interference from the Catholic Church.

They adhered to a spiritual worldview of Caridad (caring) that has not always aligned itself with the Catholic Church but has developed as a highly ritualized devotion to the Stations of the Cross, with a symbolic reenactment of the passion death and resurrection of Jesus. This is emblematic of their personal lives and has endured in this region since the introduction of Christianity in 1598. No matter how impossible life may seem to them, they have learned from the example of the Passion that there is a resurrection for a new beginning. That lent ends on Friday of Holy week is recognized with the ritual of tinieblas (darkness) signifying the moment Jesus died on the cross. This symbolically teaches us that we complete our cleansing of the sorrows and distresses we all go through in our daily lives.

This is how they came to understand and interpret Christianity, by singing the melancholy alabado that transcends to a meditative prayer. The alabados are stories of Jesus that focus on the time from his capture to the crucifixion while also venerating the blessed mother. The alabados not only served to teach the indigenous people the Spanish language but psychologically served as a pious doctrine with which to exploit the colonized.

The colonial sociopolitical conditions of that time arose as a result of European-Spanish contact that forever changed the worldview of the region. The introduction of the Catholic Church was the second phase of the colonial process. After combing the countryside for riches, the Spanish soon realized that the entire region had little to offer other than its natural resources. Once the colonizers established military dominion, they set out to dismantle the spiritual worldview of its conquered people imposing their God as superior.

They began the process of both Christianizing the indigenous population and teaching them a common language, Spanish, to have a viable working force. This begins with the deconstruction of the indigenous spiritual worldview to one that imposes their God as superior to all others for the purpose of controlling a colonized population. The indigenous people of the region were taught to pray in the colonizers' language and use of scripture as a form of indoctrination.

They legitimized piety, thereby warranting the colonizers' dominion. The alabado is based on scripture that is sung and was used as a method of teaching the conquered the language of the conqueror while at the same time teaching them a pious doctrine. But today the culture of la Hermandad and its focus on the stations of the cross has meaning in their personal lives and the lives of their community members. It encompasses self-empowerment, understanding that the life of Jesus is a microcosm of our own lives. The passion imitates the path in our life experiences. We all go through our own trials and tribulations only to resurrect and continue the spiritual red road of Jesus' teachings.

Neither Diocesan nor Parish Priests gained a foothold until the late 20th century. The Catholic Church's success in acculturating its indigenous population into Spanish-Mexican society was the first stage of colonization.

It wasn't until the 1950-60s that Nuevomexicanos were fast tracked into mainstream society. Their heritage language, Spanish, is in the process of being replaced by English (the language of the conqueror). Although this process of language differentiation began in the 16th century, the early stages of capitalist development shifted the world view of the region for both Native American Indians and the colonial empires.

A second phase occurred with the Post-Civil War era. New Mexico was and still is considered disputed territory; Nuevo México had been inhabited by Europeans and Indigenous people. It was the most densely populated area of the annexed territories. The displacement of Mexicanos was unprecedented.

In the 1890s, the war for control of the region was the most violent. Post-Civil War migration brought many former Confederate and Union soldiers into the region. New Mexico already had a well-established society of Spanish-Mexican-Indigenous peoples. This caused New Mexico to be a hotly contested territory. Nativo Nuevomexicanos' unyielding defense of their right to self-preservation and americanos' thirst for control of the region's natural resources set the stage for economic and cultural conflict. These sociopolitical and cultural conditions contributed to an independent, indigenous form of Christianity. The Cofradía began as a teaching method and evolved into a liberatory form of spiritual empowerment, independent of the Catholic Church while maintaining a cordial relationship with the Church. The Hermanos maintain their independence. The community is in charge of how they practice their faith, preserving the rituals and prayers brought with Christianity to Las Americas and becoming imbedded in their belief system as a frontier cooperative of spirituality.

The idea of the cosmic race was reborn as the civil rights movement gained momentum, inspiring Chicanos to celebrate all that is positive about their heritage. The Euro worldview had placed these people into a subordinate position. The Law of the Indies is a body of laws formed in reaction to the inhumane treatment of indigenous people, which was initiated during the early years of colonization. The sociopolitical, religious, and economic lives of the people of the Spanish territories, del nuevo mundo, decreed that the indigenous people of the New World were human. They, therefore, attained the right to citizenship. These people have been referred to as La Raza Cósmica, a phrase coined by José Vasconcelos in 1925. The word Raza (race) was used in the Old World as a reference to animals. The Spanish used the word Raza in the New World when referring to indigenous peoples. Today's worldview has embraced the word to reference all human beings, thereby making it possible for all people de la Raza Cósmica to fully participate in mainstream society. Legally, this meant they were able to acquire land and govern themselves. The origins of this idea began with Bartolomé de la Casas, a Jesuit priest, who vehemently defended the human rights of indigenous people de las Américas. He was instrumental in enacting what can be recognized as the first human rights law in the New World.

From 1592 to 1680, the Spanish attempted to establish, as they had in Mexico and Latin America, a feudal system of rancherías y encomiendas. This sociopolitical and economic system failed to succeed. Notwithstanding, one must consider that at this time New Mexico was not only Spain's most remote northern frontier but had little to offer monetarily. Coupled with indigenous religious subordination, these sociopolitical conditions led to the 1680 Pueblo Revolt. Twelve years later the Spanish negotiated a resettlement of the region with allowances for religious expression and a greater degree of economic and sociopolitical autonomy for native peoples. The Genízaro and Mestizo populations established settlements alongside the Pueblos and the further reaching indigenous communities of the frontier. The Genízaros structured their sacred space using the paradigm designed by the Spanish religious fraternity and incorporating elements of the indigenous spiritual world view, thus allowing a unique grassroots form of spirituality to emerge. As the process of Christianization evolved, the indigenous people left their tribal groups to form their own communities. The priests made occasional trips to those communities, but with the waning global power of the Spanish empire the Catholic Church was unable to send younger priests to the area. This made it difficult to provide spiritual direction to the people, and the religious vacuum created left them to fend for themselves where they developed an ideology of their own.

In reaction to this spiritual vacuum, Nuevomexicanos embraced their Christian foundation, allowing for their own spiritual worldview to emerge through a highly elaborate form of ritual expression.

The stations of the cross became a microcosmic expression of the individual tests and misfortunes of our daily lives. Those struggles we all face in our daily lives will pass, and we will resurrect anew—like a Phoenix from the ashes with an elixir in hand, the prize of strength and wisdom lies within each and every person's grasp. To share and help others, so long as one can maintain faith in the example left by

Jesus, one can work through their own hardships and move forward toward a new beginning. This is the lesson replayed every Lenten season, a purging of the past and present experiences that one may have gone through or is going through. This is the substance of faith - knowing that one's prayers have been answered is to purge any negative thoughts from our lives. One only needs the patience to allow spirit to work through each, and everyone's prayers so they may come to fruition. Through complete surrender of heart and mind—spirit and soul will offer comfort, and whatever the outcome maybe it is as it should be. Reverence is to accept it as it is. This is what is meant by walking the good red road of the creator of all that is. The indigenous worldview is that we are all connected to all that is in the world and the cosmos

One has to prepare for prayer in order for it to work. That is, one has to pray from God, not to God. The key to understanding prayer is to know how the law of cause and effect operates, knowing that whatever you set your heart's desire on, so long as it doesn't affect others negatively, will come to be. One could call this faith, not blind faith, but directed faith. This is what happens when the Hermanos pray together in this highly ritualized form, and through these practices, they do their best to lead a life of caring for their fellow human beings. Prayer may not be manifested in the form one prays for. However, the spirit will act on what one focuses their thoughts on. Therein lies the strength of prayer and meditation; one's connection to the spirit of God from within is to pray from God, not to God. This moves the human psyche into a luminous space, a threshold crossing from the ordinary world to a sacred one, where the kinetic energy in the brain—the synapses of the mind—stimulate the consciousness of thought. The process of prayer helps one cross the threshold from the ordinary world to the sacred. Ritual has the same effect. Together, these practices transcend the secular to the sacred, the mundane to the spiritual, becoming one with God in spirit, caressing the soul awakening one to follow his or her bliss.

The Hermanos' legacy is a testament to these people's continual presence in a land filled with intrigue and hardship. As the spiritual backbone of the community, La Cofradia provides a sanctuary for spiritual meditation and cleansing, a meditative space removed from the ordinary world and its many distractions from which to reset the individuals' lives and priorities. It plays a crucial role during times of sociopolitical duress. To gain a grip on the chaos that tends to disrupt their mundane lives, the dual nature of the sacred and the secular in a world of competing worldviews provides a social structure that has allowed Nuevomexicanos to survive and preserve their ethnic identity in the midst of the most powerful nation that has ever been known to the history of mankind to date. Upon his arrival to the New Mexico territory, the first American archbishop, Jean Baptiste Lamy, came to view the Hermandad as a primitive form of Catholic religious expression. As the representative of the Catholic Church for the region, he set out to eradicate the Hermandad, but he failed to realize the power of their resolve. Archbishop Lamy began by importing French priests from his native homeland, excommunicating local priests who failed to adhere to his every whim. He also imposed a French style of religion, importing statues and designing churches in a baroque architecture common in Europe, in addition to demeaning all forms of indigenous religious expressions, setting the stage for the dismantling of the Nativo Nuevomexicano spiritual worldview. The full wrath of the "American" contemporary Catholic Church continued with the second Archbishop Salpointe doing all he could to shift the focus of the church away from the Hermandad. One method they used was replacing the local Santos with the fabricated ones from the east coast and Europe, and replacing the altars, again with the baroque style so familiar to those found back east and in Europe. The Hermandad, however, vehemently held fast to its belief system despite Lamy having excommunicated all the New Mexico priests. His direct assault at the very nerve center of a people's spiritual worldview delivered a heavy blow, but despite all this adversity the Hermanos have persisted and continue to exist even today.

Although spiritual expression is a window into the soul of the human psyche, it is amplified during ceremony. The rituals express the compassion and love one has for their families and community. From this practice, one focuses on service and spiritual teachings and the well-being of community, while challenging humanity to act for the betterment of all. The challenge has been to get those people of privilege to recognize social ills as they manifest in mainstream society. Social change is always difficult. For the most part, people cling to what they are familiar with, but not necessarily what is best for them or others.

To promote productive social change one has to remain vigilant to ensure that the shackles of illusion are forever broken. As the message of the Sermon on the Mount states, "Blessed are those that stand forth and defend the persecuted and for justice." It's mankind's duty to do what is best for all involved and to follow their moral duty with truth. This is what one finds with the Hermanos as they held fast to their belief system, drawing on the power of collective behavior to confront injustice even by the Catholic Church. A most subtle form of dissident behavior sternly lay at the center of the state capital as a beacon to Lamy's legacy. The Cathedral and its lack of spires that should be rising up from the Cathedral bell towers, and its lack of a staircase leading to the balcony, are testaments to the community's defiance of the exorbitant cost of its construction and the dismantling of the people's church. Unprecedented hardship upon the indigenous, Christianized Nativo Nuevomexicano people is well-documented, particularly during the mid-19th century. The bell towers were never completed because the people of New Mexico were defiantly opposed to providing the necessary funds. Lamy passed away before the Cathedral was completed. The community was bitter towards the French bishop for the way he treated Los Hermanos and for imposing mandatory tithes for the sacraments.

# CHAPTER FOUR

## Migrant Camp

PEOPLE ARE PACKING UP their vehicles. They are following the migrant trail through Colorado. Wagons are filled with beets. The owner is behind a table, paying people standing in a line. Indio Gerónimo is behind his tío José María.

The ranch owner counts out, "Twenty, forty, sixty, eighty, a hundred, ten, one-two-three-four-five dollars and twenty-five cents.

José María, in a heavy Spanish accent, "This is not enough. You suppose to pay more."

Ranch Owner, "Not today, Pancho. You are working slow this year. I can't pay you anymore.

Now move on. I still have a lot of people behind you." Indio Gerónimo steps up beside his tío.

Indio Gerónimo, "Look, we have always been paid twenty cents a bushel. That's what you paid last year and the year before, why so little now? And you paid those whites thirty-five cents a bushel.

José María, "Vámonos, no quiero problemas." (Let's go, I don't want any problems.)

Indio Gerónimo, "¡No! Tío, he owes you more."

Tío José María, "Yes I know, let's go."

Ranche Owner, "Well, you never mind what I pay others. Your old man is slowing down, and the price of beets has gone down too."

Indio Gerónimo, "Do you know that man has a silver and bronze star from WWII. My dad gave his life saving a bunch of you gringos, "primo," in Korea and you're telling me that our work isn't worth as much as gringos."

Rancher Owner, "You never mind what I pay someone else. Now here's, your pay. Get out of here. Indio Gerónimo takes his money and grabs the Rancher by the shirt collar. Two gooneys standing beside the Rancher grab Indio Gerónimo and hit him, throw him to the ground, and kick him. He gets up and hits one of them. They retaliate by brutally beating him up. One of them slaps him in the head with a leaded leather strap. Indio Gerónimo falls over unconscious. Two other men hold José María, while the other braceros move towards the fight.

Ranch Owner, "Now, José, you get the crazy Indian out of here! I don't want to ever see you or your family around here again!"

Humiliated and dishonored, José María understands this is not the moment to fight. He helps his nephew up and takes him to the truck.

José María, "M'ija," he tells Fátima, "start up the truck. I'll be right back."

He calmly takes his whip and cane from the gun rack of the cab, leaving the rifle. Indio is sitting in the cab with a rag holding his bleeding head. José María calmly walks back while Fátima sits behind the wheel with the truck running. The goonies step towards him; he snaps the whip around the legs of the one who threw him to the ground and slashes the ranch owner across the face cutting him with the whip. The other goony backs off. The first goony gets up, and José María beats him with his cane. He turns and returns to the truck, gets in the back, and Fátima speeds off with Indio on the cab's passenger side.

It's sometime later. Indio Gerónimo is now in the back of the pickup lying on Fátima's lap; eyes closed in a half-somber sleep. She is wiping his face with a wet rag. His head is wrapped in a blood-soaked rag. She cleans his cheek of dry blood paying special attention to the scar he received so many years before. Fátima dreamily caresses his face. She bends over and kisses him on the lips. Indio, in a semiconscious state, accepts the kiss without reacting. He doesn't open his eyes, nor does he return the kiss, yet he relishes the moment. He lies there, his head resting on her lap as though asleep. Fátima looks off into the sunset gazing at the colorful horizon the yucas standing in silhouette as sentries on the expanse of the llano. She hums a soothing Spanish lullaby...

It is evening and they pull up to a gas station. Indio Gerónimo gets out of the truck to go to the bathroom. He looks up at the door of the restrooms. A sign reads, Whites only. He turns and sees the outhouse and walks in that direction.

José María is checking the engine oil on the truck - the radio is playing. Indio Gerónimo sees a drinking fountain and looks at the attendant. The attendant stares back, and Indio Gerónimo goes to the water faucet and takes a drink from the hose beside the building near the bathrooms. As he approaches the truck, he hears an announcement about an upcoming meeting on the landgrants. Fátima is coming from the outhouse. He turns to her as she gets into the truck and tells her, "When we get back to the Merced, we should get married, ¿verdad?" (right?)

Fátima responds, "¿A poco, what makes you think I would want to marry you? You're always in trouble." Tio José María pays the attendant and gets in the truck. Indio and Fátima are sitting in the bed of the truck as they drive off.

## RADIO TALK SHOW, LAS VEGAS 1963

Libertado cuts the final log while Martín loads. Libertado puts the saw on top of the woodpile and ties it down. Martín takes a canteen from the cab of the truck and drinks. Libertado lights up a cigarette. Martín takes a drink and hands the canteen to Libertado. They get in the truck and head home. On the way out of the canyon, Martín messes with the radio until he gets reception - it's the Las Vegas, New Mexico Spanish radio. "Your favorite convenience store brings you the Community Forum."

The radio station is on the second floor of the 19th century Ifield building on Main Street in Las Vegas. The forum participants are all seated around a table with microphones in front of each of them.

A large window overlooks the town, and the mountains are in the foreground.

The radio announcer says, "Señoras y caballeros, aquí tenemos con nosotros a Zara y está haciendo investigaciones sobre las Mercedes en España. (Ladies and gentlemen, we have with us Zara, and she is investigating the landgrants in Spain). Y también tenemos al Profesor de Sociología Dr. Knowlton de La Universidad de Highland, que ha escrito varios artículos sobre las razones de la pobreza de la raza mexicana." (And we also have the Sociology Professor Dr. Knowlton from the Highlands University, who has written various articles on the poverty of the people of Mexican descent).

At the same time Tío José María is on the road headed towards home from Colorado. The truck radio is on the same Spanish talk show. He pulls up to the home of his extended family.

Colonias, New Mexico. José María is with friends and family, sitting on the porch looking out over the village. Kids run about. A woman in the kitchen takes a serving bowl of chile and another bowl of beans and sets them on a table, then she returns to the house and gets the dishes. The young girls help to set the table while a young boy fiddles with the radio, tuning in to the same Las Vegas station.

Radio Program, Zara, "Gracias Héctor. Es cierto, apenas llegué de España, aunque la investigación fue bastante extensa y encontré muchos documentos y títulos de nuestras mercedes y el documento más importante fue el descubrimiento de las leyes de las Indias. En esas leyes aprendí que somos Indohispanos y tenemos los mismos derechos que cualquier otro ser humano con los mismos derechos ajenos igual que los criollos, eso quiere decir que también somos ciudadanos." (Thank you, Hector, yes, it is true, I just got back from Spain. I did a lot of research, and I found many titles of our landgrants there. The most important document was my discovery of the Laws of the Indies. In those laws I learned that we are Indohispano and we have the same rights as any other human being. Those laws give us the same rights as the Europeans and we are also citizens).

Martín and others are listening attentively to the program, as are thousands of Nuevomexicanos as far as the radio waves will reach.

The truck is loaded down with wood. Libertado is driving. Martín smokes. They are both listening to the radio.

Libertado says, "Estaba hablando con José María y quiere que nos juntemos el sábado como a las siete en La Mesa Poleo."

(I was speaking with Jose Maria and they want us to meet Saturday at 7:00PM at La Mesa Poleo)

Martín says, "¿No se escucha nada del Payne Land and Cattle?" (You haven't heard anything about the Payne Land and Cattle Company?)

Libertado responds, "No, nomás que le quieren quitar los ranchos a la gente de Ensenada." (No, no only that they want to take the ranches away from the people in Ensenada).

Martín says, "Sí, el Mundy anda en eso también." (Yes, Mundy is also involved in that.)

Libertado says, "Oh, puros ladrones, esos cabrones son nada más que puros ladrones." (Oh, they're all thieves, those sons of bitches are all nothing but real thieves)

Martín flips his cigarette out of the truck into the creek. "Sí la corporación va a llevar a la corte a la Payne Land and Cattle Company, están reclamando 12,000 acres de la merced de Tierra Amarilla. Están quitando los ranchos de todos los que viven en Ensenada." (Yes, la Corporación is taking to court the Payne Land and Cattle Company. They are claiming 12,000 acres of La Merced de Tierra Amarilla. They are taking away the ranches from everybody that lives in Ensenada)

Libertado asks, "Yee, ese Mundy, ¿cuándo se metió en Ensenada, y comó agarró esos terrenos, ¿quién se los dio?". (And, that Mundy when did he get to Ensenada, and how did he get that land, who gave it to him?)

Martín says, "Eso no te puedo decir, se me hace que lo compró de los Burns o anda acuestado con la Campania de Payne. No sé cómo lo dicen" (That I couldn't tell you, I think he bought it from Burns, or he is in bed with that Payne Company. I don't know what they call themselves.)

Libertado says, "Y, ese también fue una rata ladrona que nos robó todo. Oh no, todos estos gringos que llegan aquí nos están robando y dejándonos sin nada y nomás porque son gringos entran aquí y agarran lo que se les da la gana y la ley los apoya. Y a nosotros nos echan afuera como si fuéramos perros." (And he is also a rat thief that stole everything from us. Oh no, all these gringos that show up steal from us leaving us with nothing, and just because they are gringos they come here and take what they want, and the law supports them. And we are thrown out as though we were dogs)

In the radio station studio, there is a territorial map of the American Southwest surrounded by album jackets of popular bands, both local and from Mexico. Zara continues speaking, and Dr. Knowlton listens intently to everything Zara is saying.

Zara, "Estos gavachos nos robaron las mercedes porque el Tratado de Guadalupe Hidalgo específicamente dice que Estados Unidos iba a respetar los títulos Españoles y Mexicanos. Bueno, en mil ocho cientos cuarenta y seis cuando los gringos tomaron posesión del suroeste, pandillas de capitalistas se juntaron con el gobierno y nos quitaron los terrenos." (Those americans stole the landgrants because the Treaty of Guadalupe Hidalgo specifically states the United States was to recognize Spanish and Mexican titles to the land. Well, in eighteen hundred forty-six, when the anglos took possession of the Southwest, gangs of capitalists got together with the government to take our land.)

The radio announcer turns to the Professor, "Doctor Knowlton, what can you tell us about the plight of the Spanish-Americans of New Mexico and how it is affecting us today?"

José María is having supper on the porch. He finishes, pushes his plate away, takes a pouch of mountain tobacco from his shirt pocket, and rolls a cigarette while listening to the radio.

The professor continues, "Land enclosures accelerated after the nationalization of the forest, and many policies were set in place beginning in the 1930s on to 1950s and 60s that negatively affected particularly small local ranchers and local mills, in favor of large cattle companies and timber corporations. So, when many WWII and Korean veterans came back home, they found they could no longer graze their cattle on land that had traditionally been in the family for many generations."

"These lands were supposed to have been protected by the Treaty of Guadalupe Hidalgo. After annexation, the court of private land claims began nullifying community landgrants from people and assigning them to individuals. The federal government has continued to act in favor of corporations and individuals by passing laws and making policies that made it easier for them to extract the natural resources like timber, water rights, mining-coal for example, oil, and so forth, cutting the native Spanish-Americans from their land."

"In effect, this has displaced many 'Spanish-Americans,' forcing them to join the migrant trails and/or leave their homes and ranches altogether in search of work. It's unfortunate, but the result has had devastating effects on the people of northern New Mexico and yet has made other individuals very wealthy. And if I may, I would add that the Treaty of Guadalupe Hidalgo, ratified in 1848, states that the titles and civil liberties of all the heirs to the landgrant were to have been protected in the annexed territories."

Radio announcer, "¿Y Zara, ¿qué descubriste en tus investigaciones?" (And Zara, what did you discover in your investigation?)

Zara, "Descubrí las Leyes de las Indias, pero también el tratado de Córdoba de 1821, que fue cuando España le otorgó la independencia a México, esos mismos derechos ajenos están protegidos. Sí, esos mismos derechos civiles que se reconocieron en las Leyes de las Indias se transformaron en el tratado de Córdoba en 1821 y en el tratado de Guadalupe Hidalgo de 1848. Esos títulos Españoles y Mexicanos son válidos, la continuidad de estos tratados es la prueba de nuestros títulos. Quiere decir que sólo tenemos los mismos derechos ajenos que otras personas de los Estados Unidos, sino que se tiene que reconocer nuestra cultura e idioma. Somos Indo-Españoles, la nueva raza - una mezcla de mamás indias y papás españoles, una raza cósmica que reúne los dos continentes, Europa y las Américas. Esas mercedes no las robaron y queremos que nos las devuelvan. Esos gringos llegaron aquí e hicieron papeles diciendo que estas Mercedes son de ellos. Claro, los títulos oficiales de los gobiernos más poderosos del mundo no están reconocidos para nosotros pobres mexicanos, pero para ellos sí." (Yes, in the treaty de Córdoba of 1821, when Mexico liberated itself from Spain, those same human rights were protected. Yes, those same human rights recognized in the law of the Indies were transferred to the treaty of Guadalupe Hidalgo. It says that we not only have the same human rights as any other person of the United States, but that our culture and language are to be recognized as a new race, a mixture of Native mothers and Spanish fathers, the cosmic race that unifies Europe and the Americas. The landgrants were stolen and we want them back. Those anglos came here and did as they pleased, making "papers" (titles) saying that the landgrants were theirs. Oh, yes, our official land titles given to us by the most powerful government in the world are not recognized for us poor Mexicans but for them they are.)

Radio announcer, "Ya se nos está acabando el tiempo y antes que nos vayamos, ¿qué vas a hacer con esta información?"

(Our time is running out, but before we go, what are you going to do with this information?)

Zara, "Bueno, vamos a tener una función en Tecolote este fin de semana, están todos invitados, va a haber comida y voy a compartir más información sobre las Mercedes. Queremos formar una alianza formal que incluye todas las Mercedes. Vamos a hacer una petición al gobierno para que nos devuelvan nuestras mercedes." (Well, we are planning a function in Tecolote at the end of the week. You are all invited. We will have food, and I will share more information on the landgrants. We also want to form an Alliance with all the landgrants in New Mexico, and in this way, we can petition the government together for their return.)

Radio announcer, "Señoras y caballeros, espero que nos visiten la próxima semana en este programa." Ladies and Gentlemen, I look forward to your attendance at next week's gathering.

Libertado and Martín sit in the truck listening to the radio in front of Martín's house. "Ese rinche White no quería darnos un permiso para sacar leña de Cañones, nos quería mandar para Petaca."

"Oh no, está muy lejos." (That "rinche" (ranger) White didn't want to give us permission to take wood from Cañones. He wanted to send us to Petaca. It's too far.)

"Oh no Martín, está muy lejos y había mucha leña tirada allá por donde estábamos. No, ese rinche White no sabe lo que está pasando." (Oh no Martín, it is too far and there was plenty of wood where we were at. No, that "rinche" (ranger) White does not know what's going on.)

## José María Writes a corrido

Colonias, New Mexico. José María turns to his wife and tells her that a savior is on the horizon. The landgrants will be returned. They go to bed, but he tosses and turns late into the night until he finally gets up, goes to the kitchen and tears a piece of cardboard from a box filled with kindling.

He finds a pencil, sits down, and starts writing. By morning, he sings the corrido to his wife.

## Repiquen las Campanas

1.
*Cuando repiquen las campanas*
*Con una amorosa alegría*
*Cuando repiquen las campanas*
*La bautizamos en el nombre*
*De Santiago y Santa Ana*
*A esta tierra mía*

2.
*Por esta tierra mía*
*Cuando Dios haga el milagro*
*Y se nos sea concebido*
*Te damos un juramento*
*Nos entregamos más a tus servicios*
*Por esta tierra mía*

3.
*Cuando ya crezcan los maizales*
*Y otras frutas de la tierra*
*Cuando ya crezcan los trigales*
*A más por los ganados*
*Cumpliremos con los diezmos*
*Que el extranjero se ha llevado*
*De esta tierra mía*

4.

*Dios sabe que le han robado*
*Las frutas de su semilla*
*Dios sabe que le han robado*
*Del pan de cada día*
*De cantarles no me canso*
*Si ofendo me han de perdonar*

*Y no hago por hablar*
*Pero por la tierra mía*

1.
When the bells ring
With loving happiness
When the bells ring
We will baptize in the name
Of Santiago and Santa Ana
And this land of mine

2.
For this land of mine
When God does a miracle
And it has been granted
We give you our oath
We'll submit to you service
For this land of mine

3.
When our corn grows
And other fruits of our land
When the wheat plants grow
And more for the livestock
We will complete our title
The foreigner has taken
For this land of mine

4.

God knows they have stolen
The fruits from the seed
God knows they have stolen
Our daily bread
I do not tire of singing to you
If I offend you have to forgive me

And I do not do it to talk
But for my land

***

José María asks his wife, "¿Qué piensas?" (what do you think)

She asks him, "¿Cómo se titula el corrido?" ("What is the title of your corrido?")

"No sé, qué piensas sería un buen título," he asks. (I don't know. What do you think the title should be?)

She answers him, "Ponle, 'Repiquen las Campanas', o le pones 'A Esta Tierra Mía'. ¿Lo vas a presentar al Zara?" (Put the title The Bells are Ringing or put this sad land of mine. Are you going to present it to Zara?)

José María responds, "Sí, se lo presentaré hoy en la tarde cuando terminemos la comida, se lo presentaré cuando estemos solos, y si le gusta se lo presentaré al público cuando esté la banda, así me pueden acompañar, y entonces a ver qué título le gusta al público,". (Yes, I will present it to him in the afternoon when we finish eating. I will show it to him when we are alone, and if he likes it I will present it to the public when the band is playing. That way they can accompany me and see what title the public likes.)

## MEETING AT THE VILLAGE OF TECOLOTE

An old Army parachute provides shade. Benches and chairs are set out. A low trailer acts as a platform at one end of the staging area. Food is being set out to one side.

Zara gets up on the platform, "¿Buenos días, cuántas Mercedes tenemos aquí representadas?" (Good morning, how many landgrants do we have represented here?)

People shout out the landgrants they are from: "¡Las Vegas! ¡Tecolote! ¡Las Trampas! ¡San Joaquín de Río Chama! ¡Atrisco! ¡Tomé! ¡Sangre de Cristo! ¡Las Vegas! ¡Mora! and the list goes on..."

Zara, "Bien, me da gusto recibirlos, y entre más seamos, más poder tendremos. Déjenme darles un reporte en lo que descubrí en España. Estaba investigando en los archivos y allí descubrí Las Leyes de las Indias, no sé cuántos de ustedes me oyeron ayer por la radio donde hablé un poco sobre este tema. (Good, it gives me pleasure to receive you. The more we are the more power we have. Let me give you a report of what I discovered in Spain. I was doing research at the archives and there I discovered The Law of the Indies. I don't know how many of you heard me yesterday on the radio where I talked about this subject.)

"Antes los españoles no nos consideraban como humanos, sino como animales, como los perros mojados con la cola entre las piernas porque sabían que la palabra "Raza" se refería a animales, como caballos, vacas, y borregos. Sí, la palabra Raza se refería a los animales y con el tiempo los españoles comenzaron a referir a los indígenas de las Américas como raza - animales. No somos animales, somos hijos de Dios y tenemos los mismos derechos ajenos que cualquier otro ser humano. Somos una Raza cósmica, una nueva Raza mezclada, indígenas colonizados por sangre y cultura española." (In the past, the Spanish did not consider to be human beings. They saw us as animals, like wet dogs with our tails between our legs because they knew the word race referred to animals, like horses, cows, and sheep. Yes, the word Raza referred to animals, and when the Spanish colonized the New World, they refer to indigenous people from the Americas as that race of animals. We are not animals, we are the children of God, and we have the same human right as any other human being. We are the Cosmic Race, a new breed, a mixed breed of Indians colonized by Spanish blood and culture.)

"El tratado de Córdoba es el tratado que se firmó cuando México se liberó de España, y allí se conservaron los mismos derechos ajenos que se establecieron en las Leyes de las Indias. Y el tratado de Guadalupe Hidalgo también conservó esos derechos humanos. Lo que quiero decir es que tenemos los mismos derechos que los anglos, los que llegaron aquí y en el Tratado de Guadalupe Hidalgo dice específicamente que los Estados Unidos respetan los derechos nuestros." (The treaty de Cordoba, that treaty that Mexico signed when they liberated from Spain there, they preserved the same human rights that were preserved from the laws of the Indies. And the treaty of Guadalupe Hidalgo also conserved those same rights. My point is that we have the same rights as anglos, who came here, and in the Guadalupe Hidalgo Treaty. It says specifically the United States would respect our human rights.)

"Bueno, con eso me despido y vamos a compartir una cena. Estoy seguro de que tienen hambre y veo que la comida está lista. Después tendremos una elección para formar un cuerpo para incorporarnos, formando una Alianza Federal de Mercedes. Ésta es la única forma de que nos tomaran en serio. Así le enseñamos en números que estamos organizados y vamos en serio. Y que estamos determinados a que nos devuelvan nuestras Mercedes, entonces demandaremos que nos devuelven nuestros ejidos." (Well, in closing, let us share a meal. I am sure that we are all hungry, and I see that the food is ready. And after that, we will hold an election to incorporate the Alianza Federal de Mercedes. This way they see that we are serious. And that we are determined that they return our landgrants.)

Indio Gerónimo stands up and claps. Others follow. Zara puts his hands out and says, "Vamos a comer." Come! Let's eat!

People clap, giving him a standing ovation and cheering in agreement. He steps off the platform, shaking hands with people. Zara takes his position at the front of the line to be served.

Zara is at the table gobbling his food. Lupita, Zara's daughter, a beautiful young woman, is seated to one side of him. She locks eyes with Indio; there is immediate chemistry.

Libertado pushes Indio. "Hurry up, ese, tenemos hambre también. Leave her alone. She's spoken for. Zara has arranged for her to marry some guy from Mexico. Move it; tengo hambre."

Indio is served enchiladas and beans. He takes a tortilla and Fátima gives him a glass of Kool-Aid, looking over at Lupita. "Aquí tienes Gerónimo."

Indio Gerónimo is fixated on Lupita. Fátima spills the Kool-Aid on his arm, spilling it over onto his plate.

Libertado says, "All right, Indio Gerónimo, you get a sweet and hot plate today."

"No, Libertado, he gets no food from me," responds Fátima.

Indio Gerónimo tilts his plate, pouring off the Kool-Aid. Fátima glares at him and he drops his head and moves on.

Calixtra tells her son Libertado, "Ándale, muévete, la gente quiere comer." (Hurry, move, people want to eat).

Libertado whines, "Hey, tía, it's Indio that's holding up progress, not me." They walk away from the serving table and take a seat.

Indio Gerónimo, "Hmm, this meat is good. What is it?"

José María walks by and slaps him on the head. "Come y calla la boca." (Just eat it and shut up.)

Indio Gerónimo, "Ouch, what did you do that for?" Laughter.

Libertado, "You're not supposed to be asking where the carne (meat) came from– just eat it and shut up. You know it's elk, no te hagas el pendejo." (don't act stupid)

Indio Gerónimo, "¡Oh yeah! No." He laughs, knowing very well that it is poached game.

Libertado, "No agarraron permiso de los rinches, oh este hermano está lento. Se nota que hace mucho tiempo que ha estado afuera de aquí." (No, no, they didn't get permission from the rangers. Oh, this bro is really delayed. You can tell he's been away from home too long.) Laughter!

Indio Gerónimo, "But it don't taste like beef, vatos, ¿qué es?"

Libertado, "Hey—que pendejo, que perdiste tu cerebro en la pisca." (You really lost your mind while you were picking.)

Martín jokingly to Libertado, "He was getting high on onions." "Por eso vuelves tan buenito, buey, pushing him, verdad, Hermano," dice Libertado. More laughter.

# CHAPTER FIVE

## RETALIATION

IT IS MORNING and Dr. Knowlton walks out of his house to find his tree and bushes toilet papered, the tires on his car slashed and the windows painted. He goes back into the house and calls the police. They come out and take a report. Dr. Knowlton calms his wife down and tells her that he needs to leave for an appointment with the university president.

The police pull up. While Knowlton and his family assess the mess. the officer gets out of the patrol car, walks up to Knowlton and says, "It looks like someone is not happy with you, Professor."

Knowlton, "Yes, this is beyond a prank, isn't it?" Knowlton tells him everything looked all right at nine p.m. when he locked up and went to bed. He tells the officer that he needs to go and that his wife can fill him in on any information he needs.

Knowlton walks to campus and into the administration building and to the President's office.

Secretary, "Hello Professor. I'll tell the president you're here."

She walks over to the President's office door and knocks. "Professor Knowlton has arrived."

President, "Send him in." He shakes hands with Knowlton. Knowlton turns to the Dean of his department and shakes his hand.

The President motions him to take a seat. "Well Knowlton, I think you have some idea why we called this meeting. I got a phone call from the Governor and a number of calls from local ranchers about the radio program you appeared on a few days ago."

Knowlton looks around the room. Friendly photographs of university president Tomas Donnelly and Senator Joseph McCarthy accompanied with a young Roger Stone adorn the office.

Knowlton, "Yes, I did appear on a Spanish radio program and I talked about an article I just published on the poverty of Spanish Americans in northern New Mexico. The State needs to help these people or something is going to blow. They are being forced to endure horrendous poverty. And the natives are angered at how the Forest Service fails to respond to their needs by not allowing them to pasture their livestock. The Forest Service is making some outrageous claims that elk cannot coexist with domestic livestock."

With a thick German accent, the Dean says, "Yes, Knowlton, that's fine, but you don't go on the radio and get the Mexicans all riled up. You can't be making those types of statements, especially with a communist the likes of Zarfarano (Zara). He is already getting people all in tizzy."

Knowlton responds, "Well gentlemen, all I did was comment on my findings as a result of my research. It is my understanding that this is an institution for higher learning. My responsibility is to the intellectual development of humanity. And to do that is to make life better for all of mankind."

President, "Your ideals are lofty and that is fine, Knowlton, but you can't be getting the natives worked up. I'm getting complaints from local ranchers of destruction of property by an organization calling itself La Mano Negra in Río Arriba County, and here it seems the 1890 organization Las Gorras Blancas is doing its share of vandalism. It seems the locals have resurrected a version of the clandestine organization from the last century. If you continue stirring them up like this I assure you it will have an effect on you getting tenure. So, I am alerting you, and this is not just me but on the recommendations of many political figures and the regents, you have to stop coddling the natives. I'm telling you to lay off."

The president walks over to Knowlton and puts his hand on his shoulder, "Thank you for coming in and I hope we have taken care of this matter once and for all." He turns to the Dean, "Let's see how it goes."

The Dean responds, "The Mexican students are becoming very vocal in expressing their dissatisfaction with past historical inequities. A charter was recently submitted for a student organization calling itself the Mexican American Youth Organization (MAYO). I'm afraid we are seeing alliances being formed across the country."

University President Donnelly responds, "Well let's see what happens."

Knowlton leaves the building and walks home. He opens the front door, "Hello, anyone home?"

His wife calls out, "Yes, I'm in here."

Knowlton stands in the foyer going through mail. "How was your day honey?" he asks, walking to the kitchen.

His wife wipes her hands over the kitchen sink. Knowlton, with an envelope in his hand, kisses his wife on the cheek.

She says, "I'm really concerned about how the children are being treated at school by the local kids, Knowlton, and the incident this morning, toilet papering the hedges and slashing the tires. Things are getting dangerous."

Knowlton says, "Yes, maybe it's time to move on, as much as I like it here." He opens the envelope and reads the letter.

He looks up at his wife, "Well, it looks like I have been offered a position at Texas Western College. I guess we will be moving to El Paso."

"Oh, Knowlton, I am so relieved." She hugs and kisses him.

## ALIANCISTAS MEET WITH SÁNCHEZ

A late 1950s station wagon pulls up to a law office. The sign reads: Alfonso Sánchez, Esquire. Four men get out of the car and go into the office.

The secretary asks, "Can I help you?"

An elderly man in his late sixties, a working vaquero in jeans and a worn cowboy hat, says, "Venimos a hablar con el Señor Sánchez."

The secretary asks, "And who shall I say is calling?"

"El hermano de Calixtra, primo de su esposa. Soy José María, a sus órdenes señora, tenemos una cita." (The brother of Calixtra, cousin of his wife. My name is José María, at your disposal. We have an appointment.)

"Sí señor, le diré que está aquí—estábamos esperándole." She stands up and walks over to Sánchez's office and knocks on his door. (Yes, let me tell them you are here—we were expecting you.)

Alfonso Sánchez is on the phone with the governor. His door is ajar. The secretary says, "Excuse me, Alfonso, but your appointment is here."

"Thank you. Diles que allí voy." He takes his hand off the receiver and carries on his conversation on the phone, "Yes, my wife has family up there. I will look into it right away, governor." Governor speaking to Alfonso, "As I was telling you, Bill Mundy just had his home burned down and other ranchers are complaining of vandalism as well. We need to put a stop to this, and I mean pronto."

Alfonso Sánchez, "Yes, governor, I will look into this right away."

Alfredo hangs up the phone. Putting his hands over his face and leaning back on his chair, he rubs his eyes and gets up to greet his clients, "Hey ¿cómo estás José María? ¿Y tu hermana cómo está?

"Oh, está bien," ("Oh, she's well,") responds José María. "Déjeme presentarle a Zarfarano." ("Let me introduce Zarfarano.") He gives him his hand. "Y aquí le presento al señor Nicolás López de La Puente y este joven Gerónimo de Canjilón." ("And let me present Nicolás López de la Puente and this young man Gerónimo de Canjilón"). "Vamos a sentarnos en este cuarto, tendremos más espacio." ("Let's sit down in this room, it is more spacious."

Alfonso leads them to a conference room. Everyone takes a seat. "Bueno señores, ¿en qué les puedo servir?" (Well gentlemen, how can I serve you?)

José María, "Alfonso, queremos saber si nos puedes ayudar con los papeles para establecer una organización sin ánimos de lucro." (Yes, Alfonso, we would like to have you help us with the papers for a nonprofit corporation.)

Alfonso asks, "¿Y para qué se va usar esta corporación?" (And what will this corporation be used for?)

Zara responds, "Bueno, la razón de esta corporación es para establecer una alianza incorporando a todas las mercedes, los ejidos, que nos fueron robados, vamos a movilizarnos para que nos devuelvan las mercedes." (Okay, the reason for this corporation is to form an alliance of all the landgrants that have been stolen from us, we are going to mobilize so that they will give them back to us.)

"Pero el congreso de los Estados Unidos ya resolvió ese caso hace mucho tiempo," Alfredo responds. (But that issue has been resolved. The United States Congress resolved those issues some time ago.)

"¡No está resuelto! Esos terrenos son de nosotros. Los gringos americanos, con la ayuda del gobierno y el apoyo de la ley, nos los robaron y los van a devolver. Esas Mercedes nos pertenecen a nosotros, los Nuevomexicanos, indo-hispanos, genízaros del nuevo mundo," Zara says. (No, it's not resolved! Those lands are ours. The anglo-americans with the help of the government and the support of the law stole them and they are going to return them to us. Those landgrants belong to us, the New Mexicans the Indians, Spanish, mixed bloods of the New World.)

Alfonso Sánchez, "Zara, déjame decirte otra vez que ese caso de las Mercedes ya está resuelto. No puedes agarrar terrenos si no tienes título y si continúas con esta idea ridícula te estoy advirtiendo que yo voy a ser la persona que te va a perseguir. Repito, Y YO VOY A SER LA PERSONA QUE TE VA A PARAR." Alfredo, now standing, leans forward with his fist on the table looking stern. (Zara, I am telling you again that the issue of the landgrants has been resolved. You cannot take land that you no longer hold legal title to, and I am warning you if you pursue this ludicrous idea, I WILL BE THE PERSON TO STOP YOU").

## Junta en Placita Blanca

Several days later, in another meeting, Zara says, "Buenos días, tenemos bastante representación para formar una Alianza de Mercedes. Yo, con la ayuda de muchas personas, empezaré con el papeleo para registrarnos con el estado y así no tenemos que pagar impuestos. Ya hablé con la gente de Las Vegas y muchos otros pueblos. Ya estamos llegando al tiempo, muchachos, que el gobierno nos tiene que ver serios. Estamos creciendo en números, yo he visto la injusticia en la manera que están usando la ley a su favor y tienen que responder ante los ciudadanos Nuevomexicanos y delante de Dios. (Good morning. We have enough representation to form an Alliance of Landgrants. With a lot of help from many people we can start the paperwork to register with the state as a non-profit organization so that we don't have to pay taxes. I have spoken with the people of Las Vegas and many other pueblos. We have arrived at a place, folks, that the government has to see us serious. We are growing in numbers, I have seen the injustice in the way the law is being used in their favor, and they have to answer to the citizens of New Mexico and before God.)

Zara reaches out his arms, motioning the group to settle down and thanks them for the warm reception. He begins his speech:

"La gran hipocresía que los Estados Unidos ha cometido contra los pobres, ha causado hambre y siempre habrá hambre si seguimos aceptando estas injusticias. Queremos mantenimiento de nuestro idioma castellano—tenemos muchas riquezas en nuestra cultura para compartir con el mundo. Y la única manera de que acabaremos con el odio del racismo es denunciar sus crímenes, y sacar todos los que han cometido al público. Hacemos mal guardando la boca cerrada. Tenemos que levantar el grito en contra de todos los males que hacen en contra de los pobres." (The great hypocrisy that the United States has committed against the poor has caused the hunger, which will continue if we continue to accept this injustice. We want the maintenance of our Castilian language; we have many riches in our culture to share with the world. The only way we can overcome this racism is to denounce their crimes, and to reveal what they have done to the public. We have to call attention to their misdeeds that they do against the poor.)

## SANTA FÉ PROTEST

In front of the Alianza headquarters in Albuquerque, a caravan of cars and people are getting ready for a march from the Alianza office north on 2nd street. The road turns onto the old highway through Sandia Pueblo, Bernalillo to Algodones, San Felipe, and Santo Domingo, and on to Cochiti and Santa Fé. Hecklers and passers-by honk and yell obscenities. Others are in support.

Zara rides a mule. Indio Gerónimo and Lupe walk together and talk. She is a few years older than him. It's obvious they like one another. He is shy and innocent. The attention from an older girl is somehow forbidden but alluring. The protesters stop to make camp, and Indio, with the men setting up camp, is acutely aware of Lupita's every move, as she is of his. Zara unloads provisions and helps set up camp.

Zara says, "Terijú, ven para acá." ("Terijú, come here".) Zara's eldest son, in his twenties, walks up to his father.

Zara tells him, "Quiero que cuides a tu hermana." ("I want you to take care of your sister".)

Terijú, "Okay, Dad." He walks over to his sister and talks with her. "What is the matter with you? You know Daddy got you a husband."

Lupe says, "Yeah, but I have never met him, and he is in México."

Terijú says, "So, you can't be flirting with anyone. You know what Daddy will do."

Frustrated, Lupita turns and walks away. Indio is fetching the tent from the truck. He unties it and spreads it out, Libertado helps. Chile, beans, papas, and meat are on the campfire; tortillas warm on rocks at the edge of the fire. People talk and laugh. The mood is festive. Indio Gerónimo hammers stakes and ties down the tent, taking direction from an elder.

Flirtatious stares are exchanged as Lupita sets out dishes on a serving table. José María takes out his guitar, strums it, and warms up his voice. He begins to sing a corrido about the revolution. The sun is setting. The Sandía Mountains explode with detail from the reflection of the sun. Zara keeps an eye on him as he talks with his closest advisors well into the night. Indio Gerónimo and Lupita stand next to one another as everyone gathers around the campfire.

Fátima stays home taking care of her grandmother and going to school, while Indio Gerónimo joins the protesters in front of the State Capitol to demand an audience with the governor. Governor Campbell refuses to meet with them. Only after several hours does he send out a local "Hispanic" representative to appease the crowd.

An elder from the crowd yells out, "No venimos a pedirles cosas gratis." (We didn't come asking for anything free of charge.)

Gregorita yells out from the crowd, "No queremos leche de polvo, queremos justicia, queremos nuestras Mercedes. Esos terrenos son de nosotros." (We don't want powdered milk, we want justice. We want our landgrants. That land is ours.)

José María agrees, "¡Sí, no venimos pidiendo estampas, sino lo que es de nosotros!" (Yes, we have not come to ask for food stamps, but for what is ours!)

The State Representative says, "I understand - but the governor is still not in the building."

Gregorita shouts out from the crowd, "Well then, where is he? We want to talk with him right now!"

The State Representative says, "He is on his way to Washington D.C. and will be back next week. I am sure he will meet with you then."

Gregorita responds, "That is a lie. He knew we were coming." People are angry, yelling. Others break up into small groups. Restlessly they start tossing objects at the speaker.

Zara, high on the Capitol steps, speaks, "No se preocupen por el gobernador, vamos a seguir la lucha y vamos a hacer que el gobierno nos preste atención." (Do not concern yourselves with the governor. We will continue to fight and make the government listen.)

Zara has his hands stretched forward in a gesture to quiet down the crowd. People listen to what he has to say. His piercing eyes stare down the crowd as though to cast a spell over the hundreds of people.

Zara says, "El gobernador nos tiene miedo, se está escondiendo, como un ratoncito escapándose de una trampa, no nos quiere enfrentar. Le llamaremos otro día. No se enojen, tenemos el derecho, y no puede parar la justicia." (The governor is afraid and is hiding. Like a mouse sneaking out of a trap, he does not want to face us. We will call him on another day. Do not be angry, we have the right, and he can't stop justice.)

Hundreds of people, only moments before ready to riot, are now calm.

Zara tells them, "Somos como una garrapata en la oreja de un león que anda molestando y molestando al león, y el león se rasguñaba hasta que el mismo se rompó la oreja porque sabe que lo que hace está mal. Se robaron nuestras tierras y el gobierno nos está tratando injustamente. Y nosotros como la garrapata no lo vamos a dejar. El gobierno mismo va a caer por el daño que nos causa." (We are like the tick in a lion's ear that was bothering and bothering the lion, and the lion would scratch until he tears his ear because he knows he was wrong. They stole our lands and the government is treating us unjustly. And we, like the tick, will not let them. The government will come down because of the wrong they are doing.)

Indio stands next to Zara, guarding him. He shouts out, "Tierra Y Justicia, Tierra Y Justicia, Tierra Y Justicia." The crowd follows, repeating, "Tierra y Justicia, Tierra y Justicia." (land and justice)

The crowd hoots and hollers. Mariachis start playing, and José María picks up his guitar and begins to sing the corrido, Carabina 30-30. The crowd follows along. The mood is festive. People clap while others gather their things and head back home. Indio Gerónimo walks with the boys. Lupe is nearby with a group of girls as they make their way back through the crowd. The boys joke. Indio Gerónimo, shy, walks up alongside Lupe. Terijú, a short distance away, is watching his sister.

Lupita says, "You know I am promised."

Indio asks, "Can we still be friends?"

Terijú walks up to Indio Gerónimo and puts his hand on his shoulder.

Terijú says, "Come on, let's go, you need to leave my sister alone."

Lupita says, "I don't know ... I mean no!"

### La Mesa Cósmica

The leadership has gathered at Alianza headquarters in Albuquerque. The Alianza building had been a warehouse, and the council chambers was once where frozen meat had been kept. A seven-foot round cement slab table on a single pedestal stands at the center of this large room. La Mesa Cósmica is Zara's version of King Arthur's round table where King Arthur's sat with his twelve knights, the most coveted. This was the foundation from which Zara imagined la Mesa Cósmica and his twelve Apostles. He combined Arthur's legend with Jesus's and his twelve Apostles. The idea of the Knights of the Round Table was that there was no head: all men were equal as members of the Round Table. Like King Arthur's quorum, the idea was that la Alianza's governing body was a landgrant Alliance whose members were all equal participants. King Arthur's Knights of the Round Table complemented the Alianza mythology and their unwavering commitment to the retrieval of the landgrants. This idea also coincided with references made about John and Jackie Kennedy and the utopian life of Camelot. Borrowing from "America's royalty" and "idyllic couple" as well as from the legend of King Arthur's Camelot, Zara connected the utopian world of his prophecy with the utopian landgrant community, thus building their Alianza's mythology. The Aliancistas' unwavering commitment to the retrieval of the landgrants determined the most trustworthy Apostles to hold the coveted seats at la Mesa Cósmica and to lead the idealistic life of bygone days before American annexation.

The Apostles are making their way up the narrow stairwell; their shoulders rub the cold concrete walls that lead to the council meeting room. From the ceiling hangs a rustic rod iron chandelier with hand-blown deep golden goblets in the shape of flames. The twelve apostles, los Apóstoles, take their places around la Mesa Cósmica, occupying the twelve ornate hand-carved chairs surrounding a thirteenth chair that looms over the others. This is the largest chair of all, Zara's throne, from where he presides. Some of the men talk among themselves while others shuffle papers they are trying to get in order. The serious mood is shifted by a joyful José María walking in. "Buenas Hermanos, ¿cómo amanecieron?" (Good morning, Hermanos, how are you today?)

Los Apóstoles respond, "muy bien Hermano, ¿y tú?" (Good, Hermano, what about you?)

José María complains, "Bien, nomás que amanecí descobijado y solo." (Well, although I woke up feeling cold and lonely).

Hermano Aguilar chuckles, "Oh no Hermano, eso no debería de pasar nunca. ¿Por qué no me acompañas entonces?" (Oh! This should never happen, Hermano. Why don't you sleep with me then?)

Everyone starts laughing.

"¿Ay, Hermano por qué te comportas tan grosero?" responds Hermano José María in a crusty gruff. (Brother, why are you being so rude?)

The other Hermanos laugh and make additional remarks to one another but loud enough for the rest of them to hear them poking fun at José María.

Zarfarano turns the corner and begins to walk up the narrow stairs when Lupita calls out to him, "Daddy, Uvaldo quiere hablar contigo: tiene noticia que nos van a dejar usar espacio en la escuela en Coyote pa' la conferencia." (Uvaldo wants to talk to you: apparently, we will be able to use the Coyote school as a conference venue)

Zara takes the phone, "Sí, bueno, ¿dime qué pasa?" Uvaldo explains that he got approval to use the school cafeteria and kitchen for the Alianza meetings. He hangs up the phone and races upstairs. He is late for the council meeting. Everyone is there. Zarfarano takes his throne and the Apostles settle down. He slams a wooden crude handmade gavel on a block of wood and says, "Bueno, llamo esta junta al orden. La primera cosa que tenemos en la agenda de esta junta, a día de 16 de septiembre de 1966, es la siguiente: necesitamos seguir presionando al gobierno que nos sean devueltas las Mercedes, y hemos de conseguir la atención del público. El segundo punto es relativo a la búsqueda de un espacio para la conferencia de este verano en el norte, y el tercer punto es el reporte del tesorero. Bueno, el primer punto de la agenda: ¿cómo llamar la atención del gobierno para que nos tomen en serio y nos regresen las Mercedes?" (Okay—I call this meeting to order. The first thing we have on the agenda on this day of the 16th of September 1966 is how we can keep pressing the government to get our landgrants back and find a way for the public to listen to us. The second discussion topic is our search for a space in the north for our summer conference, and the third is the treasurer's report. Okay, the first point on the agenda: what can we do to get the attention of the government to take us seriously about returning our landgrants?)

First Apostle José María responds, "Tenemos que hacer algo que les llame la atención, como una marcha-protesta más grande de la que ya tuvimos en Santa Fé." (We need to do something dramatic, like a protest march to the courthouse, bigger than the one in Santa Fé.)

Apostle Manuel Aguilar says, "No, ya hicimos eso. Necesitamos algo más dramático como tomar posesión de unas tierras que nos han quitado. Ocupar la floresta con nuestros animales y dejarlos pastar allí." (No, we have already done that ... something more dramatic, like taking possession of some of the lands they have taken from us. Occupy the forest with our animals to graze freely.)

José María says, "No, señores, con eso sólo lograremos que nos quiten las bestias y nos cobren una multa." (No, gentlemen, they will only take our animals from us and charge us a fine.)

Zara speaks, "Necesitamos un lugar bastante transitado para que nos vea la gente." (We need a place where there is traffic, so people will see us.)

Miguel replies, "Podemos poner campamento allí en el Banco del Burro." (We can put a camp there at el Banco del Burro.)

Libertado says, "Sí, los rinches pusieron campos con mesas."

(Yes, the rangers put tables at the camp site.)

Nicolás asks, "¿Dónde dices?"

Cruz, Miguel's twin brother, answers, "Allí, donde le dicen el Echo Amphitheatre, allí cerca del Banco del Burro." (Over there where they named the Echo Amphitheater, close to el Banco del Burro.)

"Si, eso estaría bien. Por allí está el zoológico con animales locales en jaulas chiquitas," responds Cruz. (Yes, it would be a good place. The zoo is out there, with local animals in small cages)

"Sí verdad, ¡tienen hasta los animales encarcelados!," everyone laughs. (Yeah, right, they even throw the animals in jail!)

"Así como nos tratan a nuestra raza, verdad..." responds José María. (The way they treat us, la raza)

Zara, "¿Bueno, estamos de acuerdo entonces? Está bien. Vamos a ocupar el Anfiteatro Eco el último fin de semana del mes de octubre." (So, do we agree then? Very well. We will occupy the Echo Amphitheater the last weekend of this month.) He slams his gavel. "Bueno, eso nos trae al segundo punto y de allí seguimos con las medidas de presión con acciones en la floresta para demostrar que esos terrenos son de nosotros. (So now to the next point. We need to talk about the what we can do to keep the pressure on the forest to show them those lands are ours.)

# CHAPTER SIX

## INDIO GERÓNIMO AND LUPITA

LUPITA IS ON HER WAY home from high school. Indio Gerónimo meets her.

Lupita asks, "Hey, what are you doing here?"

Indio says, "I came down with my Tío José María. He dropped me off while he went to pick up some parts for the tractor."

Lupita has her books in hand.

Indio offers, "Let me carry your books."

She hands them over with deference. They walk, enjoying each other's company. When they get to her front yard, her father, Zara, peeks through the window, watching them. José María pulls up in a pickup truck. Indio Gerónimo says his goodbyes and gives her a candy bar. He leaves, and she goes to the front door, giddy. Her father waits at the door.

Zara asks, "What are you doing? I told you to stay away from that boy!"

Lupita says, "Daddy, look at what Indio gave me."

Zara says, "What do you think? He can win you over with a candy bar, is that what you think?

All he wants is to take you away from me. Is that what you want?"

"But Daddy, he was just being nice to me," responds Lupita.

Zara responds angrily, "Here, then!" He takes the candy bar from her and shoves it in her mouth, wrapper and all. "There you go—eat it, eat it all, go on swallow, I said swallow it all," Zara orders her.

## Parque Eco Anfiteatro

La Alianza meets at its headquarters in Albuquerque to plan a second protest. The building had once been a warehouse and has thick concrete walls that were used for cold storage. Zara walks in and takes his "throne," a large ornate hand-carved chair. Los Apóstoles are talking about the recent Santa Fé protest and what their next move is going to be.

José María walks in, takes off his Stetson and sits down to assess the discussions.

Nicolás turns to José María, "¿Cómo le ha ido, Hermano?" (How did it go, Hermano?)

Zara picks-up a rustic wooden mallet and bangs it on a wooden block, "Orden Apósteles, orden. El primer caso en la agenda es del alboroto en Santa Fé. Apóstol José María nos va a dar su reporte." (Order Apostles, order. The first thing on our agenda is the protest in Santa Fé. Apostle José María will give us his report.)

José María, "Bien, salimos tarde de la casa, con su permiso," (Well, we left the house late, with your permission.) he announces and turns to address everyone. "Hermanos, quisiera darles un reporte de la junta con el gobernador, hicimos la lucha de presentar nuestras quejas de injusticias al gobierno y no nos hizo caso. Me parece que tenemos que hacer algo más intenso, dramático, como lo que hicieron las Gorras Blancas en aquellos tiempos.

Sí, claro, algunas de las acciones que tomaron fueron violentas, pero ¿qué era el significado de sus acciones de cortar cercos y destruir propiedades como aquí más recientemente con las gorras negras? Bueno, los americanos estaban y están diciendo que las propiedades son de ellos porque levantaron ranchos, construyeron algún campo, como el banco del burro ahí donde los rinches hicieron el campamento en El Parque de Eco Anfiteatro. No estoy proponiendo que hagamos lo que han hecho nuestros antepasados de destruir propiedades americanas, pero tenemos que hacer una ocupación simbólica de La Merced

(Brothers, I would like to give you a report on our meeting with the governor. We made the attempt to present our concerns of injustices with the government, and they didn't want to listen to us. I believe we need to do something more intense, dramatic, like Las Gorras Blancas did in those times and La Mano Negra. Of course, some of their actions that they took were violent, but what was the significance of their actions by cutting down fences and destroying property? Well, the americanos are saying that the property is theirs because they have built on it like farm. They constructed something like El Banco del Burro, where the ranges made the campsite Echo Amphitheater Park. I am not saying that we do what our ancestors have done destroying property that the Americans have done, but symbolically occupy La Merced.)

"Lo que estamos proponiendo, o sea en el nombre de La Corporación de Abiquiú - Merced de Tierra Amarilla, es que ocupemos simbólicamente el Echo Park, situado en la frontera de La Merced de Tierra Amarilla, y La Merced de San Joaquín de Río Chama." (What we are proposing, in another words, La Corporación de Abiquiú-Merced de Tierra Amarilla that we symbolically take possession of the Echo

Park. It is situated on the border of La Merced de Tierra Amarilla y La Merced de San Joaquín de Río Chama.)

Everyone agrees that it is a good idea, settles on a date, and the Apóstoles work out the details.

A month and half later...

José María, Calixtra, Indio, and Fátima are on the highway headed north towards Echo Amphitheater Park near Abiquiú. They are part of a caravan that started in Albuquerque. Another started in San Luis, Colorado, and yet another in Las Vegas, New Mexico.

"Why do they call this place, Ghost Ranch, tío?" Indio Gerónimo asks as they pass Abiquiu.

"Cuando se robaron la tierra los 'cowboys' que trabajaban allí tomaron posesión de la Morada (When the land was stolen, the anglo cowboys that worked in the area took possession of la Morada.) TD Burns y Tomás Catrón had their cowboys stay at la Morada. There weren't any Hermanos there. The cowboys would stay there until winter. It is said that during Cuaresma, Los Hermano difuntos se aparesían (Lent, the deceased Hermanos would awaken.) Ghosts would show up and they would do ejercicios (sacred exercise). They would pray for the living and the dead, paying penitencía and giving their blessing for all that they had and didn't have. The Presbyterian Church later took possession of this section of the Piedra Lumbre Grant, and they named it Ghost Ranch because there was never a title except for the one they made for themselves.

Fátima inquires, "Tío, ¿do the Hermanos still go to that Morada?"

"I don't know. The Morada is gone, it has melted away into a pile of caliche, rotting vigas and window frames, but los difuntos todavía están allí con las cruces pudriéndose, rotting from neglect, but during holy week they say you can hear Hermanos singing Alabados echoing through el cañón de los fantasmas."

They pull over to the shoulder a mile or so before the entrance to Echo Park where the forest has a walkway with a bobcat, a coyote, and other wildlife in cages for the public's view. Another caravan comes from the north. Convoys of cars gather along the shoulder of the road. Zara stands in the bed of a pickup truck. "Prepárense. Vamos a hacer la entrada, los valientes primero porque ellos no le temen a la muerte. En este día vamos a reclamar nuestra tierra y el Pueblo libre de San Joaquín de Rio Chama—Merced de Tierra Amarrilla. Todos son valientes, pues estamos haciendo historia reclamando lo que es nuestra tierra y dignidad." (Prepare yourselves. We are going to make our entrance, the brave ones first because they do not fear death. On this day, we are going to reclaim our land and the village of San Joaquin de Rio Chama - Merced de Tierra Amarilla. We are all brave, for we are making history, reclaiming what is our land and dignity.)

Cars honk, people shout. Two U.S. Forest Service Rangers stand at the entrance. They attempt to stop the Aliancistas as they cross the cattle guard. The Rangers jump out of the way, narrowly avoiding being run down. La Gente make their entrance, circling around the campgrounds like wagons forming a circle. The automobiles stop. The Aliancistas get out of their vehicles and plant a flag, declaring Echo Park the free city-state de las Mercedes.

The overcast sky makes the landscape surreal, the sunset light shadowed by the clouds brings out the contrasting earthen, green, and floral colors creating a dreamlike ambiance as though in another world. The reflections from the sandstone mesa cast an orange and yellow light, making the canyon walls pulsate with life. The National Forest Park Rangers, Evans and White, both known to have reputations for their animosity towards Mexicans, approach the picnic area. The Aliancistas are setting up their camp. Ranger White, in a gruff voice, demands they pay for a picnic permit. The men and women tell the ranger that it is they who are trespassing, and it is they who need to pay them for being on their land. José María tells the ranger, "You are the one in violation! And both of you are under arrest for trespassing en La Merced de San Joaquín de Río Chama - Merced de Tierra Amarilla." Gregorita, "Yes! Youu...you are under arrest, mister! You are trespassing on our land. This is our Merced our abuelos were awarded by the Mexican government!"

Indio Gerónimo, Terijú, Libertado and others grab the rangers by the arm, telling them that they are under arrest by the authority of La Merced de San Joaquín de Río Chama. A scuffle ensues as the rinches resist, and several Aliancistas forcibly arrest them. They escort them to a nearby pickup truck with high cattle railings that act as a makeshift jail while a jury is formed. Women and youth take branches from trees and make switches. They slap and poke the rinches, Calixtra pinches them. Jerry Noll, a self-proclaimed descendant of the King of Spain and failed law student, acts as judge. He speaks in flowery language using legal vocabulary. The women and children continue to poke and prod the rinches. San Joaquin police escort them from their makeshift cell up the hill to a picnic table on a rise which serves as a judge's bench. Aliancistas, women and bystanders yell obscenities.

A woman asks sarcastically, "Now who is in charge? ¡Apestosos rinches!" (rangers)

The Alianza guards make a futile attempt to keep the people away. Jerry Noll sits at the picnic table using a hatchet and block of wood as a gavel. The jury is seated to one side of him as he calls the court proceeding into session.

Jerry Noll announces, "The court is now in session. Please bring the defendants forth." José María is the defense attorney, and with a swagger, steps forward mockingly.

The Defense Attorney states, "Judge, my clients are innocent. They did nothing wrong. They were only doing their job."

Jerry Noll says, "Will the defendants please respond." Ranger White refuses to respond and is extremely infuriated.

Ranger Evans, "You people have no idea what you are getting yourselves into."

Judge Noll turns to the defense attorney, "Will you please have the defendant answer the question, or he will be held in contempt."

The Defense Attorney José María has a word with his client, "You listen here, Mister, you had better treat this court of law with more respect, o te van a mandar a la cárcel." ("...or you are going to jail".)

Judge Noll asks again, "How do you respond to the charges, sir?"

Ranger White retorts, "Why you goddamn Mesicans!' Bam!

The Judge slams the gavel, and states, "Bailiff, will you please remove him from the courtroom."

The Judge slams the gavel again. Bam! "What does the prosecution have to say?"

Prosecuting Attorney Santiago Anaya, a slightly shorter rugged rancher, "Yes, your honor...these gentlemen, they are trespassing. They do not have permission from any of the citizens of La Merced de San Joaquín de Río Chama and Tierra Amarilla to be here. And we ask the court to prosecute to the fullest extent of the law."

Judge Noll says, "The jury has heard the charges. I ask the jury to deliberate and inform the court of your verdict as soon as possible."

The jury gets up and walks towards the vehicles to deliberate. They come back and take their seats on the hilly knoll surrounded by piñón trees... piñones (seeds) cover the ground.

Jury Foreman Gregorita stands, "Judge, we find the rinches guilty as charged. They violated our laws. They trespassed on our land."

The judge slams the gavel. "You are hereby found guilty of trespassing on La Merced de San Joaquín de Río Chama, Merced de Tierra Amarilla. We, the court, will forfeit custody to the State Police and suspend the fines of five hundred dollars.

The Aliancistas escort the prisoners down the hill to Captain Vigil of the New Mexico State Police, where he has been observing the entire incident from a distance. News reporters begin to arrive.

They turn the prisoners over to Captain Vigil, and he walks them to a patrol car. The officer puts them in the back seat and whisks them away north to Tierra Amarilla.

The Aliancistas' emblematic victory is confirmed by news reporters crowding Zara and asking him questions. He appears on the next day's local television and newspaper headline news as well as in local and national newspapers and radio. The Alianza has entered another stage, gaining much publicity.

It is sunset. People are celebrating their victory. Zara, with a group of men, turns and calls Indio Gerónimo.

Zara, "Indio, ven pa'cá. Quiero que te pongas de atalaya allí arriba de la mesa y nos avises si ves la patrulla o bien hóstiles o quien sea que llegue. (I want you to be the lookout on top of La Mesa. Keep an eye out for the police or hostiles, or anyone else that may come.)

Indio goes to the tent, gets his things and bids Fátima good night with a kiss. He mounts a mustang. Lupita is in the shadow of an árbol de piñón (pine tree) watching Indio. The horse rears up, kicking its front legs in the air. Indio rides towards a crevice in the mesa, turns and sees Lupita. They smile at one another and he makes his way to the top of the mesa, overlooking the valley, where he has a clear view of the highway in both directions for many miles, the campsite just below. The women prepare to settle the children in for the night. Indio starts a fire to keep warm for the evening and sets out a bed roll.

Standing proud, rifle butt setting on his thigh, he is in silhouette as the sun is setting. He looks down upon the campsite where people celebrate; music echoes into the twilight.

Nicolás is at a table, writing furiously.

José María asks, "¿Qué andas haciendo, Hermano?" ("What are you doing, Hermano?")

Nicolás says, "¿Cómo suena esto?" (How does this sound?)

He clears his throat to sing the corrido he has just composed of the day's events. José María joins in with the guitar. The mood is festive. They celebrate their victory. Indio sits next to a campfire on the mesa top, rifle next to him, listening to the activity below. He rolls mountain tobacco and smokes a cigarette as the melodies linger on the night wind along with the rustic voice of Nicolás, as his tío plucks and strums the guitar.

**Corrido de Eco Anfiteatro**

| | |
|---|---|
| 1. | 1. |
| *Escuchen señores la famosa historia* | Listen people to the famous story |
| *De un hombre sabio y valiente* | Of a wise and valiant man |
| *Puso en peligro su vida* | His life he put in danger |
| *Por defender a su gente* | To defend his people |
| *Con su bandera en su mano* | With his flag in his hand |
| *Al gobierno le hizo frente* | He confronted the government |
| 2. | 2. |
| *La historia se refiere al nombre* | History refers to the name |
| *Nombre de muy grande estima* | A name of high esteem |
| *El fundador de la Alianza* | The founder of the Alianza |
| *Zarfarano* | Zarfarano |
| *Por defender a su raza* | To defend his race |
| *Su vida para nada la estima* | His life he does not esteem |

3.
*Dice Zarfarano*
*El que confirmó la Alianza*

*Es hombre de gran confianza*
*Y miembro que no falla*

*Es valiente y bondadoso*
*Su nombre es Santiago Anaya*

3.
Zarfarano says
Whoever confirmed the Alianza
Is a trustworthy man
And a member who does not fail
His is valiant and kind
His name is Santiago Anaya

4.
*Zarfarano hombre valiente*
*Sin mi sol subió a la luna*

*En la ciudad de Alburquerque*
*Tiene su nido y su cuna*
*Amonesta la verdad*
*Y a nadie le queda duda*

4.
Zarfarano, a valiant man
Without my sun climbed to the moon
In the city of Albuquerque
He has his nest and his crib
He admonishes the truth
And no one doubts it

5.
*Año de mil novecientos*
*Sesenta y seis en octubre*
*Dice Zarfarano*
*Les voy a encender la lumbre*
*Voy a quitarles el orgullo*
*Que han tenido por costumbre*

5.
In the year nineteen hundred
Sixty-six in October
Zarfarano says
I will strike fire on them
I will take away their pride
That they are accustomed to

6.
*Sale Zarfarano*
*Rumbo al norte con su gente*
*Para el condado de Río Arriba*
*A desafiar a la muerte*
*Dándole prueba a su pueblo*
*Que cumple lo que promete*

6.
Zarfarano heads out
To the north with his people
To the county of Río Arriba
Defying death
Giving his people proof
That his keeps his promises

Coro
*Clarines y cajas*
*Música de viento*
*Vengan a tocar para la Alianza*

Chorus
Bugles and drums
And wind music
Come to play for the Alianza

*Con su noble caravana*

7.
*Cuando se iban acercando*
*Detuvo a toda su gente*
*"Ya vamos hacer la entrada*

*Prepárense los valientes"*

*Zafarano va adelante*
*Porque él no teme la muerte*

8.
*Hermanos de Zarfarano*
*Valientes y decididos*
*Le dicen "Donde tú mueras*

*Moriremos junto contigo*
*Es preferible la muerte*
*Mejor que quedar cautivos"*

9.
*Hombres, mujeres, y niños*
*Acompañando la marcha*
*Dice la hispana valiente*

*"Está no es cosa de chanza*
*A ver si las mujeres arreglan*

*Ahora se ríe y se ancha*

10.
*Porque ya se llegó el día*
*Pregúntaselo a la Alianza*
*¿Quieren pan con mantequilla?*

*Vengan a poner la panza*
*La hispana está lista*

With his noble caravan

7.
When they were getting close
He stopped all his people
"We are going to make our entrance
Prepare yourselves, valiant ones"
Zafarano is at the front
Because he doesn't fear death

8.
Brothers of Zarfarano
Valiant and decided
They tell him, "Wherever you die
We will die along with you
Death is preferable
It's better than being captives"

9.
Men, women, and children
Accompanying the march
The brave Hispanic woman says
"This is not by chance
Let's see if the women will fix things"
Now she swells with laughter

10.
Because the day has come
Just ask the Alianza
Do you want bread with butter?
Come and put your stomach
The Hispanic woman is ready

| | |
|---|---|
| *Hoy comenzó su venganza* | Today her vengeance has begun |
| 11. | 11. |
| *La Merced de San Joaquín*<br>*Es la primera en la listaIs*<br>*Hoy la vamos a tomar*<br>*A ver si el gobierno chispa* | The landgrant of San Joaquín<br>The first on the list<br>Today we're going to take it<br>Let's see if the government backs down |
| *Por lo que hacen a los demás* | For what you do to everyone else |
| *Yo no los pierdo de vista* | I won't lose sight of them |
| 12. | 12. |
| *La Merced de San Joaquín*<br>*Fue la primera escogida*<br>*Situada en el corazón*<br>*Del condado Río Arriba*<br>*La primera que ofreció*<br>*A su pueblo nueva vida* | The San Joaquín landgrant<br>Was the first one chosen<br>Situated in the heart<br>Of Río Arriba county<br>The first that offered<br>New life to its people |
| *Coro (Se canta cada seis versos)* | Chorus (Sung every six verses) |
| 13. | 13. |
| *Dice el pueblo a Zarfarano*<br>*"Tienes muchos adversarios*<br>*Tenemos que seguir adelante* | The people say to Zarfarano<br>"You have many adversaries<br>We need to keep moving forward |
| *El Pueblo está atrás de tí*<br>*A nadie llevas a fuerzas*<br>*Todos somos voluntarios"* | The people are behind you<br>You are not forcing anyone<br>We are all volunteers" |
| 14. | 14. |
| *Cuando se iban acercando*<br>*Detuvo a toda su gente*<br>*"Ya vamos a hacer la entrada* | When they were getting close<br>He stopped all his people<br>"We're going to make our entrance |

*Prepárense los valientes"*
*Zafarano va adelante*
*Porque él no teme la muerte*

Prepare yourselves, brave ones
Zafarano is at the front
Because he does not fear death

15.

*Hermanos de Zarfarano*
*Valientes y decididos*
*Le dicen "Donde tú mueras*
*Moriremos junto contigo*
*Mejor que quedar cautivos"*

15.

Brothers of Zarfarano
Brave and decided
They tell him, "Wherever you die
We will die alongside you
It's better than being captives"

16.

*Cuando quebramos el frente*
*Te vimos a la carrera*
*El primer paso que dimos*
*Fue plantar nuestra bandera*
*Proclamando libertad*
*Hasta el último que muera*

16.

When we broke through the front
We saw you at full pace
The first step we made
Was to raise our flag
Proclaiming liberty
Until the last of us is dead

17.

*Oficiales de gobierno*
*Estaban ya preparados*
*Para arrestar a la Alianza*
*Pero fueron arrestados*
*Siendo hijitos del gobierno*
*Quedaron avergonzados*

17.

Government officials
Were already prepared
To arrest the Alianza
But they were arrested
Being sons of the government
They were left humiliated

18.

*Ya tomamos posesión*
*De nuestra anhelada tierra*
*Rindamos un saludo*
*A nuestra hermosa bandera*

18.

We have taken possession
Of our beloved land
Let us render a salute
To our beautiful flag

*Coro (Se canta cada seis versos)*

Chorus (Every six verses)

19.
*Que hermosa es nuestra bandera*
*Azul color como el cielo*
*Con letras de oro grabados*
*A cincelado con mucho esmero*
*Proclamando en su grabado*
*El Hispano no es limosnero*

19.
How beautiful is our flag
Blue like the color of the sky
With golden engraved letters
Chiseled with great care
Proclaiming in its engraving
The Hispanic is not a beggar

20.
*La misión de Zafarano*
*Tiene un gran poder*
*Pregonero de justiciar*
*Por inspiración de justicia*
*Los que sus ojos no veían*
*Su corazón lo adivina*

20.
The mission of Zafarano
Has great power
Town crier of justice
Inspired by justice
What his eyes did not see
His heart would guess

21.
*La misión de Zafarano*
*Tiene un gran poder*
*Con su fé y su inteligencia*

*Y su noble corazón*
*Traspasaría las barreras del mundo*

*Sin ninguna intervención*

21.
The mission of Zafarano
Has great power
With his faith and his intelligence
And his noble heart
Surpassing all the barriers of the world
Without any intervention

22.
*Y ésta es la historia famosa*
*Aquí le voy a dar fin*
*Cuenta cómo fue tomado*
*La Merced de San Joaquín*
*Entre música de viento*
*Y como jefe el clarín*

22.
And this is the famous story
Here I will bring it to an end
It tells about how it was taken
The San Joaquín landgrant
In the midst of wind music
And with the bugle as chief

***

Indio lies next to the fire and he huddles up in the fetal position and falls asleep to the sounds of glee and music.

# CHAPTER SEVEN

## LA CUARESMA

INDIO AND HIS TÍO José María pull up to the Morada. Hermanos are cleaning in preparation for Cuaresma (Lent), "Buenas, Hermanos. ¿Cómo les va?" (Good day brothers. How is it going?) Hermano José María shakes the hand of several Hermanos.

Hermano Mayor hands Indio a broom, "Pues muy buenas tardes Hermanito" (Well, good afternoon, little brother.) Indio takes the broom and starts to dance with it, "¿Qué estás haciendo, Hermano? Te vamos a castigar por bailar en este tiempo cuaresmal, Hermanito." (What are you doing, brother? We are going to discipline you for dancing now during Lent, little Brother.)

"Oh, no sabía lo que querías. Pensé que esperabas que te enseñara a bailar, hermano. Además, la Cuaresma sólo empieza dentro de una semana," responds Indio. (Oh no, I didn't know what you wanted me to do. I thought you wanted me to teach you how to dance, Brother. Anyway, Lent doesn't start for another week.)

Other Hermanos laugh. "Como se esta poniendo sabio este Hermanitio," more laughter.

"Oh no, Hermano, ya estás comenzando mal, vamos a tener que darte un castigo," answers Hermano Mayor. (Oh no, Hermano, you are already starting out wrong, we are going to have to discipline you.)

"Okay Hermano, ¿dónde quieres que empiece? Nomás que me da tanto gusto verlos y de que va a empezar la cuaresma, por eso estoy así, Hermano," Indio responds in a humbled voice and posture. (Ok, where do you want me to start? It's just that I am so happy to see you guys and that Lent is going to start, that's why I am like this, Hermano.)

"¿Por qué no empiezas limpiando el altar?" (Why don't you start by cleaning the altar?) Hermano Mayor tells him.

Indio puts the broom to one side and gets a dust cloth and busies himself dusting the Santos. As more women arrive and take over the cleaning Indio goes outside to help. Fátima arrives and begins cleaning the candleholders. Other women sweep the floor and wipe the altar as members of the community continue to show up to help taking rakes and shovels.

Time passes. People begin to arrive with food and set up. Hermano Mayor announces to everyone the food is ready,

"Vengan a comer" (Come and eat.) The Hermanos wash up. Others gather the tools and begin to sit at the table. Hermano Mayor asks Hermano Francisco to lead the prayer for the comida.

## Rezo para la Comida

*La persignación: En el nombre del Padre, del Hijo, y del Espíritu Santo*

| | |
|---|---|
| *Bendice Señor nuestros alimentos* | Bless our food, Father |
| *Que vamos a recibir por obra* | That we're going to receive by deed |
| *Y gracia del Espíritu Santo* | And the grace of the Holy Spirit |
| *Y el rey de la eterna Gloria ha hecho* | And the King of eternal Glory has done |
| *Y participamos en su mesa celestial* | And we participate in his divine table |
| *Donde están los Ángeles y Santos* | Where Angels and Saints live |
| *Y el cuerpo de nuestro señor Jesucristo* | And the body of Jesus Christ |

***

Los Hermanos take turns singing while everyone is having their meal. Peaceful silence decends.

## El Mejor Hombre

| | |
|---|---|
| 1. | 1. |
| *El mejor hombre del mundo* | The best man of the world |
| *En la cruz fue clavado* | On the cross was nailed |
| *En santa Jerusalén* | In holy Jerusalem |
| *Alabado y ensalzado* | May he be praised and exhalted |
| 2. | 2. |
| *A orillas de un ojo de agua* | At the edge of a spring of water |
| *Estaba un Ángel llorando* | An Angel was crying |
| *De ver que se condenó* | To know He was condemned |
| *El alma que traía cuidando* | The soul of which he was watching over |

3.
*La Virgen le dice al Ángel*
*No llores Ángel varón*
*Que yo le rogaré a Cristo*
*Que esta alma tenga perdón*
4.
*La Virgen le dice a Cristo*
*Ay, hijo de mi corazón*
*Por la leche que mamaste*
*Saca este alma del fuego ardor*

3.
The virgin says to the Angel
Don't cry, male Angel
For I shall pray to Christ
That this soul is pardoned
4.
The Virgin tells Christ
Oh, son of my heart
By the milk that you suckled
Free this soul from the fire
ardor

5.
*Cristo le dice a la Virgen*
*Madre de mi corazón*
*¿Para qué quieres esta alma*
*Si tanto nos ofendió*

5.
Christ tells the Virgin
Mother of my heart
Why do you want this soul
Who so often offended us?

6.
*La Virgen le dice a Cristo*
*Hijo de mi corazón*
*Pastoreando sus ovejas*
*Mi Rosario me rezó*

6.
The Virgin speaks to Christ
Son of my heart
While tending his sheep
He prayed my Rosary

7.
*Cristo dice a la Virgen*
*Madre de mi corazón*
*Si tanto quieres esta alma*
*Sácala del fuego ardiendo*

7.
Christ responds to the Virgin
Mother of my heart
If you want this soul so much
Take it out of the burning
flames

8.
*La Virgen como piadosa*
*Al infierno se arrojó*
*Con su santo escapulario*
*A su devoto sacó*

8.
The Virgin so pious
Cast herself into hell
With her holy Scapular
Her devotee she rescued

9.
*Sale el diablo embravecido*
*Hasta el cielo subió*
*Señor, el alma que me distes*
*Tu Madre me lo quitó*

9.
The Devil comes forth in a rage
To Heaven he rose
Lord, the soul that you gave me
Your Mother took it away

10.
*Quítate de aquí maligno*
*Quítate de aquí traidor*
*Que lo que mi Madre ha hecho*
*Por bien hecho lo daré yo*

10.
Depart from here wicked one
Depart from here, traitor
For what my Mother has done
As well done I shall consider it

11.
*Daremos gracias a Dios*
*Que esta alma se salvó*
*Que Dios le dará la Gloria*
*Como al Pastor se la dió*

11.
Let us give thanks to God
For this soul that has been saved
For God shall give it Glory
Just as he gave it to the Shepherd

12.
*Señor mío Jesucristo*
*Yo te ofrezco este alabado*
*Por las ánimas benditas*
*Y las que están en pecado*

12.
My Lord, Jesus Christ
I offer you this song of praise
For the blessed souls
And those who are in sin

***

An aura of peace and solemnity has enveloped all present. People turn to one another and comment on the alabado, how it made them feel. As people finish up, chatter takes over, jokes are shared, and people catch up with one another's lives telling stories of their ancestors and gossip both past and present as they finish their meal.

Elder Hermano Apolonio declares, "¡Ave María Purísima!"

Everyone stops talking and responds, "Que sea concebida sin pecado original." Hermano Apolonio begins the closing prayer, a blessing for the lunch and the Hermanas who prepared it.

**Un Rezo**

| | |
|---|---|
| *Gracias te damos señor mío Jesucristo* | We give you thanks my lord Jesus |
| *Por el sustento que nos has dado* | For this sustenance You have given us |
| *Sin ser merecido* | Without being worthy of it |
| *Tú, cuando anduviste en el mundo* | You, when you walked the Earth |
| *Comistes y bebistes por obra* | You ate and drank by deed |
| *De tu Padre eterno* | Of your Eternal Father |
| *Y para bien del linaje humano* | And for the good of the human lineage |
| *Y así como has participado* | And the way you have participated |
| *En esta mesa temporal* | In this temporary table |
| *Participamos en su mesa celestial* | We participate in his Divine table |
| *Donde están los Ángeles y Santos* | Where the Angels and Saints are |
| *Para toda la eternidad* | For all of eternity |
| *Amén Jesús* | Amen, Jesus |

Un ave María, para las Hermanas y todos los que ayudaron a preparar esta comida y para quien nos han ayudado con el mantenimiento de esta santa Morada. Y un sudario para todos los Hermanos de esta Morada y sus familias y a todos nuestros conocidos difuntos. Ave María purísima. (An Ave Maria, for all those Hermanas that prepared this food and those that have helped in the maintenance of la Morada. And a prayer to all those Hermanos of this Morada and their families and loved ones that have made their transition.)

"Ave María Purísima," (Holy Mother of God) announces Hermano Mayor...

The other Hermanos respond, "Que sea concebida." (May She be conceived.) "Sin pecado original," (Without original sin.) other Hermanos respond.

"Santa María, madre de Dios, santificado sea su nombre, vénganos a tú reino, hágase su voluntad aquí en la tierra como en el cielo, el pan nuestro de cada día danos hoy Señor perdona nuestra deudas así como has perdonado a nuestras deudores, no nos dejes caer en tentaciones más líbranos de todo mal. Amen."

(Hail Mary full of grace, sanctified is your name, comes your reign do your will here on earth as you do in Heaven. Give us our daily bread every day dear Lord, forgive our debts here like you have forgiven our debtors. Do not allow us to fall into temptation, but liberate us from all that is not good. Amen.).

Por las ánimas benditas todos debemos rogar. (For all the souls we pray). Responden los demás. (The rest respond.)

"Qué Dios les saca de pena y los lleve a descansar." (May God take their pain away and lay them to rest.)

"Señor Dios que nos dejaste la señal de tu divina pasión y muerte: la sábana santa en la cual fue envuelto tu cuerpo santísimo cuando José fuiste bajado de la cruz. Concédenos Señor o piadosísimo Salvador que por tu muerte y sepultura santa te hayas llevado las benditas almas del purgatorio de todo los Hermanos de esta Morada y sus familiares, y conocidos a descansar a la gloria de la resurrección, a donde tú, señor, vives y reinas con Dios Padre, en la unidad del Espíritu Santo Dios por todos los siglos de los siglos santos. Amén." (Lord God, who left us the sign of your divine passion and death: the holy sheet in which was wrapped your holy body when Joseph lowered you down from the cross. Grant us Lord o pious Savior, that by your death and sacred burial you have taken the blessed souls of purgatory to rest in the glory of the resurrection., where you live and reign with God the Father in the Holy Spirit. God for all ages of the holy ages. Amen.)

Everyone pitches in to clean. Los particulares (the regular people) express their appreciation and donate to help pay for candles and the maintenance of the Morada as they leave. Las Hermanas pack up pots and pans, and utensils, and bid their goodbyes. The Hermanos bring in firewood and water and prepare for an all-night vigil. The Hermano Mayor calls for everyone's attention, "Ave María, Hermanos."

"Que sea concebida sin pecado original," responden los otros Hermanos. (may it be conceived without original sin.)

Hermano Mayor, "Hermanos, les quiero dar las sinceras gracias por el trabajo que han hecho hoy. Ya saben la importancia de tener nuestra casa en orden, y no nomás la Morada, sino también nuestro espíritu en este tiempo sagrado. Nuestra Hermandad se dedica a la pasión y muerte de Nuestro Jesús el Nazareno. Dedicamos nuestros rezos a las almas difuntas y a nuestros vivos. El reconocimiento de la pasión y muerte de Nuestro Padre Jesús es una reflexión del camino en que cada uno de nosotros andamos. Es un tiempo de meditación para que miremos como van nuestras vidas que nos quedemos en la presencia de Dios. Que nos comportemos con integridad en todo lo que hagamos, con nuestras familias, y cualquier ser particular," explains the Hermano Mayor.

("Brothers, I want to give you my sincere thank you for the work you have done today. You already know the importance of having our house in order, and not only the Morada, but our spirit during this sacred time. This Brotherhood dedicates itself to the passion, death, and resurrection of Jesus of Nazareth. We dedicate our prayer to those souls that have passed and those still alive. The recognition of the passion and death of our father Jesus reflects of the road that we all have to take. It's a time of meditation so we can see how our lives are going and stay in the presence of our Creator. We should conduct ourselves with integrity in all that we do, with our family and anyone we encounter.")

"Bueno, en este momento vamos a abrir la casa para una discusión. Hermano Herman quiere compartir con nosotros una explicación del por qué somos Hermanos Nuevomexicanos y por qué nos dedicamos a la Cuaresma para rejuvenecer el espíritu." (Okay, at this time the house will be open for a discussion. Hermano Herman would like to share with us an explanation for why we are Nuevomexicanos brothers and why we dedicate this time to Lent to rejuvenate the spirit.)

"Y también, Hermanos," continúa Hermano Mayor, "quisiera que comenzáramos a meditar y reflexionar sobre nuestras vidas, particularmente qué nos ha pasado este año. Practiquen los rezos y piensen en lo que dicen, lo que nos quieren enseñar. Bueno, con eso le voy a dar la palabra al Hermano Herman." (And also, Hermanos, I would like you to think and reflect on our lives, particularly what has happened to us this past year. Practice your prayers and think about what they are saying and what they are telling you. Well, with that I will pass the floor over to Hermano Herman.)

"Buenas tardes, Hermanos. Que la paz de Nuestro Señor Jesucristo siempre esté entre nosotros," says Hermano Herman. (Good afternoon, may the peace of Jesus Christ always be with us.) "Así sea," answer the other Hermanos." (May it be.)

"Bueno, vamos a hablar de lo que hacemos durante este tiempo cuaresmal, como ya dijo el Hermano Mayor, nuestra Fraternidad se dedica a las últimas horas que Jesucristo estuvo en este mundo como ser humano, desde el momento que bajó del Monte Calvario hasta la crucifixión. Yo he aprendido que uno tiene que preparase para este tiempo, digo psicológicamente, de nuestra jornada espiritual y cómo se relaciona con lo que hacemos en este tiempo cuaresmal. (Okay, let's talk about what we do during this time of Lent. As Hermano Mayor already said, our Fraternity dedicates itself to the last hours that Jesus Christ was in this world as a human being, from the time he came down from Mount Calvary to the crucifixion. I have learned that one has to prepare oneself for this time, I mean physiologically, for our spiritual journey and how it relates with what we do in this time of Lent.)

"¿Qué es lo que significa la pasión y muerte de Jesucristo?" (What is the meaning of the passion and death of Jesus Christ?)

"Bueno, como lo aprendí yo de nuestros antepasados, lo que quería Dios Espíritu que aprendiéramos de la pasión de Jesucristo es que cada paso de las catorce estaciones son ejemplos de lo que pasamos a través de la vida, nuestro sufrimiento y dolor, pero tenemos que tener en mente que siempre va a haber luz, no importa qué nos pasa, por lo bueno o lo malo. Así como había luz después del sufrimiento, cuando murió en la cruz, y la resurrección de Jesús, hay luz y después de la agonía, como hay vida después de la euforia. La resurrección de Jesús nos enseña que la vida sigue. El Espíritu es abundante, amoroso, sin duda no hay que sentir falla en nuestras vidas, mientras podamos mantener en nuestras mentes que el Espíritu siempre está con nosotros, y mientras nos mantengamos justos, nuestros sueños se escucharán." (Well, like I learned from our ancestors, what God Spirit wanted us to understand from the passion of Jesus Christ is that every fourteen stations are examples of what we all go through in life, our suffering or pain, but we have to keep in mind there will always be light. It doesn't matter what happens to us, good or bad. Just as there was light after Jesus' suffering, when he died on the cross, and his resurrection, there is light after agony as there is life after euphoria. The resurrection of Jesus shows us that life goes on. Spirit is abundant, loving, without doubt there is no need to feel we lack anything in our lives so long as we can keep in mind that Spirit is always with us and we stay true, our dreams will be heard.)

"Yo sé que esas palabras se oyen vacías, todo el mundo dice eso. ¿Cómo podemos sacar de esas palabras alguna cosa de sustancia? ¿Cómo llegamos a un lugar donde podamos creer que Dios nos está ayudando cuando el concepto de Dios es una cosa tan abstracta? Otros también nos dicen que tenemos que tener Fé, el cual es otro concepto abstracto, y también escuchamos esto, pero a la misma vez, al ser seres humanos, tenemos que actuar como tal. Entonces ¿qué es la Fé?" (I know that those words sound hollow, everybody says so. How can we get any substance from those words? How do we get to a place where we can believe that God is helping us when the concept of God is so abstract? Others tell us to have faith, which is also an abstract concept, and we also hear this, but at the same time being human beings we have to act like such. So then what is faith?)

"Fé es la ausencia de miedo y confianza en la vida, si uno anda con miedo es necesario que se tranquilice la mente, que mire y sienta lo que es, ¿qué es el origen de lo que siente uno? ¿Dónde está tu refugio? Esto yace en el subconsciente y una vez que uno se da cuenta de eso, se vuelve consciente y luego uno puede guiar sus pensamientos a la acción; sin embargo, cuando uno está inconsciente, uno opera con miedo porque no conoce el propósito de sus acciones." (Faith is the absence of fear and the confidence in life. If one walks in fear, it is necessary to get peace of mind, know what one is feeling. What is the origin of fear? Where is your refuge? This lies in the subconscious, and once one has come to that realization it becomes conscious and then one can guide those thoughts into action; however, when one is unconscious then one operates in fear for you do not know the purpose of your actions.)

"Una vez que uno entiende por qué está preocupado con esa creencia, ya no tiene que preocuparse del pasado, por lo tanto, no hay necesidad de estar ansioso en cuanto al futuro, sino que hay que mantenerse en el presente. Eso es estar en el amor de Dios y en su gloria de abundancia y protección porque él se acuesta desde dentro, el espíritu el fuego de vida." (Once you understand why you are preoccupied with that belief, you no longer need to worry about the past. Therefore, there is no need for being anxious about the future. Stay in the present, that is to be in God's love and His glory of abundance and protection for He lays from within, the spirit the flame of life.)

"Y cuando uno esté rezando encontrará un espacio de paz, reconociendo que Dios Espíritu es todo bien y armonía, no hay discordia, Dios Espíritu es todo puro, no hay carencia material en la soledad universal de Dios sagrado espíritu." (And when one is praying you will find that space of peace recognizing that God's Spirit is all good and harmony. There is no discord. God's Spirit is all pure. There is no material lack in God the Holy Spirit, for to be with Him in the present is universal solitude.)

"¿Por eso hacemos los ritos? y ¿qué no todos caminamos por el mismo camino de las estaciones de la cruz ricos y pobres ya sea monetaria, emocional o espiritualmente? Esto es lo que significan las estaciones de la cruz, todos terminamos en el mismo lugar, acostado o acciones buenas o malas para descansar, esto es lo que significa la resurrección. Listos para seguir la vida comenzando con un nuevo capítulo en nuestras vidas, pero con la sabiduría que vino del sufrimiento, que se convierte en nuestra fortaleza al conquistar las batallas de nuestras vidas. Por eso nunca dejamos de seguir adelante, siempre tenemos que movernos y dejar lo que nos pasa en la vida exasperado y nunca rendirse uno." (Why do we do these rituals? And do we not all walk the same road of the stations of the cross, rich and poor, whether it be monetarily, emotionally, or spiritually? That is what the stations of the cross mean. We all end up in the same place, laying our actions good or bad to rest. This is what is meant by the resurrection. Ready to go on with our lives. Not only beginning a new chapter in our lives, but having the wisdom that comes with our suffering, which becomes our strength by conquering the struggles in our lives. That is why we must move forward. we must keep moving and leave behind what happens in our past with our lives although one may be exasperated never, never give up.

"Bueno, eso es todo lo que tengo que decir porque así me lo enseñaron a mí," Hermano Herman termina. (Okay, that is all that I have to say because that is the way I was taught.)

Eusebio, an elder with a prosthetic leg stands up, forcing himself to straighten up, and proposes a question as he gradually falls into a stooped position while he is speaking.

"Ave María, Hermano." (Holy Mother of God), announces Hermano Eusebio.

"Que sea concebida." (As She was Conceived), respond other brothers, while still others reply, "Sin pecado original" (Without original sin.)

Hermano Eusebio goes on to say, "Si vivimos, vamos a tener experiencias en la vida que nos lastiman emocionalmente, vamos a perder a personas que amamos, así es la vida, y por eso nos dedicamos a rezar por esas almas que ya no están aquí con nosotros. Pero también rezamos por los vivos, por su buena salud, para una buena vida para nosotros. Eso es parte de nuestro trabajo también." (If we live we are going to have experiences in life that hurt us emotionally.

We are going to lose people that we love. That is life, and that is what we dedicate our lives to. To pray for those souls that are no longer with us. But we also pray for the living, for their good health, for a good life for us. That is part of our work as well.)

"Hermanos, como ya dije tengo rato pensando en la Sagrada Trinidad. Quisiera abrir con una discusión de lo que significa la Sagrada Trinidad. Dice la iglesia católica que ya no está bien que reconocemos la Sagrada Trinidad porque es como venerar diferentes Dioses, pero como yo la entiendo y como la he aprendido de nuestros Hermanos antepasados, la Sagrada Trinidad representa las tres características de Dios, o sea El Padre, El Hijo, y El Espíritu Santo. Nos quiere decir que el padre es el poderoso de la mente, la sabiduría, la razón, la sobrevivencia y el conocimiento. El hijo es el salvador y la acción moral del mundo. El Espíritu Santo es la compasión divina, la intuición y el amor. Nuestra acción creativa del mundo es nuestra conexión con el mundo y nuestra conciencia colectiva del libre albedrío. Bueno, ahora estamos abiertos para la discusión." (Hermanos, Like I just said I have spent some time thinking about the Holy Trinity. I would like to open a discussion about what the significance of the Holy Trinity is. The Catholic Church says that it is not good to venerate the Holy Trinity because it is venerating different Gods. But the way I understand it, and how I have learned it from our deceased brothers, the Holy Trinity represents the three characteristics of God, that is, the Father, the Son, and the Holy Spirit. It wants to tell us the Father is powerfulness of mind, wisdom, reason, survival, and knowledge. The son is the savior, the moral action of the world. The Holy Spirit is divine compassion, intuition, and love. Our creative action of the world is our connection to the world and our collective consciousness of freewill. Ok, we are open for discussion.)

El Hermano Eusebio sits down.

"El Espíritu Santo es la compasión divina, la intuición, y el amor expresado como las tres caras de Dios. La acción creativa del mundo es la conexión entre nosotros mismos y el espíritu," answers El Hermano Santos." (The Holy Spirit is divine compassion, intuition, and love expressed as three faces of God. It is the creative action of the world and its connection between ourselves and spirit.)

Hermano Eusebio, "Bueno, déjeme a explicar cómo entiendo yo La Sagrada Trinidad, no digo que soy autoridad—soy un ser humano humilde de la sierra, pero como lo he pensado, y lo que he aprendido de otros hermanos después de mucha discusión, esta es la manera que lo entiendo yo." (Well, let me explain how I understand the Holy Trinity, I don't mean I am an authority - I am a humble man of the mountains, but the way I think about it, and what I have learned from other brothers after much discussion, this is the way I understand it.)

"La cabeza del Espíritu Santo es donde se comienzan los pensamientos y la intuición. Sus pensamientos pueden ser de Dios, quiere decir amor, armonía, y abundancia, o al mismo tiempo puede ser lo contrario de lo que tú decides, o lo que pienses, esto es libre albedrío. Las acciones físicas del cuerpo, como Jesús vino al mundo y sintió el dolor y la agonía que todos experimentamos, el egoísmo, miedo por falta de recursos en esta cosa que decimos la vida y la discordia entre nosotros mismos. Dios mandó a Jesús al mundo para ser un ejemplo, para dejarnos una guía para seguir por buen camino, y para que aprendiéramos como tener la mejor vida posible." (The head of the Holy Spirit is where the thoughts and intuition begin. Your thoughts can be God's, which means love, harmony, and abundance, or at the same time it can be the contrary of what you decide, or think about, this is freewill. The physical actions of the body, like Jesus came to the world and felt the pain and agony that we all experience, ego, and fear of not having the resources to survive in this thing we call life, and this creates the discord amongst us. God sent Jesus to be an example, to guide us down a good path, and so we could learn how to have the best life possible.)

"La segunda cara de Dios se expresa en forma del Alma, es la subconsciencia y el espíritu es la conciencia. El Espíritu como la conciencia manifiesta en nuestros pensamientos y el Alma lo hace sin discordia; no discrimina, hace lo que el pensamiento le dice, y esos pensamientos se expresan mediante el cuerpo, o como se forma simbolizada mediante el camino de Jesús en el mundo experimentando todo lo que experimentamos como humanos. El camino de Jesús es un símbolo que da forma, expresión, acción, y reacción aquí en nuestra tierra." (The second face of God is expressed as the soul; it is the subconscious and the spirit is the conscious. The spirit is the conscious that manifests our thoughts and the soul does what it is told, without discord, it doesn't discriminate, it does what subconscious sets into motion - original thought tells it, and those thoughts are expressed through the body, or as form symbolized through Jesus' path in the world experiencing all that we experience as humans. The path of Jesus is the symbol that gives form, expression, actions, and reactions here on Earth.)

"Con eso les doy las sinceras gracias y si les he ofendido, agraviado, o escandalizado, no fue intencionalmente. Y con eso, Hermanos, me despido si tienen preguntas o algún comentario, estoy para servirles. (With that I give you thanks and if I have offended, aggravated, or scandalized anyone, I didn't do it intentionally. And with that Brothers I close, but if you have any questions or commentary you would like to add, I am here to serve you.)

"Bueno, Hermanos, si nadie tiene algo mas que decir tocante este tema, sé que todos tenemos obligaciones de familia y trabajo. Quiero que estemos listos para la Cuaresma, y todos deberían estar pensando en lo que ha sucedido en nuestras vidas y en lo que nos ha sucedido en el pasado reciente y en el presente mientras nos preparamos para esta temporada de Cuaresma. Creo que estamos listos para terminar esta reunión. Vamos a rezar un Ave María, un Padre Nuestro, un rezo para aquellos que han fallecido, un rezo para todas las Almas difuntas de la Morada, o familiares, amigos y todas las almas sagradas en el mundo. Sabemos que Jesús murió en el monte por nosotros y nosotros somos los guerrilleros humildes de Dios. Y todos hemos hecho el compromiso a nuestro Dios Espíritu y hemos hecho el compromiso de hacerlo juntos en esta casa, mis hermanos, y con la fortaleza de nuestro amoroso Dios, nuestras obligaciones morales y espirituales," explica el Hermano Mayor. (Well Brothers, if no one has anything else to say about this theme I know that we all have obligations with our families and work. I want us to be ready for the Lenten season, and all should be thinking about what has happened in our lives and what has happened to us in the recent past and the present as we prepare ourselves for this Lenten season. I believe that we are ready to end the meeting. Let us pray a Hail Mary, an Our Father, a prayer for those that have passed away, a prayer for the souls of the deceased in our Morada, or family, friends and all those sacred souls of the world. We know that Jesus died on the hill for us, for we are the humble warriors of God. And we have all made a commitment to our God, and we have made that commitment to do it together in this house, my brothers, and with the strength of our loving God, our moral obligations and spiritual ones.)

Everyone goes to their knees to receive the blessing from the Hermano Mayor. The Hermano Mayor stands, "En el nombre del Padre, del Hijo, y del Espíritu Santo, la de tu madre María Santísima y después la mía que le alcance y le aumente su santa devoción y que los lleve por buen camino."

Hermanos responde, "Y yo lo recibo en el nombre del Padre, del Hijo, y del Espíritu Santo."

The Hermanos stand and the Hermano Mayor goes to his knees, "La bendición Hermanos."

The Hermanos give the blessing to the Hermano Mayor. The Hermano Mayor stands, everyone says their good-byes, gathers their things and leaves.

# CHAPTER EIGHT

## NUESTRA SEÑORA DE LOS DOLORES

THE CULMINATION OF SACRED time for La Cuaresma has arrived. Indio Gerónimo and José María leave for Santa Fé to pick up el Santo Entierro, Doña Sebastiana, y otros Santos in safe keeping with the Archbishops archive. The height of Lent begins on this day. The second to the last Friday of Lent, a week before Easter Sunday, the resurrection of Jesus is observed. It is a time for all to begin anew, to put closure to sorrow and incidents that have weighed one down from past experiences—a time for letting go and celebration. It is also the symbolic initiation of the spring equinox, so people are planting. El día de Nuestra Señora de los Dolores, the day of our Blessed Mother of Sorrows, José María is driving the rugged back road that leads to the highway and on to Santa Fé to retrieve the beloved treasures. The Holy relics are in storage because of a rash of burglaries on the Moradas. Collectors have discovered the sacred artifacts and are paying good money for them.

A good relationship between the Archbishop and the Hermandad has been evolving since the late 1940s and a Concilio (Council) of Hermanos had been formed to address issues between them and the

Church. It was during this time that the Moradas were experiencing a plethora of burglaries. Los Hermanos del Consejo (a council of Penitente brothers) approached Archbishop Davis to allow the Santos to be stored with him, and the Archbishop agreed to store them in the church archive. It was during this time that there was a shift in the North American psyche, recognizing the value that the Hermandad had in the history of New Mexico and their unique style of religious expression. The sudden shift in appreciation for New Mexico religious folk art also changed the way people viewed Los Hermanos; now people looked upon them as possessing stoic dignity. These Santos, primitive woodcarvings painted with natural pigments donning human hair, added to the unique characteristic of this Northern New Mexico folk art. The Smithsonian Folk Art Museum as well as various Universities began their own collections. Private collectors created an even higher demand for any and all items associated with the Hermandad, causing the allure of these artifacts to soar. These items came to be so sought out that an entire art industry emerged. An annual folk-art fair started to be held in Santa Fe, attracting thousands of buyers from throughout the world. As a result, the Morada felt hollow without its beloved Saints to pray to.

Lent is a time for Penitentes to make their pilgrimage home, to La Morada, stopping along the way, visiting other Moradas and rekindling brotherly friendships. As Indio Gerónimo and José María make their way from Santa Fé to Tramperos, known today as a suburb of Mora called Cleveland, named after the americano postmaster of the 1920s and a subliminal colonial expression renaming of an indigenous community as a subtle form of dominion. Indio Gerónimo and José María are talking about who the next Archbishop will be, and how it will affect the state of affairs with the Hermandad.

"Ahora que van a poner un arzobispo nuevo, ¿a quién crees que van a poner, tío?" (Now that they're going to name a new Archbishop, who do you think he will be, uncle?)

"No sé m'ijo, he oído del Padre Sánchez de la plaza vieja en Alburquerque, pero prefiero el Padre Jaramillo de Las Vegas, es más progresivo. El Sánchez es más conservador y por esa razón me parece que Sánchez tiene mejor chanza. Aunque me cae más Jaramillo, el punto es que en este momento de la historia vamos a tener el primer Arzobispo Nuevomexicano. Lo que tenemos que acordar es que, pues el arzobispo Davis ha sido muy bueno con nosotros. Históricamente, como ya lo he dicho, nunca hemos tenido tan buena relación entre la iglesia católica y la Hermandad como ahora. Ya sabes que los americanos instalaron el primer arzobispo de Santa Fé. M'ijo, ya te he dicho que en aquellos tiempos la mayoría de los hombres del pueblo eran Hermanos y la mayoría de los padrecitos eran franceses, y cómo nos han tratado mal. Los demás gringos se creen superiores a nosotros y nos hallaban repugnantes. No querían la Hermandad por la razón de que teníamos más poder en la comunidad que ellos, los sacerdotes, o sea, que la mayoría de la gente en nuestros pueblos estaban accionados con la Hermandad. Los padrecitos no querían reconocernos como una fraternidad religiosa, pero sí querían comenzar una parroquia. Ellos tenían que reconocernos, o no iban a tener tanto éxito recuperando gente para la parroquia. Eso nomás fue inicialmente, con los años y más las mujeres que los hombres, comenzaron a ir a la iglesia, y con el tiempo la iglesia siguió arrimando a la gente y la gente comenzó a tener más confianza con la iglesia. Y por eso me parece que nos tenían odio, por el poder que teníamos en la comunidad porque los de nuestro Pueblo nos tenían más confianza. Los padrecitos nos miraban como salvajes por el modo en que nos expresábamos espiritualmente. Estábamos bien organizados y muy hechos a nuestras tradiciones y modos de práctica espiritual, no queríamos practicar como nos estaban demandando los padrecitos franceses. No estábamos de acuerdo en todo lo que nos ordenaba el arzobispo, y nuestra gente prefería ir a Semana Santa con nosotros, y participar en nuestras ceremonias, como el encuentro y tinieblas en vez de ir a la iglesia con ellos. Hasta nos echaron la culpa por matar un sacerdote allí en la parroquia de Santa Gertrudis." (I don't know, son, I have heard that Father Sánchez of Old Town in Albuquerque, but I prefer Luis Jaramillo from Las Vegas. He is more progressive. Sánchez is more conservative and for that reason I think that Sánchez has a better chance. Even though I like Jaramillo the point is that in this moment of history we are going to have our first New Mexican Archbishop. The thing is we need to remember is that Archbishop Davis has been very good to us, and historically, as I have said before, we have never had such a good relationship with the Catholic Church and the Hermandad as we do now. You know that the americanos installed the first archbishop in Santa Fé. M'ijo, I have already told you that in those times the majority of the men of the town were Hermanos and the majority of the padrecitos were French, and how they have treated us poorly. The rest of the gringos think they are superior to us and they found us repugnant. They didn't like the Hermandad because of the reason that we had more power in the community than them, the sacerdotes (priest), in other words, the majority of the people in our towns were active with the Hermandad. The padrecitos didn't want to recognize us as a religious fraternity, but if they wanted to start a parish, they had to recognize us, or they wouldn't have very much success in bringing people to the church. That was just initially. With the years, and the women more than the men, started to go to the church, and with time, the church kept bringing people in and the people started to have more trust. And that is why I believe that they hated us, because of the power that we had in the community, because the people of our towns had more trust in us. The padrecitos looked at us as savages because of the manner that we would express ourselves spiritually. We were well organized and very used to our traditions and ways of spiritual practice, and we didn't want to practice the way the French padrecitos were demanding us to. We weren't in agreement with everything that the archbishop ordered us to do, and our people preferred to participate in our ceremonies, like the encuentro y tinieblas, when Jesus met our lady of sorrows during the passion and the moment Christ died, instead of going with them. They even blamed us for killing a priest there in the Santa Gertrudis parish.)

"Oh sí, ¿cómo fue eso, tío?" Indio Gerónimo asks. (Oh yeah, how did that happen, uncle?)

"Sí, en ese tiempo, para el Lamy, le estaba yendo muy mal con nosotros y excomulgó a todos los sacerdotes Mexicanos que se alineaban con nosotros. El arzobispo Lamy fue a Francia a reclutar sacerdotes franceses, asignándolos a los pueblos donde la Hermandad estaba más fuerte. Como en Mora, es un ejemplo, no había quien no era Hermano, m'ijo, en aquellos tiempos había más de veinte Moradas en el Valle de Mora. Ahora parece que la iglesia católica reconoce el valor de la Hermandad entre la comunidad," says José María. (Yes, at that time, for Lamy, it was going very bad for him with us and he had excommunicated all the Mexican priests that would support us. Archbishop Lamy went to France to recruit priests, assigning them to the towns where the Hermanos were strongest. Like in Mora, for example, there wasn't anybody who wasn't an Hermano, son, in those days there were more than twenty Moradas in the valley of Mora. Now it looks like the catholic church recognizes the value of the Hermandad within the community.) "Y parece que el clima sociopolítico está listo para aceptar un Hispanohablante para la posición de arzobispo. Va a ser un gran honor y placer para el pueblo Mexicano tener el líder de la iglesia católica que es de aquí, uno que es nuestro paisano nuevomexicano." (And it looks like the sociopolitical climate is ready to accept a Spanish speaker for the position of archbishop. It's going to be a great honor and pleasure for the Mexican people to have a leader of the Catholic Church that is from here, one that is a New Mexico Native.)

"Sí, ahora vamos a tener voz en la casa de nuestra Fé Católica, al fin nuestra cultura Nuevomexicana va a tener respeto y ser reconocida por nuestras contribuciones a la sociedad. Todo el daño que hemos experimentado por los gringos queriendo eliminar nuestra cultura comenzó aquí y terminó aquí con nosotros, los Hermanos de esta Cofradía, la mera alma, la cuna de nuestra ideología de quienes somos como Nuevomexicanos surgió de la Hermandad. Y así es como nuestra cultura, nuestra herencia y nuestras Mercedes siempre van a ser de nosotros. Acuérdese del verso del alabado de la tierra: de la tierra fuimos formados, y a la tierra regresaremos, así es como es, nunca vamos a dejar esta tierra. "(Yes, we are now going to have a voice in the house of our Catholic faith, finally our New Mexican culture is going to have respect and be recognized for our contributions to society. All of the harm that we have experienced by the anglos wanting to eliminate our culture started here and ended here with us, the Hermanos of this Fraternity, are the very soul of our ideology of who we are as Nuevomexicanos emerges from the Hermandad. And that's how our culture, heritage, and landgrants will always be ours. Remember this verse in the alabado de la tierra, the alabado of the land: of the earth we are made, and to the earth we will return, this is the way it is and so be it: we will never leave this earth)

"Tío, platícame cómo maltrataron al padrecito francés, "declara Indio Gerónimo.

"Bueno, cuando el sacerdote francés fue asesinado en Mora, no sé quién lo hizo. Alguien envenenó el vino en el cáliz durante la misa. Cayó muerto, allí en el altar, y nunca se supo por qué. Algunos dicen que fueron los Hermanos, otros dicen que andaba detrás de mujeres. Eso lo que yo sé, no sé qué pasó, nomás lo que he escuchado. Allí mero cayó en el altar. Y así es como me dijeron a mí." There is a long pause... (Okay, when the French priest was murdered in Mora, I don't know who did it. Someone poisoned the wine in the chalice during mass. He fell dead, there on the altar, and it was never known why. Some say that it was the Hermanos, others say that he was chasing women. That is what I know. He fell right there at the altar. And that's the way the story was told to me.)

Tío José María, "Sí, es cierto, en muchas maneras la iglesia católica ha causado mucho daño bajo el liderazgo de los arzobispos gavachos, no aprecian lo que somos, y durante el tiempo de los arzobispos Lamy y Salpointe, excomulgaron a todos los sacerdotes que no alineaban su ideología con la de ellos. Sentían que los Santos Nuevomexicanos no tenían valor, que eran primitivos y una vergüenza para la iglesia. Preferían que usáramos los que estaban hecho de yeso de las fábricas del este." (Yes, that's true, in a lot of ways the Catholic Church has caused much pain, they don't appreciate who we are. Under the leadership of the American Archbishops, and during the time of Archbishops Lamy and Salpointe, they excommunicated all the priests who would not align their ideology with theirs. They felt that the New Mexican Santos had no value, that they were primitive and an embarrassment to the church. They preferred that we use the ones made of plaster from the factories back east.)

They are driving past the Morada del Talco, approaching the highway.

"M'ijo, este camino en el que andamos es la carretera original para la entrada al pueblo de Mora. ¿Ves la Morada del Talco? En aquellos días los americanos atacaron Mora en 1847 por habernos defendido en contra de la ocupación de nuestros territorios Mexicanos. La primera vez que nos atacaron ganamos y matamos a ocho americanos y se retiraron para ocupar más refuerzos. La siguiente vez vinieron con dos cañones, y vinieron por la carretera detrás del Talco, aquí por este camino, y bombardearon la plaza, destruyendo nuestra comunidad. En esta batalla murieron veinte personas de Mora. Y querían acabar con nosotros, y mira, aquí estamos fuertes con nuestra herencia intacta y con treinta Moradas en esta región. Y con nuestro idioma intacto. Esto también es una forma de rebeldía: no siendo violento, pero sino luchando por mantener nuestra herencia. Así es como hemos derrotado la invasión de nuestros territorios y sobrevivido el genocidio cultural manteniendo nuestras creencias y ritos." (Son, this road we are on is the original road used to come into the town of Mora. Do you see the Morada del Talco? In those days when the gringos attacked Mora in 1847 for defending ourselves against the occupation of our Mexican territories. The first time they attacked, and we won and killed eight gringos and they retreated for reinforcements. And when they came back, the second time they came with two canons. They came on the road behind el Talco and they bombed the plaza, destroying our community. In this fight twenty people from Mora died. And they wanted to do away with us, and look here, we are strong with our heritage intact and thirty Moradas in this region. And with our language intact, which is also being rebellious, not to be violent but to fight to maintain our heritage. That is how we have defeated the invasion of our territories and have survived cultural genocide, is by holding on to our spiritual beliefs and rituals.)

Tío José María continues, "Ahora que van a instalar a Sánchez como Arzobispo, un nativo, estamos anunciando al mundo quienes somos, que nuestra Fé es una expresión de esta región, una expresión de quienes somos como Nuevomexicanos." (Now that they are going to install Archbishop Sánchez, a native, we will announce to the world who we are, that our faith is an expression of this region, an expression of who we are as Nuevomexicanos.)

# CHAPTER NINE

## THE ORDINATION OF THE ARCHBISHOP

ROBERTO SÁNCHEZ, a NUEVOMEXICANO, was ordained Archbishop of Santa Fé, New Mexico, with an estimated 14,000 people in attendance. He was the first "Hispano" Archbishop from the United States. The jubilant celebration, with Mariachis and Spanish folk dancers, was observed across the nation as Nativo Nuevomexicanos in particular looked forward to one of their own assuming leadership of the Catholic Church in their homeland. This event coincided with the honeymoon period of the civil rights movement. The Chicano Movement had gained momentum, challenging the specter of racism and making advances for an equitable society. People were now rejoicing in anticipation of better days to come, recognizing the religious contributions made by the first Christians in North America. Not unlike other oppressed communities throughout the country and abroad, New Mexicans were expressing their elation mainly by reviving the arts and traditions that had been suppressed and that expressed the best of their culture. They saw their beloved Archbishop as a symbol of their New World brand of

Catholicism, a symbol of their permanence in North America that had begun with the first permanent colony in 1598.

Una comisión de Hermanos met with the archbishop. They wished to officially advance the status of La Hermandad as a Catholic, faith-based community. The Hermandad had historically been seen as archaic and a public embarrassment. Archbishop Sánchez saw them as the pinnacle of New Mexico Catholic expression. For americanos today the "Penitentes" are seen as a curiosity, exotic, unlike when previously when they were seen as backward. When the American Catholic Church established itself in New Mexico it didn't recognize this frontier brand of religious Christianity. It was seen as a remnant of the 15th century form of spiritual expression and the hold Hermanos had on the communities' worldviews.

The newly appointed 19th. Century French Archbishop was appalled by the religious practices de La Cofradia de Nuestro Jesús de Nazareno, the official title of the religious fraternity founded at the time of Oñate's colonization of Nuevo Mexico. The Hermanos held to their principles of caring for their communities and today are revered by the public and recognized for who and what they represent. The newly appointed Archbishop, in 1974, acknowledged Los Hermanos' perseverance to hold on to their unwavering spiritual expression, affirming their existence and expressing themselves through a folk ritual unique to North America.

The Hermanos focus on the rosary Dolorosa, one of five rosaries. Each rosary focuses on a different aspect of scripture and is an intense form of meditative prayer practiced as one prepares for the rituals that follow. In praying the rosary, one is also praying a series of mysteries that make up the entirety of the rosary. The repetitive nature of the rosary is meant as a meditation to settle the mind. At the beginning of each mystery, one prays the Our Father and introduces what that mystery is and what one should meditate on according to the explanation provided in that mystery. Each bead of the rosary is held to ensure that ten Hail Marys are prayed for each mystery. At the beginning of each mystery there is an explanation of what that mystery is. Between each of the mysteries one contemplates what happened at each stage of the Passion. The ten Hail Marys are a veneration to the Sacred Mother (Virgin Mary) meant to bring one deep into meditations on the Passion from the moment Jesus is captured by the Romans to the crucifixion. But the practice of the rosary is meant to focus not only on the way of the cross but as a means to provide a sacred space for reflection on the trials and tribulations in one's life. What is unique to the Penitential rosary is in the detail of the Gregorian chants sung throughout, embellishing the scripture with an intense cinematic image sung in verse.

Many ceremonies found in the Catholic church have taken on the characteristics of the culture of the community it is evangelizing while teaching that community the language of the colonizer. As is the case throughout the American Continent, Native Indian and Spanish Mexican culture, today influenced by North American culture, is a result of both the miscegenation of these distinctive ethnic communities and sociopolitical amalgamation. This makes for a truly North American Christian expression. This evolution began in the 16$^{th}$ century in this region and like an organic, living being, it lives and dies only to resurrect again, holding fast to its archaic rituals and forms of prayer.

Beyond the Spanish introduction of livestock and steel to New Mexico, for example, the use of the Spanish language served as a coherent language for communication between native Indians and the Spanish colonizer. As a result of being able to communicate with one another, the Spanish were able to organize a labor force and exploit indigenous peoples throughout the American continent. That is, the process of Christianizing the indigenous population introduced a form of hierarchy unknown before, transforming the people's spiritual and linguistic identity. The Hispanized Mestizo Mexicanos had been in the region for nearly a hundred years when the Native Indians, along with detribalized Indians (Genízaro) and Mestizos, fomented a revolt against the intruding colonial regime. Raza was born—a people who had not only impacted the development of the American Southwest for three millennia but whose impact continues to evolve today.

Throughout the history of the United States, as in any developing nation, the downtrodden challenge those who exploit them and the natural resources in the region they have colonized. The people in the subordinate position are the first to experience the pains of living in a colonial environment littered with socioeconomic disparity. Minor concessions are made by those in power, but racism towards those people who are in the minority still exists, and they are still faced with limited access to social mobility.

Those accommodating the status quo and calling themselves "Hispanics" lie on the periphery of the sociopolitical foray. They are able to take advantage of opportunities unavailable to them previously. They unconsciously believe they are able to attain social mobility on their own, failing to realize that if it were not for the sociopolitical changes resulting from social protest those opportunities would not be available to them. A groundswell of popular support coalesced. Racial and ethnic alliances were made by those communities facing similar experiences, and people empathetic to the cause unconsciously participated in what has now become a national Civil Rights Movement challenging those exploiting the downtrodden. Many took advantage of the co-optive opportunities offered by the group in power but, in essence. these programs, such as preschool, bilingual education, and sanitary conditions in neighborhoods, distracted those at the forefront of social protest. It was those activists who challenged the racial, ethnic, sociopolitical, and economic order which was escalating to a revolutionary fervor.

During this period church leaders brought the Hermandad into the vanguard as the archetypal Hispanic-Christian-Catholics of North America. The Church recognized the Hermanos with accolades, publicly holding them in the highest regard. The Church's gracious treatment of the Hermandad brought it out publicly, reminding the community of its little-known history. By this time La Hermandad had been lost to memory, for many Nuevomexicanos failed to realize that such a cultural treasure had ever existed. Appointing Archbishop Sánchez as Hermano Supremo de La Cofradía de Nuestro Jesús Nazareno led to the restructuring of the age-old religious fraternity that had evolved organically. This did not go uncontested. The rank-and-file felt that there was nothing wrong with the organic nature from which the Hermandad had evolved, and they didn't agree with the political restructuring of the last contested beacon of foreign intrusion of their sacred space.

## La Constitución

La Constitución de 1857, which made La Hermandad officially independent of the Church, was authored by Padre Martínez and his associates, all of whom had been excommunicated. This 1821 document was discovered in 2015 by Hermano Gilbert Archuleta when he met Hermano Orlando Ortega del Pueblito del Duende who had inherited the prayer book from his father. The book included what Father Jose Martinez called La Constitución. What we call Las Reglas, or what he called La Constitución, is essentially a guide to how to live a life of carida (a life of caring). The document outlines the assignments of its officers. Since 1821, the bylaws of Las Reglas have evolved.

Although Los Hermanos Comisarios unwittingly went along with the changes, they surrendered the heart and soul of La Hermandad to the Archdiocese. This completely contradicted the ideological posture that had given rise to the Hermandad in the first place. At the time of modification, *los particulares* (people of the ordinary world) were caught up in the honeymoon period of the Civil Rights Movement, which celebrated their ethnicity and all its positive aspects. They thus became susceptible to the Nativo Nuevomexicano Archdioceses and forfeited their independence. The Hermanos who led the change sought to bestow honor on their native New Mexican Archbishop. Still, they failed to consider the long-range effects of disempowering the organization which had advanced a community-based spiritual worldview on the Spanish Frontier. The Hermanos who led the restructuring failed to consider the future of the Cofradia when Sánchez would no longer be the archbishop. At the time the commission was assigned to reorganize the Cofradia. It reasoned that this was an opportunity to be officially recognized by the church and a chance for their brand of spirituality to be treated with honor. On the downside, Los Hermanos relinquished their power of self-determination to the Church. They did, however, maintain their archaic way of prayer and the practice of rituals distinctive to Catholicism and the ways of Saint Frances. The ideological shift to the Archdioceses took the power away from the community-based organization and put it in the hands of the autocracy. The Hermanos found themselves guided by the church hierarchy and led by an institution that had little understanding of the inner workings of community spirituality.

This maneuver placed the spirit of the Hermandad into question. In theory, the Moradas were to do what the archbishop ordered, thereby surrendering their right of self-determination. In effect self-determination no longer existed. The church now had official dominion over what and how the Hermandad viewed themselves and now guided their ideology. Since the time of Lamy and to the present day, the struggle between the Church and the Hermandad has been one for control of how Nuevomexicanos express their spirituality. The first step when colonizing a people is to take control militarily; the second step is to take control of the region's natural resources; the third involves gaining psychological control to maintain the status quo of the conquered. This is initially accomplished by dismantling the spiritual worldview of the subordinate group by imposing the God of the conqueror as superior to no other. The new sociopolitical structure design makes the conquered complacent in their subordinate status. Archbishop Lamy made that position clear when he excommunicated Padre Martínez and other Nuevomexicano priests for failing to rebuke the Hermandad and insisted that they follow the Catholic doctrine as laid out by the institution of the church and according to the spiritual worldview of French born and raised Lamy in the mid-19th century.

From the time of United States annexation to the present, Nuevomexicanos have reacted to the tides of capitalist development and the land enclosures of the North American frontier. In effect the dispossession of marginalized, indigenous people, even though the Hermandad commission acted in good faith, dismantled their organic structure.

In reaction to the rules imposed on them by a government not of their own making, many Nuevomexicanos protested. At the same time, other factions attempted to work within the restraints of a newly imposed sociopolitical system. Others participated in symbolic protests. Still, others found solace by becoming active in the Morada, the spiritual sanctuary de Los Hermanos. The latter found strength by drawing on spirit and ritual from both themselves and their ancestors to resolve the sociopolitical impasses in which they found themselves.

The americano colonizers did not understand the spiritual rituals of these frontier people, and Nuevomexicanos became introverted, practicing their frontier Catholicism in secret. They were left with little recourse but to become invisible during their ritual practices. This resulted in separation from their extended secular communities. The organic nature of the rise of this religious ritual allowed for their survival by isolating themselves. The indirect result was a dwindling identity, for they no longer had the public exposure once enjoyed during the Mexican period. Although they maintained a quasi-relationship with neighboring Moradas, people saw less and less of the Hermanos publicly, coupled with the increasing influence of the institutional church. This shifting sociopolitical terrain left a void in village life, and fewer people were exposed to the cultural rituals in context. In contrast, during the Mexican period the Catholic Church tolerated the sometimes-excessive penitential practices. One must also consider that Nuevo Mexico was the most remote Northern Euro-Mexican frontier, and years would pass before communication would arrive from other regions of the world.

A new Archdiocese was established after the annexation of what became the American Southwest. When this happened the intellectual development of Nuevomexicanos to a more invasive prejudicial environment was affected. Had the archdiocese remained with the Durango archdiocese, Nuevomexicanos would have had an opportunity to continue to evolve naturally and linguistically, to the point of even establishing a university and a form of public education fashioned to suit the culture of New Mexico. This would have strengthened their Mexicano identity to one more closely associated with who they were and how they were developing naturally. However, Nuevomexicanos would have also been affected by the historical-political developments in México, and who knows how that would have affected Nuevomexicanos.

Considering this, we can better understand the battleground as Nuevomexicanos fought to hold onto their spiritual autonomy as another means of self-preservation. The intent of the 1857 Constitución de La Hermandad was to protect La Cofradia from church interference, thereby guaranteeing their autonomy. These Articles of Incorporation constitute the embryo of a declaration, a social contract—a caring of community—laying the foundation for an ideology that provides structure and a life of thoughtful contemplation. The document defines the purpose of their existence, and the by-laws of governance provide a methodology or system of ritual practices that express their values and spiritual worldviews in the form of a narrative that is exemplified in the ways of Jesus. It sets the parameters of how mankind should conduct their lives. Though this document is seen as an Article of Incorporation, by today's standards, it can also be seen as the beginning of thoughts of nationhood. That is, from this document, one reads about the formation of ethnic identity, a critical first step towards nation-building.

It must also be understood that an unstated power comes to those who put pen to paper in a case such as this. Those involved in the rewriting of Las Reglas should understand the history so as to embody the principles of the people it represents. Padre José Martínez had just returned from the monastery in Durango, Mexico where he studied for the priesthood. While there he found a Mexicano version of la Cofradía de Nuestro Jesús Nazareno near the monastery.

Padre Martínez was in México in the 1820s during the post-revolutionary era for Independence from Spain. He was most certainly influenced by the revolutionary fervor in Mexico and by the thoughts of nationalism coupled with the inevitability of U.S.A. expansionism. Surely Padre Martinez understood the right to self-determination. The annexation of the North American southwest set the stage for unprecedented sociopolitical and economic change in the region. It ignited Nuevomexicanos' view of nationhood and created a refined North American identity. Padre Martínez understood the importance ritual has on the human psyche to mitigate change. When people are under duress it causes them to draw from inner strength. Ritual provides a sacred space of self-empowerment and expression of the worldviews of ethnic communities. Martínez understood this. He formed an alliance with the Hermandad, established the first public schools, and acquired the first printing press in the area. He recognized the importance of literacy and education.

As a result of prolonged acculturation, Nuevo Mexicanos, with the exception of recent-generation Hispano-Hablantes, have lost much of their language, and much of Spanish-speaking heritage is now influenced by North American culture. At the same time la cultura Hispano-Hablante-Indigina-Americano is being reinforced with consistent migration from Mexico and Latin America.

La Hermandad continues to play a significant role in the preservation of the culture and language of New Mexico, they struggle to be known and understood to the greater community. The unique elements of their culture, such as their mannerisms and expressions, are being forgotten and replaced by contemporary ones suitable to the times and of mainstream society. Acculturation today is influenced by the communications revolution as we undergo a worldview articulated by a United States culture driven by new sociopolitical nuances. This has equally stifled Nativo Nuevomexicanos' identity and has been taken over by a consumer ideology. The Mexicano ideology of selfhood began in the fifteenth century and has continued to evolve to the present. It has been a process of evolution which, unfortunately, is in an inevitable state of decline due to becoming Angelized. The culture of New Mexico has been more tolerant of racial-ethnic differences at every level of society than its counterpart, White American Protestantism. However, one cannot negate the elements of race, ethnicity, language, gender biases and the ever-elusive color bar.

Like the events that led to the crucifixion of Jesus, both the Church and the secular community shunned the Hermanos because they were seen as contrary to the Protestant belief system of ethnocentricity. Anglos imposed an ideology of Manifest Destiny, which professed a worldview based on their perceived superiority. Nuevomexicanos reacted by defending their worldviews. It was those progressive Hermanos who resisted the imposition of americano dominion on their sacred space in spite of the salacious propaganda aimed at discrediting them. They persisted in their sacred practices in secret, much like the Jewish people during the Inquisition. The organic emergence of a New Mexico form of Christianity challenged the Catholic Doctrine, and the Anglo-Protestant ideology of the God-given right to dominion set forth the stage for a prodigious conflict between competing political powers for control of its people, its culture, and its territory.

The view of America's Protestant God and its belief in Manifest Destiny, of Anglican-Protestant doctrines, included a spiritual and cultural cleansing of the North American continent. There was a time when whenever a scandalous incident occurred in the region that involved Nativo Nuevomexicanos, the "Penitentes" were blamed. They were said to practice blood-letting rituals, directly or indirectly implicating them in immoral behavior. This form of ethnic cleansing is an example of how colonized people are cowed. The cultural genocide manifested here is an example of how the conqueror kept the colonized in a subordinate position.

New Mexico's history is replete with stories of ethnogenocide. One such story is of a young boy who was accused of killing a university adjunct professor in the mid-20th century. This led to his conviction and a life sentence for this 14-year-old Nuevomexicano. The village of Tijeras, New Mexico was up in arms. The residents collected hundreds of signatures petitioning for the boy's release. As the story has it, the young houseboy was preparing a bath for the adjunct professor when he attempted to force the boy into inappropriate behavior. Although no documents say this directly, it can be implied, especially after a review of the court transcripts and when one considers the sociopolitical climate at the time. The humiliated boy went home, got a gun, went back, and shot the adjunct professor. The story played itself out much differently in the U.S. newspapers, however. The newspapers made the boy out to be a crazed bloodthirsty "Mexican Penitente." They said that such heathen behavior could only be explained through their genetic makeup and their ritual practices. The court system came down hard, sentencing the young boy to life in prison. The news media speculated that it was because the "Professor" had written an article about the Hermandad that the young Penitente murdered him. It is views of this sort that held the Hermanos and all Nuevo Mexicanos y Indios under considerable scrutiny (*Hidden Chicano Cinema*. A. Gabriel Melendez).

Throughout the early part of the 20th century people stalked the Penitentes to get photographs and continued to write contemptuous stories. This was in reaction to what is unfamiliar to the pervading culture of domination. In spite of this early history, it seems today that a somewhat idealized alliance has finally come to be in lieu of the ill-fated restructuring of La Hermandad. The result has been an identity crisis that has affected the very soul of Nuevomexicanos. The manufacturing of consent by the oligarchy through the use of propaganda makes for the preponderance of a worldview that disempowers the commoner. This conflict results in a struggle for who controls the modes of production and accumulation of wealth, therefore influencing the way we see ourselves.

All People need to create binding agents that bring them together. For ethnic communities to view themselves accurately is to unfold the layers of their colonial experience and how it has affected their ability for social mobility. To practice ritual is to balance spirit, soul, and body. This is what we find in the ritual practices of the Hermandad. Human dynamics between ethnic communities affect the collective consciousness of humanity.

To comprehend how colonialism disrupts the organic order of how we structure ourselves as communities, societies, nations, and empires is to understand how colonialism influences people's view of themselves and its ripple effect on them. This is expressed through ethnocultural rituals. Nuevomexicano's sociopolitical history can be found within the practices of La Hermandad. Their collective worldview influences how Nuevomexicanos react to the larger community.

## THE ARCHBISHOP MEETS WITH THE HERMANDAD

In this scene a commission of Hermanos has been formed to establish communications with the newly appointed Archbishop, Robert Sánchez. There are four dignified but humble workmen, some dressed in cowboy boots, hats, and western shirts. They are rugged weathered, worn men. One is wearing dress pants and a fedora. They are escorted to a conference room, where they wait for a moment. The Archbishop enters, and they all stand up and greet him, shaking his hand. One Hermano, Juan Sandocal, kisses the hand of the Archbishop. Archbishop Sánchez introduces Father Jerome.

Archbishop, "Buenas, Hermanos, ¿Cómo están? I believe you all know Father Jerome from El Rito, New Mexico."

Father Jerome smiles at the familiar faces, "¿Cómo están Juan, Cosme, Santos, y José María? Espero que sus familias estén todos en buena salud," everyone exchanges salutations.

The Archbishop sits down. "Well gentlemen, I want to say that I am not only deeply honored but pleased to have you here today. I understand that we are going to pick up where Archbishop Byrne left off and that we have an opportunity to work towards further reconciliation between the Church and the Penitentes."

"Dispense, Sr. Arzobispo, pero nos referimos como Hermanos," says Hermano José María. (Excuse me, Archbishop, but we refer to ourselves as Hermanos.)

The Arzobispo feels embarrassed, clears his throat and sits down. The others take their seats.

"Sí, Sr. Arzobispo, nos sentimos honrados y nos da mucho gusto estar en su presencia," Hermano Sandoval responds. (Yes, Archbishop. we are honored and very pleased to be in your presence.)

"Ave María, Hermano," another brother responds. "Que se concebida." (As she was conceived.)

The other Hermanos respond, "Sin pecado original." (Without original sin.)

Hermano Cosmes, "Honorable Arzobispo te mandamos una carta explicando sobre la razón ¿porque estamos in su presencia? Queremos a ver si podíamos establecer una relación más cerca a la iglesia." (Honorable Archbishop, we sent you a letter explaining why we would like to meet with you. We would like to establish a closer relationship with the church.)

Juan Sandoval, "Arzobispo, así es, estamos aquí porque queremos tener mejor relación con la Iglesia, ya sabe que siempre hemos tenido relaciones duras históricamente, pero, como en 1947, con el Hermano Archibeque, establecimos una posición sin confirmación oficial, y hora quisiéramos, con su bendición y dirección, establecernos oficialmente con la Iglesia Católica Romana." (Archbishop, we are here because we want to have a better relationship with the church, and you know historically it has been tense. But since 1947, with Hermano Archibeque, we have established an official understanding. We would like to, with your direction, establish an official one with the Roman Catholic Church.)

"Yes, I think it would be a very good idea and all of you know Father Jerome," responds the archbishop.

In a superior posture and speaking in slow and deliberate pronunciation of both English and Spanish el Padre Jerome responds, "Si, pienso que sería muy bien, los Hermanos han sido importantes para mantener la Fé católica." (Yes, I believe this is a good idea. The brotherhood has been critical to maintaining the Catholic faith.)

Archbishop Sánchez, "¿En qué les pudiéramos servir, Hermanos?" (How can we help you, Brothers?)

Father Jerome had well-mannered deportment. He had grown up in El Rito, a village north of Española, and had the good Spanish enunciation of the region. Archbishop Sánchez on the other hand had been reared in Albuquerque and had been influenced by American urban culture. His refined religious training gave him an air of superiority.

"Queremos darle al arzobispo un puesto honrado," says Hermano Cosmes. (We would like to give the archbishop an honored position.) "Sí, como el Hermano Supremo Mayor de todas las Moradas," responds Hermano Sandoval. (Yes, as Supreme brother of all the Moradas.)

"And what would be the responsibilities of this position?" Asks the archbishop.

"Pues, eso es lo que tenemos que discutir, arzobispo. No lo tenemos claro aún, pero como lo miramos a usted, sería encargado de nosotros en todos los negocios como líder, dirigiéndonos espiritualmente como Hermano Supremo. Y ahora que es arzobispo, quisiéramos ponerle en un cargo honrado," el Hermano Juan responde. (Well, that is what we want to talk about, Archbishop. We are not clear, but the way we look at it you would be in charge of us in all our business, with our leader directing us spiritually. And now that you are archbishop, we would like to give you this honorary position.)

"Quisiera decir, que es para mí, un honor. ¿Por qué no formamos una comisión para que Ustedes definan mis responsabilidades como Hermano Supremo? Padre Jerome, lo voy a poner a cargo y si necesita ayuda, le doy mi permiso para hacerlo." (I am honored by your proposal. Why don't we form a commission which will define my responsibilities as Supreme Brother? Father Jerome, I will put you in charge, and if you need help I give you permission to get it.)

# CHAPTER TEN

## COYOTE CONFERENCE

AT THE ALIANZA HEADQUARTERS, which used to be a warehouse, people are busy. The ditto machine flips out copies of the upcoming conference to be held in Coyote, New Mexico. Eduardo, the caretaker of la Alianza, greets people as they come in, directing the core membership to the meeting room. Valentina, a young woman of seventeen, is in the office to answer the phone. She folds and stamps flyers to mail. Porfirio, much older than Valentina, walks in, bends at the waist, and kisses his girlfriend on the cheek. Beside her desk is a flight of narrow stairs which leads up to the concert council chamber. The room, with its thick concrete walls, used to be a refrigerated storage room. The concrete Mesa Cósmica is in the center of the room lit by a wrought iron chandelier hanging over the middle of the table. The lights are covered with hand-blown goblets casting a subdued golden glow which adds to the eerie ambiance of the inner sanctum of La Alianza. Downstairs in the office Lupita finishes typing the agenda and hands it to her father, Zara. He looks it over and the phone rings. Lupita answers and hands the phone to her father.

Zara, "That's good, we can use the cafeteria and the gym."

Zara hangs up the phone and heads up to the council chamber. The narrow, cold hallway leads to a dimly lit room, the Alianza command post. Zara takes his prominent place.

Zara begins, "Bueno, tenemos permiso para usar la cocina en la escuela allí en Coyote para la conferencia. Y tenemos que hacer planes para cómo vamos a coordinar y finalizar los objetivos de la conferencia." (Well, we got permission to use the kitchen at the school there in Coyote for the conference. And we need to make plans for how we will coordinate and finalize the objectives of the conference.)

José María, "Sí, pienso que debemos tener una oficina en el norte, es que viene mucha gente por aquí y no conocen la zona." (Yes, I think that we should have an office in the north. Many people are coming and they don't know their way around.)

Nicolás, "Tengo un lugar en Hernández, allí en un lado del camino. Tiene fácil acceso, y acabamos de comprar una de esas barracas militares de Los Álamos. Podemos usarla como una oficina." (I have a place in Hernandez, there on the side of the road. It is easy to find, and we just bought one of those army barracks from Los Alamos. We can use it for an office.)

### DETECTIVES TALK WITH PORFIRIO

State Police Detectives Facundo Martinez and Romero Jaquez are parked on the side of the road just before the turn to the Hernández Alianza office. They are watching with binoculars the activities of the Aliancistas as they settle into the new office. Surveillance goes on for quite some time before they decide to approach the Alianza headquarters.

They knock on the door. Feliciano Martínez, an Aliancista, opens it. He is startled. Everyone freezes. Weapons lie in plain sight, but no one makes a move to pick them up. State Police Detective Facundo takes a step towards the weapons. Indio takes the automatic rifle leaning against the wall within his reach and loads a round in the chamber. Detective Facundo freezes and steps back cautiously. He tells the other policeman to follow suit. Feliciano Martínez also picks up a weapon. Zara slips out a back window from another room.

Detective Romero, "Queremos hablar contigo, Porfirio." (We want to talk with you, Porfirio.)

The three of them walk out to the police car. The police invite him to get in the car so that they can talk.

Detective Romero asks, "¿Que están haciendo?" (What are you guys doing?)

Porfirio responds, "Vamos a ocupar La Merced." (We are going to occupy the landgrant.)

Detective Romero takes out a pack of cigarettes and offers him a smoke. He says, "¿Quieres un cigarro?" (Want a smoke?)

Porfirio says, "No, te hace daño." (No, it's not good for you.)

Detective Romero asks, "¿Y cómo van a hacer esto?" (And how are you going to do this?)

Porfirio says, "Bueno, ya pasamos por la primera fase." (Well, we have gone through the first phase.)

Detective Romero inquires, "¿Y qué es la primera parte del plan?" (And what was the first part of the plan?)

Porfirio says, "Hemos tratado de negociar con el estado legalmente y hemos hecho todo lo posible y nadie nos ha puesto atención, ahora vamos a comenzar la segunda fase y eso es tomar posesión de La Merced. La Merced está en nuestra jurisdicción y está dentro de nuestro derecho de no dejar que nadie pase por nuestros terrenos. Si quieren pasar van a tener que pagar una cuota. Estos terrenos son de nosotros. Si los quieren usar, tienen que pagar." (We have attempted to deal with the problem legally. We have done everything possible, and no one has paid attention. Now we are in the second phase, and that is to take La Merced back. The landgrant is in our jurisdiction, and it's within our right to keep people from coming through our land. If they want to come through they need to pay a toll. These lands belong to us. If they want to use them they need to pay.)

Arson is on the rise. Buildings and haystacks are set ablaze, fences cut, cattle shot. Ranchers and businesses are threatened, and vehicles are vandalized. District Attorney Alfonso Sánchez works tirelessly in an attempt to avoid further conflict. He does a background check and finds Zara's police record from Arizona, so he contacts the FBI.

### PLAZA DINER

An unmarked Black 1967 Impala pulls up in front of the Diner on the Santa Fé Plaza. A State police officer, Police Chief Black and Captain Vigil get out and go into the diner.

The District Attorney, Alfonso Sánchez, and his assistant are sitting at a center table. Sánchez is reading the newspaper, "Look at this. That damn Zara made the paper again, and he is calling me out, challenging the State to defend their right to the National Forest."

Chief Joe Black, an orphaned mixed-blood who was raised Chicano, walks in with Captain Vigil and hands Sánchez a file. They sit down. The waitress approaches with a pot of coffee.

The waitress is an attractive young local native girl, "Would you like some coffee?" She hands them menus.

"Yes, and a glass of milk," responds Chief Joe Black. "Here is the background check on Zara. It looks as though he is a fugitive in Arizona. He fled while the court was in recess. He was facing charges for burglary and theft.

Captain Vigil says, "Me and Detective Romero talked to Porfirio a few days ago. It's all in the report."

Alfonso Sánchez smiles, "Good, good, I see here that they are planning to charge people to drive through the Merced. Let's have the judge issue a warrant for Zara's arrest."

Captin Vigil retorts, "¿Por qué? No ha hecho nada mal aquí. No ha violado la ley aquí en Nuevo México. ¿Con qué delito le acusamos?" (Why? He hasn't done anything wrong here. He hasn't broken the law here in New Mexico. What infraction can we charge him with?)

Alfonso Sánchez responds, "Well, he failed to appear on that civil lawsuit permanently prohibiting him and his followers from taking any properties that don't belong to them. That's what he's talking about right here in the paper, and that's what Porfirio told you, right? We can have him and his followers arrested for conspiracy to take property that isn't theirs and then later have him extradited to Arizona. They plan on taking what isn't theirs, which is against the law."

He turns to his assistant, "I want you to write up the warrant. Charges will range from extortion to illegal meetings and the killing of wild game out of season as well. Haven't you guys been telling me that these people have been killing game out of season? Hell, I even got a phone call from some people in Canjilón telling me that they had seen them with the carcass of an elk. I want you and Captain Vigil to pick up the signed warrants and head up there. Find them and bring them in. Upon having the Alianza leadership arrested we'll take them into court and get to the bottom of this once and for all. So, I want you to come up with a list of Aliancistas and give the list to the judge. We will have Judge Tackit sign the warrants. I want you to put up roadblocks on all roads leading to Coyote. You got it, Chief. Meanwhile, I will get a hold of Uvaldo in Coyote, the director of the Home Education and

Livelihood Program, and have a talk with him just to let him know of the possible repercussions of the program he directs if he continues to cooperate with Zara. If he continues his involvement with the Alianza and communist activities his program may suffer. These are my orders, gentlemen." Chief Black and the other officers leave.

## LAW ENFORCEMENT ARRESTS ALIANCISTAS

Porfirio and Valentina are coordinating the upcoming conference for the Coyote Conference from the temporary Alianza office and living quarters. People are expected to come from as far away as California and other parts of the country. On the morning of June 1, 1967, at about 6:00 a.m., the police come to the Hernández office where several Aliancistas are staying and preparing for the conference. It's early in the morning. Valentina and Porfirio are still in bed. Detective Facundo knocks at the door. Startled, Porfirio gets up and answers.

Detective Facundo says, "We have a warrant for your arrest, Porfirio."

Porfirio asks, "¿Por qué?"

Detective Facundo tells him, "Conspiracy against the United States. Come on. Let's go."

Porfirio says, "Espérese, déjame rasurarme y ponerme una camisa limpia." (Ok, let me shave and put a clean shirt on.)

Detective Facundo follows Porfirio to the bathroom. The door remains open while he shaves.

Valentina, "You can't arrest Porfirio!!! He hasn't done anything. ¿Cómo puedes arrestarlo si no ha hecho nada? You're nothing but a bunch of vendidos! Can't you guys see that you are helping the gringos take our land?" ¡Desgraciados! ¡Sin vergüenzas!"

Detective Facundo nervously paces the floor as Valentina yells, waving her hands at the police officer. Porfirio is in the bathroom calmly shaving.

Facundo nervously says, "Cálmate, cálmate, Porfirio, cálmate...." Porfirio very calmly continues to get ready.

Captain Vigil, "Tenemos que llevar esos archivos." (We're going to have to take those files.) Facundo steps towards the files.

Terijú tells them, "Hey! Wait a minute! Do you have a warrant for those? You can't take those files unless you have a warrant."

Captain Vigil responds, "Well, I'm going to have to arrest you, too," he tells Terijú.

Valentina says defiantly, "If you arrest him, you're going to have to take us all in because we are not going to let the files out of here."

The Aliancistas band together, bravely challenging the police. Some of the police reach for their weapons. Captain Vigil orders them to hold down. Everybody freezes, piercing stares glare across the room.

Captain Vigil, "Bueno, dicen bien, pero déjenme decirles una cosa, voy a ir por una orden y regresaré luego para agarrar esos archivos. Les estoy diciendo que es lo que voy a hacer. Es cosa de ustedes lo que hagan con esa información." (Okay, you're right, but let me tell you guys something. I'm going to go get a warrant and come right back and get those files. I'm just telling you what I am going to do. It's up to you, what you do with that information.)

Captain Vigil turns to Feliciano Martínez, "¿Eres Feliciano verdad?" (You are Feliciano, aren't you?) Feliciano answers that he is.

Captain Vigil says, "Tenemos una orden de arresto para ti también." (We have an order to take you in as well.)

The police take both Feliciano and Porfirio to jail.

At the ranch of Uvaldo's father at Youngsville there is much activity. The name of the village had been changed from Encino to Youngsville in the 1940's. The post office had been named after a mailman, one of many changes that had taken place in New Mexico during that time. This is one example of the Americanization of the region in an attempt to erase the history of the colonized. Zara, Terijú, Indio, Jerry Noll, Lidertado, and José María are in hiding. They are talking strategy to figure out how to react to the actions taken by the State.

Aliancistas are being arrested at all hours of the day and night. Guns and rifles are confiscated. Valentina and others are at the headquarters. People show up. The phone rings. There is a great deal of confusion. Valentina is on the phone, "I don't know. The cops showed up this morning and arrested Porfirio and Feliciano. We're trying to figure out where they took them. We don't know, we just don't know. We don't know whether or not to have the Coyote Conference."

## LARRY CALLOWAY HEADS NORTH

Larry Calloway, a reporter for the *Journal North* is with friends in Albuquerque. The evening news is on TV with the day's headlines. Alfonso Sánchez talks while pictures of the State are shown.

Police are arresting Aliancistas. A hearing is to be held the next day. The Associated Press (AP), his competitor, got the drop on the story. That weekend he became aware of what was going on in the north. Calloway understands that the people of Northern New Mexico are getting pushed into a corner. He knows enough about Zara's psychology to know that Al Sánchez' actions are not going to go unheeded.

Sunday's newspaper headline reads, "It's a Showdown!". Articles cover the upcoming conference with photos of the Alianza on 2nd Street in Albuquerque. There is much activity, flyers are being printed for the scheduled conference in Coyote on the weekend of June 3 and 4. Zara uses the phrase, "It's time for a showdown," referring to the Forest Service and DA Alfonso Sánchez.

A US Forest Ranger on horseback rides up to the ranger's station in Canjilón.

The ranger says, "These damn locals think this Forest is theirs. They think they can come and take trees and fallen wood as they please. Hell, their poaching is out of hand."

It's daytime. In the village of Hernández women with their families show up at the Alianza office wanting to know what is going on.

Alfonso Sánchez is making an emergency announcement over the radio, "I implore all those who plan to attend the Coyote Conference to turn back. Anyone found to be collaborating in these communist acts of taking land that doesn't belong to them will be arrested for conspiracy against the United States. I implore the people of New Mexico to not cooperate."

Aliancistas throughout New Mexico listen to the radio and are noticeably upset. People are on the phone and on the streets. Everybody is talking about it.

Valentina says, "It isn't right; the police do not have the right to arrest people for planning to have a meeting! Unlawful assembly...how can the conference be an unlawful assembly when we haven't even met? We have to do something. This is an attack on the landgrants and on us as citizens."

Gregorita responds uncompromisingly, "De todos modos deberíamos tener la conferencia." (We should have the conference anyway.)

Valentina suggests, "Let's start telling people to meet in Canjilón."

The leadership, for the most part, has been arrested or is at large and in hiding. Confused, the younger Aliancistas suddenly find themselves thrust into leadership. They stay put and provide information as people contact them.

# CHAPTER ELEVEN

## RESPONSE TO ARREST

CRUZITA, LUPITA'S SISTER, and Valentina walk into the Española police station. Valentina wants to find out what is going to happen to her husband, Porfirio, his compañero Feliciano, and the others who have been arrested. Captain Vigil steps out of his office to talk to them.

Captain Vigil asks, "How are you girls? Malcriadas" (badly raised, without respect for elders). "Now it's my chance to misbehave like you did with me." They all laugh. "No, in all seriousness, you were right about those files. They were not on the warrant. It's a good thing you did that." The girls look at one another feeling a sense of pride.

Valentina asks, "We came to find out when you are going to let Porfirio and Feliciano out of jail."

Captain Vigil, "They are in T.A. (Tierra Amarilla) now. The judge should let them go on their own recognizance. I would just wait for them. They will be released by this afternoon."

The Aliancistas are hiding out at the home of Uvaldo's grandfather. They are milling around, talking about what is happening and what action they should take when Jerry Noll mumbles, "It is within our constitutional right to free assembly. Yes, our constitution stipulates that we have the right to have this conference, and Sánchez is violating that right. It is within our right to make a citizen's arrest on the District Attorney.

José María, Indio, and Libertado are sitting at the kitchen table. Zara is in the bathroom combing his hair. Indio draws a geographic map of the area with possible places to establish checkpoints and charge a toll fee on all highways that go through Las Mercedes de San Joaquín y Merced de Tierra Amarilla.

Jerry Noll comments on the grounds for making a citizen's arrest. Everyone stops cold and listens.

"¿Qué quiere decir eso?" (What does that mean?), pregunta Libertado.

"Well, the Constitution of the United States says that when any public servant is doing something illegal ordinary citizens have the right to arrest said official," explains Jerry Noll. "And the way I see it the District Attorney is violating our first constitutional right to free assembly. We have the right to have a public assembly. We have the constitutional right to have a Coyote Conference."

Indio Gerónimo stands up and walks over to the kitchen sink to get himself a glass of water. He walks over to the table and points out where he thinks the roadblocks may be. They discuss other possibilities and finalize where the proposed checkpoints should best be established.

Zara says, "We need to regroup."

José María says, "Podemos tener la junta en mi lugar." (We can have a meeting at my place.)

Zara says, "Sí, voy para allá esta noche." (Yes, I will go there tonight.)

"Bueno, entonces vale más irme para la casa y prepararme," says José María as he leaves. Libertado leaves with him. (Okay, I better leave so I can get ready.) He leaves in his 1948 Dodge.

Later that afternoon Indio Gerónimo is standing over the kitchen sink looking out the window when he notices an unmarked police vehicle. He doesn't see anyone. He grabs the rifle that he'd left leaning against the kitchen cabinet and runs out the back door and around the house, catching the police as they step onto the porch. With his rifle to his shoulder he pulls back the hammer. Zara hides in the bedroom closet.

Indio Gerónimo, in a heavy Spanish accent, asks, "Excuse me, can I help you?"

The State Police turn and put up their hands. Indio Gerónimo calls out to those inside, "¡Hey!, Mira lo que tengo aquí." The others are startled and grab their weapons. Uvaldo opens the door and walks out, closing it behind him.

Uvaldo addresses the police in a dignified posture and with Spanish decorum and asks in English, "Can we help you sir?"

The policemen, startled, step back with hands in the air.

The police say, "Aha, we are looking for Zara and some of the other Aliancistas. Have you seen them?"

Uvaldo looks at Indio, they both turn, and stare sternly at the police.

Uvaldo, standing straight and distinguished, "No, no one is here, and I haven't seen any Aliancistas. What is an Aliancista anyway? I don't know what you're talking about. Who or what is an Aliancista?" He relaxes in confidence.

Indio holds his rifle to his shoulder, finger on the trigger.

The police hold their ground. Uvaldo says, "Well, we were told that Zara was seen in the area. Are you sure you haven't seen him?" ask the police

Uvaldo responds, "No, no—I haven't seen anything unusual—if we do, I assure you that we will notify the authorities." Zara is intently listening to this conversation. His heart is pounding, and he is sweating profusely as he hides in the adjacent room.

"Well, if you do see something will you give us a call?" The officer hands him a card, "Call this number and they will get you to the proper officer."

"Of course. I will, officer. Thank you, now I have to go. Thank you. Now, why don't you get off my property? I got to go now."

Indio keeps Detective Facundo in his sights as he backs away slowly. Uvaldo, in a stiff, upright posture says, "I believe it would be a good idea for you to get off my property." He tells them in Spanish, "Me parece que deberían irse, ahora." The officers step away cautiously to their vehicle. Indio Gerónimo guardedly steps towards them with the rifle to his shoulder.

The police open the car door carefully. They get in and slowly drive away.

Indio Gerónimo, rifle to his shoulder, keeps them in his sights as they make their way up the rutted mountain road. Indio and Libertado stand in proud defiance.

Terijú goes into the bedroom and tells his father, Zara, that it's clear. Zara is hiding in the armoire, an antique piece of furniture with a mirror on the door. Zara pushes the door open and steps out.

Zara, "Más vale irnos de aquí ahora." (We'd better get out of here now.)

## INCIDENT IN THE TROCHIL

In Placita Blanca, a short distance northwest of Tierra Amarilla along the Río Chama, the police turn down a long winding dirt road leading to a ranch house. Gregorita's husband, Apostle Cruz Aguilar, has just finished feeding the pigs at the back of the house. Standing with an empty bucket, he hears someone drive up.

The police walk up to the front door and knock, not noticing Cruz. Gregorita answers the door. The police ask, "Buenas tardes señora, ¿vive Cruz Aguilar aquí?" (Good morning madame. Does Cruz Aguilar live here?)

Gregorita says, "Sí, ésta es la casa de nosotros, ¿y porqué buscan a mi esposo?" (Yes, this is our Home. Why are you looking for my husband?)

Cruz walks around the corner, "Sí, ¿en qué les puedo ayudar? (Yeah, how can I help you?)

The police say, "Cruz, you have to come with us."

Cruz asks defiantly, "¿Por qué? No he hecho nada." (Why? I haven't done anything.)

The police persist, "You are an Aliancista, right? And you're with Zara, right? And you are organizing a meeting, right? Then you need to come with us. We have a warrant for your arrest."

Cruz asks, "¿Y qué?", and then in heavily accented Spanish, "I am not violating the law."

The police ask, "You are a part of that group planning the meeting in Coyote, aren't you?"

Cruz responds, "¿Y qué? Tenemos el derecho a tener junta, como ciudadanos de este país." (So what? We have the right to have a meeting as U.S. citizens, citizens of this country.)

The police respond, "You can tell that to the judge. You have to come with us." Cruz's wife gets between her husband and the officers.

Gregorita tells them, "¡No pueden llevar se a mi esposo...él no ha hecho nada!" (You can't take my husband! He hasn't done anything!)

Their son, Daniel, a young boy of 13 years old, runs to the house and up the stairs. He grabs the 30-30 and looks for bullets. He can't find any, but he goes back downstairs anyway with rifle in hand and points it at the police. Daniel backs them up into the trochil (the pig's pen). Gregorita takes the 22-rifle from the truck's gun rack.

The police yell, "Put those guns down! We don't want anyone to get hurt!"

Gregorita tells them, "No se van a llevar a mi esposo ni a ninguna persona de aquí, ¿entienden?" (You are not going to take my husband or anyone from here, do you understand?)

Cruz realizes the danger and is afraid that his family may get hurt, so he gives in.

Cruz tells the cop, "Ya, ya. Voy contigo pero no me pongan las puños de mano." (Okay, okay, I will go, but don't put on the handcuffs).

At José María's ranch house, Indio Gerónimo stands guard outside under the portal while Zara's wife and their new baby settle in for the night. José María holds a cup of coffee in his hand as he listens to the radio station from Juárez, México.

From the Coyote Elementary School gate, State Police send people back home.

Alfonso Sánchez is on KOB radio, the only English-language radio station that reaches throughout the state. José María listens to the radio as State District Attorney Alfonso Sánchez pleads with the public not to attend the meeting at Coyote:

"I implore those people who plan to attend the landgrant meeting in Coyote to stay home and tend to your families and animals. It is not a good idea for anyone to attend this meeting. Again, I ask all the people of Coyote and Río Arriba County and all New Mexicans not to participate with the Alianza - and do not, I repeat, do not go to the Coyote meeting. Please stay home."

José María is on his way to Coyote.

The radio announcer comments, "Well, it seems that the Spanish Americans believe they own the National Forest. I'm telling you ever since that Zara came into town our 'gente de razón' have been in a tizzy."

## Roadblock at Abiquiú Dam

It is June 4. Libertado is stopped at a roadblock on Abiquiú dam, José María is some cars behind him. Officers Alex Quintana and Nick Sais are questioning people. Libertado gets out of his truck. A rifle hangs on a gun rack over the back window. Sais rummages through the vehicle and finds a pistol under the seat.

Quintana asks Libertado, "Where are you headed?"

"Oh, tengo trabajo en Coyote, estoy componiendo cercos para unos americanos." (Oh, I have work in Coyote, I am fixing fences for some americanos).

"Está bien, Libertado, pero si vas a la junta de la Alianza, tenemos la orden de decirte que no vayas, el abogado del distrito declaró que es una asamblea ilegal." (It's OK, Libertado, but if you are going to the Alianza meeting we have orders to tell you not to attend. The District Attorney says that it is an illegal assembly.)

Libertado, stuttering, says, "No, no,no—na, nada, yo, yo, yo voy pa, pa, para Coyote, nomás pa Coyote." (No, no, nnnothing, I, I, I am going to Coyote, just to Coyote.)

Officer Quintana, "¿Y qué vas a hacer allí?" (What are you going to do there?)

Libertado, "Ya te dije. Voy a ayudar a Heron a componer su cerco." (I already told you. I'm going to help Heron fix some fencing.)

Officer Quintana, "There's been a lot of fence cutting going on. Do you know anything about it?"

Libertado, "Sí...sí...sí estoy agarrando mucho trabajo componiendo cercos." (Yeah, yeah, yeah... I've been getting a lot of work mending fences.)

Sais hands him his pistola, "Ya vete y ten cuidado."

José María is in his pickup truck a vehicle behind Libertado. He backs up his pickup, turns around and heads back home.

Officer Quintana says, "Go on," and hands Libertado his pistol and waves him through the checkpoint.

# CHAPTER TWELVE

## La Toma de Tierra Amarilla

It's Monday morning, June 5, 1967. In Santa Fe, reporter Larry Calloway gets ready for work at the United Press International (UPI) Bureau office at the State Capitol. He smokes nervously, listening to the radio, anxious and alert. He knows something big is brewing. The whole state is buzzing. Calloway knows there is going to be a bond hearing of some kind for the Aliancistas who had been picked up over the weekend. He jumps in his car and heads to the office.

It is the calm before the storm. The Alianza camp at the ranch of José María is just waking up. The campsite is situated just above a vega, an open grassy pasture covered with white flowers.

Zara, in the house, pours himself a cup of coffee and goes outside to greet people as they wake up. People are washing their faces over a dish basin and brushing their teeth. José María, in the house, stokes the fire in the wood stove and pours himself a cup of coffee. His wife makes a native sweet blue cornmeal, atole, over the wooden stove.

"¿Quieren atole? Vayan para fuera y agarren capulín." The grandchildren are at the table. (Do you want atole? Go outside and pick some wild blackberries)

José María answers, "No, gracias." The kids run outside, bowls in hand. José María walks outside to the campsite with a cup of coffee and meets Zara, "Sabes que me quedé pensando en una cosa que dijo el Noll ayer, que es posible hacer un arresto ciudadano a Sánchez por la violación de nuestros derechos humanos." (You know I was thinking about something Noll said yesterday, that it is possible to arrest Sánchez for violating our human rights.)

Libertado drives up in his 1948 Dodge pickup. He gets out and walks up to the campsite.

"Sí, José María, yo también lo estaba pensando," answers Zara.

Libertado walks up and says, "Buenos días. ¿Cómo amanecieron?" (Good morning. How is everyone?) He greets Zara and José María while getting a cup from a table to pour himself some coffee. The coffee pot is on a rock against the fire.

Zara says, "Libertado, le estaba diciendo a José María de un sueño y en ese sueño arrestamos a Sánchez por violar nuestros derechos civiles." (I was telling José María about a dream I had, and in that dream, we arrested Sánchez for violating our Civil Rights.)

Jerry Noll walks up, listening to the conversation. A second vehicle pulls up. It's Martín.

## THE CALM BEFORE THE STORM

A car pulls up to the Journal office in Santa Fé. Calloway gets out and flips a cigarette to the ground. He rushes into the building and then to his desk. He makes a phone call, trying to find out where and when the Alianza hearings are going to be held. No luck. He lights up another cigarette.

Langley, owner of the *Albuquerque Journal*, is on the phone with Bullock, a wealthy rancher from an oil family in Farmington, New Mexico. "Langley, I just spoke with Scarborough and they're going to get those people out of there as soon as possible before the Mexicans make a fuss.

The phone rings. Langley is making a call, "Get to TA (Tierra Amarilla) right away! We found out they're going to have a hearing this morning. They're trying to keep a low profile, but they want to rush through the bond hearing and get those people out of there before the locals make a commotion. So, get up there!" Langley tells Calloway.

District Captain Vigil is briefing three patrolmen in the conference room of the Tierra Amarilla courthouse.

Captain Vigil tells them, "Be on the alert! The hearing will begin soon. Now we have tried to keep this out of the news. But you never know, so I can't emphasize to you enough to stay on the alert!" He takes his folders and puts them in a briefcase. "Now I'm heading back to Española. Report to me as soon as the hearings are over. Again, I need the three of you to be vigilant. We're bringing in those Aliancistas apprehended this weekend and there may be a crowd. We don't know how Zara and his people are going to react, so be on the alert. Again, the judge wants to get them in and out of here before anyone can figure out what is going on."

Under a cloudy, overcast sky with drizzling rain Calloway heads north to Tierra Amarilla, a place unknown to him. He stops at the Lotta Burger on his way out of Santa Fé and gets a double burger. He eats while driving in what has now become a rainstorm. The hearing is already underway by the time he gets to the courthouse. It beats down on the tin roof, clacking like a heard of deer. He can't hear, so he moves up as close as he can to the judge. This puts him in the jury box.

Calloway looks around and notices that a lot of people are in the audience. There is a mixture of locals with a spattering of anglo activists. Judge Scarborough, a crusty old southerner, calls on Benny Naranjo, the Sheriff, to translate.

Detectives Facundo and Romero are in their patrol car pulling up to Española, New Mexico, about a half hour south of Tierra Amarilla. They pull up to the courthouse to take care of some police business, then head north in search of Zara and other Aliancistas not yet apprehended.

## Canjilón

José María asks Martín to do him a favor, "Martín, go to Española and get some provisions that we need before the people start arriving. Aquí tienes 50 dólares. Pronto, corre." (Here is $50.00. Hurry, run.)

Martín is accompanied by a pretty girl, a Chicana with long black hair, coal black eyes, and a light olive complexion. She has short bangs in a large curl over her forehead, a pompadour. They leave. On their way back they hear on the radio that the bond hearing to release the Aliancistas will be held sometime today at the Tierra Amarilla Courthouse. They hurry back to Canjilón. It was understood that DA Sánchez would be there. They pull into the campsite and Martín goes into the house to tell Zara and the others what he heard on the radio.

Zara says, "Ésta es la oportunidad que esperábamos. Ahora podemos hacer el arresto civil delante del juez. Martín, ¿por qué no te vas a la corte, a ver si está Sánchez y llámanos." (This is the opportunity we have been waiting for. Now we can make a citizen's arrest in front of the judge. Martín, why don't you go to the courthouse and see if Sánchez is there and call us.)

A two-lane highway cuts over the top of Tierra Amarilla hill, a yellow outcropping. It's a cloudy day with a steady drizzle. Martín, in his repaired 66 Chevy Super Sport, is driving down the middle of the road. He's approaching the top of Tierra Amarilla hill overlooking the Chama valley when he suddenly speeds up towards Tierra Amarilla. El Cerro known as Los Brazos, a mini version of the Rock of Gibraltar, is in the foreground, and a torrent of water is spilling over the top. A 19th century courthouse with a large U.S. flag flapping in the wind appears in the middle of town.

The car turns right at the gas station and follows the road as it winds into town. Martín pulls up to the front of the courthouse as the rain picks up. They park the car across the street from the courthouse. Martín, in his late teens, nervously flips a cigarette out the window. It fizzles out on the wet yellow earth. A rifle leans against the front seat. His compañera fidgets beside him, anxious over what is going on.

Martín yells, "¡Vámonos!"

He opens the car door and she follows. She covers her head with a newspaper, and they hurry inside the courthouse. They approach the clerk who recognizes them.

The clerk asks, "¿Cómo estás, Martín?" (How are you, Martín?)

Martín responds, "¿Están teniendo la audiencia para nuestros compatriotas?" (Are they having the hearing for our compatriots?)

The clerk, startled by his brashness, replies, "Sí."

Martín tells her, "Bueno, gracias."

They leave the courthouse as quickly as they arrived. They go to a nearby relative's house and hurry inside.

Martín sees his tía and asks, "Tía, déjeme usar su teléfono." (Aunty, let me use the phone.) He walks over to the phone and dials. The phone rings. On the other end a man answers, "¿Bueno?"

"Tío, soy yo, Martín, sí están aquí."

José María turns to the others, "Allí están."

Zara says, "Dile que nos espere." He turns to the others. "Bueno señores, ésta es la última oportunidad para salir sin vergüenza. En este día el mundo va oír el grito por la injusticia que se ha cometido con los robos de las mercedes, todos lo van a saber hoy." (Okay men here we are. This is your last chance to back out without embarrassment. This is our day to tell the world of the injustice committed to us in the robbery of the landgrants. All will be known to all today.)

Libertado, Indio Gerónimo, and others look at one another, realizing this is their day of reckoning. They will arrest Sánchez at the courthouse. The mayor of La Merced de San Joaquín de Río Chama deputizes them and other Aliancistas.

The Mayordomo addresses them, "We, the people of La Alianza de todas Las Mercedes, les deputamos, we deputize you to uphold the law of our people and decree that you act as our representatives protecting our human rights."

Zara says, "Libertado, tú vas primero." (You go first.)

Shy because of his stuttering, Libertado is unaccustomed to being in a leadership role. Indio Gerónimo volunteers, "¡Yo entro primero!"

Zara tells him, "Indio, you're too quick to react. Libertado, it has to be you. You are the best choice. Eres más calmado. (You are more calm.)

Indio Gerónimo gives his leader a cold stare. He is humiliated. However, there is an atmosphere of strength and determination with an aura of fear and resolve. They are all convinced that they are doing what is just. No longer timid and afraid like they were in the past, they feel empowered and determined to right the wrongs done to their community. An air of solemnity engulfs them as they prepare for battle. They are about to face their enemy as they gather their weapons. The alcalde (mayor) of La Merced de San Joaquín de Río

Chama hands Zara a handwritten warrant. With weapons in hand, they get into their vehicles to make the long trek into the belly of their adversary and prepare for the 20-minute journey from Canjilón to Tierra Amarilla.

Meanwhile at the Courthouse the State Police get a call. Officer Quintana answers, "Yes, okay, we will send someone up there." Quintana tells Nick Sais and another junior officer to go investigate what seems to be a disturbance north of Ensenada, a ranching village not far from Tierra Amarilla.

Nick Sais says, "I already have a lot of reports to write. Why don't you and Roberto go?"

Quintana says, "Okay, you stay. We'll be right back. Vámonos, Roberto."

The hearing goes without incident. After setting a court date to answer the charges, Judge Scarborough sends the Aliancistas home on their own recognizance. He turns to the bailiff: "I'm still unsure what they did wrong."

Calloway is still taking notes of the proceedings. The judge shakes his head and goes on to tell the bailiff. "The Aliancistas are upset. I still can't figure out whether or not they committed any crime." The bailiff takes the paper from the judge. Calloway asks, "What do you mean, Judge?"

Judge Scarborough, "I'm not sure Al (Alfonso Sánchez) didn't cook up charges that bordered on unlawful assembly or something like that, and court procedure dictates that the DA submit discovery and evidence. I wish him the best of luck."

Calloway thanks the judge and leaves the courtroom. He goes downstairs to the main floor and enters a phone booth to call United Press International (UPI).

The sky is grey. The slow, steady rain gives off an aura of doom. Brazos Peak lays on the horizon. The cascading water falls into the Chama River and winds itself through the bottomland of the open vastness of the Chama basin. Clusters of villages are scattered about in the foreground. The courthouse towers over all other man-made structures. It is 2:00 in the afternoon.

Zara announces, "Bueno, señores, ha llegado el tiempo. Desde este punto en adelante ya no vamos a poder cambiar nuestro destino. Hoy es el día que van a oír nuestro Grito de Justicia, como el Grito del Águila, fuerte y poderoso. Éste es un día de infamia para la historia de nuestra Raza Nuevomexicana. Vamos a anunciar al Pueblo la liberación de nuestras Mercedes, vamos a liberar a nuestros cuerpos de la esclavitud de discriminación y rechazar la explotación de nuestra Raza y comunidades delante de todo el mundo." (Okay, men, the time has come. From this point on we cannot change our identity. Today is the day that they will hear our cry for justice, like the cry of the eagle, strong and powerful. This is a day of infamy for the history of our New Mexican race. We are going to announce the liberation of our landgrants to the People. We are going to liberate our bodies from the slavery of discrimination and reject the exploitation of our People and community before the world.)

A large group of Aliancistas leave the José María ranch. They get in their vehicles. A 1960 Chevy station wagon and a '48 Dodge pickup lead a caravan of other vehicles heading to Tierra Amarilla. The warm summer rain thumps against the canvas-covered bed of Libertado's pickup truck. The long narrow road is like a slithering snake making its way to the beacon of anglo omnipotence, the Río Arriba County Courthouse. The U.S. flag waves over the courthouse, flapping easily in the summer breeze. The Aliancistas turn right at the gas station and take the road that winds into town. Martín is parked across the street from the courthouse.

Martín, in his car, stares into oblivion. He smokes nervously, rifle next to him, his girl on the passenger side, and the rain thumping on the car. Martín rolls down his window and flips another cigarette out the window. The orange butt of the cigarette fizzles out among other cigarette butts on the ground. A truck pulls up. Zara rolls down his window.

## THE STORMING OF THE COURTHOUSE

Zara asks, "¿Están adentro, no ha salido nadie?" (Are they inside? Has anyone come out?) Libertado lights up another cigarette, listening. Lupita is frightened.

Martín says, "No, no ha salido nadie." (Nobody has come out.)

Zara tells Libertado, "Bueno, aquí estamos, Lupita va contigo y así le dan la atención a ella y no se fijan en ti, como si viniste a hacer negocio." (Okay, here we are. Lupita will go in with you and that way they pay attention to her and not to you, as if you came to do some business.)

"No, no. Nunca hablamos de eso.... Yee yee ye-it It's not a good idea, Zzza...Zara," Libertado stuttering nervously. (No, no. We never spoke of that. Ehe...e... It, it's not a good idea, Zara.)

The summer rain has slowed and lightly taps on the canvas-covered bed of Libertado's truck. Suddenly it stops. Libertado gets out, looks at Zara, and takes his pistol from under the seat. He unwraps the holster and straps it on. He stares at Zara intensely and looks down, shaking his head, tying the holster to his leg beneath a trench coat. "No es buena idea. No me parece que ella deba venir." (It's not a good idea. I don't think she should come.)

Zara turns to his daughter, Lupe, next to him. He puts his hand on her thigh, she is frightened and he squeezes her thigh.

"M'ija, váyase con Libertado." (Daughter, go with Libertado.)

Fearful, she reluctantly obeys. Libertado shakes his head and goes to the back of the truck. He unties and lifts the canvas flap. Indio Gerónimo sits against the cab, looking at Libertado while the others sit along the side. They stare intently at one another. Indio Gerónimo is the last to get out. He wears a red beret, denim jeans, spray-painted camouflage, and black military boots. The other men stand around the vehicles, some in winter coats to conceal their weapons, some wearing cowboy hats, and still others baseball caps as they prepare to enter the courthouse.

Zara tells them, "Señores, cubran sus caras con los pañuelos. Así no nos pueden identificar." (Men, cover your faces with the handkerchiefs. That way no one will identify you.)

Everyone is focused on what they are doing. No one pays attention to Zara. Libertado stealthily walks across the street, his rifle hidden beneath a long black western rider's trench coat. Zara nudges his daughter and says, "Váyase m'ija." (Go daughter.)

Lupe reluctantly follows Libertado. They walk past a green '67 GTO. The sheriff, Benny Naranjo, is inside fiddling with the car radio searching for clear reception. He hears on the radio, "3,000 Israeli infantry attack Jerusalem with minimum losses. Two hundred and fifty Palestinians killed in the heartland of the religious world."

The sheriff notices someone walk by but pays little attention. A shapely young girl in tight-fitting lime green knickers follows Libertado into the courthouse. The sheriff continues to mess with the radio for better reception, but stops to watch her walk past. He looks in the rearview mirror and notices a crowd. He turns off the radio and follows the girl. Libertado and Lupe enter the front door and walk up the few stairs to the foyer, the sheriff behind them. State Police Officer Nick Sais' back is to the entrance. He faces the bulletin board. Lupe steps to the right near the telephone booth to avoid being noticed. The Sheriff turns left into his office, and Eulogio Salazar, the jailer, comes up the stairs from the jail and follows the sheriff into his office. State Policeman Nick Sais pays little attention. He reads a flyer and takes down a phone number for a tractor that is for sale. Libertado puts his pistol to Nick's side.

Libertado tells him, "You are under citizen's arrest."

Officer Nick Sais is startled and moves abruptly, reaching for his pistol. Libertado fires and shoots Nick under his arm. The gunshot punctures his lung. Nick drops, and a pool of blood quickly forms. Lupita melts against the wall and then slips outside. Upon hearing the shot the Aliancistas rush into the courthouse. Lupita runs down the dirt road without being noticed.

As the Aliancistas rush into the courthouse Zara turns to Indio Gerónimo and tells him, "Stay outside and keep watch. Keep people away and warn us if the police are coming."

Calloway is in the telephone booth, which has a broken latch. It looks more like a closet with windows around the upper half than a telephone booth. He is dictating the proceedings to UPI: "Leaders of the Alianza were released on their own recognizance early this afternoon..."

Calloway hears the gunshot. He turns and drops to the floor of the phone booth and sees a police officer lying in a pool of blood. Libertado is stunned. He goes to the clerk's counter, grabs the phone and calls an ambulance. Calloway is still holding on to the phone, reporting the incident as it unfolds. He peeks through a crack between the door and the jam, holding it open with his fingers just enough to see what is happening. More Aliancistas storm into the courthouse. As they scatter, more gunshots are heard. Zara stands at the doorway of the sheriff's office as other Aliancistas gather people, pushing them into the conference room. The courthouse is now under the control of the landgrant activists. Pandemonium ensues. Gunshots are fired; the sheriff ducks under his desk. Jailer Eulogio Salazar is climbing out the window. There is more gunfire. Eulogio topples to the ground and stumbles up from beneath the window, blood running down his face. More gunshots. Indio pulls the telephone wire from the wall and bolts into the courthouse. Eulogio makes his way down the street towards his sister's house. Indio Gerónimo looks to his left at the sheriff's office and then to his right. Aliancistas head up to the next floor. More shots are fired.

Calloway is still on the phone, his fingers holding the door shut. He sees a man wearing a handkerchief across his face holding a vintage Peacemaker Smith & Wesson in his hand. The man is standing near the Sheriff's office. Suddenly there's a thud. Something falls against the door and smashes Calloway's fingers. He yells, "Ohoo Shit! Ohooo!"

Indio Gerónimo hears something. He pulls the unconscious elder from the door. It swings open and Calloway is discovered.

Indio asks, "What do you think you're doing?"

Calloway says, "I'm talking to my boss."

Indio says, "The hell you are!" He tears the phone off the wall, grabs Calloway by the shirt collar, and drags him into the conference room where they hold the people working there. Indio Gerónimo stands over the fallen State Police Officer. Indio Gerónimo points the rifle at the cop and pulls the trigger. The gun misfires and he reloads a shell in the chamber. Indio kicks the policeman's shoulder.

Libertado yells at Indio Gerónimo, "¡No! ¡No! ¿Qué estás haciendo? Déjalo solo. ¿Qué no ves que ya se está muriendo? (No! No! What are you doing? Leave him alone. Can't you see he's already dying?)

At the same time, Aliancistas are making their way up the stairs to the courtroom. The chamber door closes and locks. José María attempts to open the large oak door. He can't, so he stands back and kicks it several times. He still can't open it. Zara fires a flurry of bullets around the door latch, and José María kicks the door again, but someone is keeping it shut from the inside.

Undersheriff Daniel Rivera is doing everything he can to hold the door shut but to no avail. The Aliancistas open the door. Judge Scarborough is climbing up the fire escape. The Aliancistas storm into the Judge's chambers, and Rivera gets rifle butted. Libertado pulls another Aliancista away from Rivera and orders him to take him downstairs to the conference room with the others and stand guard. Dan Rivera is bleeding profusely from the face. Zara's handkerchief is down around his neck and, pistol in hand, he issues orders.

Zara yells, "¡Ándenle muchachos, vámonos!" (Everyone out! Let's go!)

Indio Gerónimo finds an employee at his desk holding a pistol. Indio asks, "Are you with us or not?"

The employee responds, "I am with no one."

Indio Gerónimo takes the pistol away, "Okay. Get over there with the others."

Indio Gerónimo and other Aliancistas continue to roam the halls, moving from one room to another.

Judge Scarborough climbs out the window first onto the fire escape and then onto the courthouse roof. He walks over to the flagpole and lowers the U.S. flag, turning it upside down to indicate distress. He then hoists it to half-mast. He faces a summer wind and heavy storm clouds hang over the courthouse. The intensity of the drizzle increases. The sun is covered in a gray overcast blocking the sun, and the summer breeze blows the judge's long salt-and-pepper hair back. His black robe is blowing back, revealing a Colt-45 pistol strapped to his hip. The oversized soaked U.S. flag hangs on the pole as though illuminating defeat. Lightning streaks and thunder crackles over Brazos Peak. The waterfall spills violently, and the shadowed sun and grey clouds make the water look dark red, like blood flowing into the Río Chama as it runs through the valley. Judge Scarborough hears the ambulance in the distance and walks over to the edge of the roof, tripping on his robe.

The ambulance pulls up. The driver takes out the gurney and goes inside the courthouse. Libertado helps put the wounded officer onto the gurney and helps take the downed officer out and load him into the ambulance. Indio Gerónimo takes the ambulance keys out of the ignition and tosses them out into the field. He then goes over to the police vehicles. The driver of the ambulance discovers she hasn't any keys. Libertado walks out into the field, finds them, and hands them to her, sending her on her way.

The Aliancistas pile into their vehicles. Zara, on the passenger side of the '57 Chrysler station wagon, turns at the bow in the road leading to the highway. Libertado follows. They turn south and head up Tierra Amarilla Hill. State patrolmen drive north, headed towards Tierra Amarilla from Chama. Indio Gerónimo realizes that he and WWI veteran Baltazar Apodaca are the only ones there.

Señor Apodaca calls out to him, "¡Vámonos!"

Indio Gerónimo goes into the conference room. He motions to Calloway, telling him in Spanish to get up and come with him. Calloway looks at the others and stays seated on the floor. He has no clue what is being said to him.

Indio Gerónimo tells him, "¡Levántate pendejo!" He steps towards Calloway and points his rifle at his head.

Someone in the room tells Calloway in English, "He is telling you to get up!"

Indio Gerónimo is agitated and very nearly shoots Calloway. Dumbfounded, Calloway gets up.

Señor Apodaca has an electrical cord he took from a coffeepot that he uses to tie Calloway's hands behind his back. Indio Gerónimo then tells Officer Prado to get up. He takes the officer's handcuffs, puts them on him and they make their way outside.

Libertado is speeding south to Canjilón in his 1948 Dodge truck loaded with his comrades in arms. Martín passes him in his '66 Super Sport. He looks over at Libertado and smirks as he passes. Libertado is intense and concerned. Jerry Noll sits in the back of the truck. José Madril, José María, and others sit silently, going over in their minds what they had done. Detectives Facundo and Romero are in an unmarked state patrol car on their way to Canjilón from the Española Courthouse. Facundo surmises, "Let's see if we can catch them in Canjilón." Romero responds, "Who told you that they were up there?" "I don't know; let's just say I got my ways," says Facundo. "We're getting close, we are getting really close. I can feel it! We have been on their trail for how many days now?"

"Three or four, ¿qué no ... when did Sánchez issue the warrants?" asks Facundo.

They approach the turn to Canjilón. They make a right turn and follow the road as it snakes down into the pueblito. They pull up to a service station at the crossroads and ask the owner, "Can you tell us where the home of José María is?"

The attendant points, "It's up there on the top of that hill. See it. There is a corral just above it. What are you up to?"

Detective Facundo says, "We're looking for Zara and some other people. Have you seen them?"

Attendant says, "Yea, they were in a station wagon, a pickup truck, and a couple of cars. They were armed and headed up towards the main highway."

Detective Romero asks, "Do you know where they were going?"

The attendant answers, "I believe to Tierra Amarilla."

The police turn the car around and head towards Tierra Amarilla. Indio Gerónimo and Apodaca exit the conference room with their hostages. Indio Gerónimo orders them to stop at the stairs leading down to the front door and out of the courthouse. He is behind Calloway; he backs up and raises his rifle. Calloway believes he is going to be shot execution-style. He trembles. Indio Gerónimo steps back and points his rifle towards Calloway, standing in front of the door. He takes aim, pulls the hammer, and shoots off several rounds. Bullets whizz by Calloway's ear. Indio Gerónimo is attempting to shoot the latch out of the door but he misses with each shot. Another volley of shots shatters the glass. Indio Gerónimo gets angry and kicks the door open.

Judge Scarborough is still on the courthouse roof. A State Police vehicle approaches. Indio Gerónimo opens the trunk of a police car. He takes weapons from the trunk and puts them in the back of a beat-up Toyota pick -up. He then notices the Sheriff's GTO and transfers his booty to the trunk of the GTO. Apodaca puts the hostages in the back seat of the car. Indio Gerónimo puts Undersheriff Jaramillo in the front seat and starts shooting at the other police vehicles. People step out into the street. Indio Gerónimo takes potshots at them as they duck and hide.

Officers Roberto Chávez and Quintana are coming from Chama. The police slow down to turn at the gas station. They wind around towards the courthouse. Suddenly they are fired upon. Officer Alex Quintana throws the car into reverse. They are under fire as they turn the corner. The car backs into an embankment. They abandon the vehicle and run down a hill and across a field towards the schoolhouse. They look back to find mayhem. Cars are ablaze. Gunshots are being fired. They stand on a hill overlooking Tierra Amarilla. In silhouette, they observe the ransacked police vehicles and hear more gunfire. There is not a soul to be seen. The scene looks like something between a Western and a gangster movie right out of the Wild West, with modern-day automobiles haphazardly parked along the road, the town mysteriously abandoned like a ghost town.

# CHAPTER THIRTEEN

## THE RETURN HOME

Baltazar Apodaca puts his hostage, Calloway, in the back seat of the GTO and stuffs a vintage long-barreled pistol in his neck. Indio takes potshots in the direction of onlookers down the dirt road in front of the Victory Bar. They duck and hide. He puts Deputy Sheriff Prado in the front seat, and Indio gets behind the wheel of the 1967 Green GTO. Indio Gerónimo is not in any particular hurry, and at that moment he is in charge of the town. He drives towards his tía's house. Other people stand out on the road in front of the pool hall to see where the gunshots are coming from. Indio Gerónimo takes his carbine and shoots again—POP, POP, POP, and POP POP—over their heads. They scatter like quail. He is having a lot of fun. Whenever he sees something that he has a hankering to shoot at, he shoots at it. He is in charge. Calloway and Deputy Undersheriff Sheriff Prado are scared. Indio Gerónimo pulls up to his tía's house and she comes out.

Indio Gerónimo, "¡Mira lo que teŋgo aquí tía!" (Look at what I have here auntie!) He shows off his hostages and the new car.

La tía responds, "Está bien m'ijo, ahora los puedes colgar." (That's fine son. Now you can hang them.)

Calloway, dumbfounded, has no clue what is being said or what is going to happen to him. Indio Gerónimo leaves and on his way out of town, pulls into a gas station. The attendant is tucked back inside the garage in the dark. Indio Gerónimo gets out with his rifle and calls to the attendant, "Marcío, llénalo." (Fill her up!)"

The attendant fills the tank with gas, and Indio Gerónimo asks the man, "¿Cuánto le debo?" (How much do I owe you?)

The attendant is frightened and says, "Está bien, Indio, nomás vete." (That's fine, Indio, just go.)

Indio Gerónimo responds angrily, "¡No! yo pago, voy apagar!" (No! I am going to pay. No! I pay! I will pay!)"

The attendant nervously says, "¡Está bien, cinco dólares!"

A sign shows that gas is $.22 per gallon. Indio goes over to the car, opens the back door, and tells Calloway, "Give me money."

Calloway leans forward so that Indio Gerónimo can take his wallet. He fishes it out of his hip pocket and takes a twenty-dollar bill from the wallet. He puts the wallet back in Calloway's coat pocket, gives the twenty dollars to the attendant, and grabs some sodas. The attendant gives him the change. Indio Gerónimo puts the change in Calloway's shirt pocket. Then he takes the driver's seat. Deputy Jaramillo is sitting on the passenger's side and Apodaca is in the back with a pistol to Calloway's neck. Apodaca gives Calloway a sip of Coke. Indio Gerónimo pulls out from the gas station kicking up dust and gravel. He heads up T.A. hill. The highway levels off as they head toward La Cebolla and then home to Canjilón. Indio Gerónimo is driving down the middle of the road on the yellow stripe. The highway is deserted. Officers Quintana and Chávez are standing high on the mountain slope across from the courthouse watching the ignominy unfold. Indio Gerónimo takes the microphone of the CB radio and clicks it on.

Indio Gerónimo, "We got hostages. I don't want to see no cops! And I am not going to the gas chamber."

Indio Gerónimo is driving Sheriff Naranjo's GTO and speeding south on the highway. The unmarked State Police car is coming down a long hill through an area known to the locals as Las Nutrias towards Tierra Amarilla. They see a vehicle coming toward them. They pass one another but act as though they don't recognize each other. Officers Facundo and Romero stare straight ahead as they pass the other car, calmly acting as though everything is normal. They continue for a short distance and then make a U-turn, following the Aliancistas into Canjilón, careful to keep their distance. It's raining, and the roads are slick. The station wagon swerves in the mud and gets stuck at the top of a small rise on the road. Officers Facundo and Romero watch from a distance on the main road.

They pass a little church and get up as far as they can.

They straddle the car across the road, blocking it. A big pile of wood is just below them.

Officer Facundo suggests, "Let's go behind that pile of wood until they come back down." With binoculars, they patiently wait.

After a while they see a group of people get into the station wagon with weapons.

Romero says, "Here they come."

The Aliancistas stop and get out of their vehicle. There is no one in sight. They look over at the police car blocking the road. The doors are locked. Detectives Facundo and Romero are behind the woodpile watching them. The scene is surreal - dreamlike. Time has stopped. The Aliancistas are gathered at the campsite above José María's ranch house under some aspen trees and scrub oak. The detectives get back in their car. Someone gets on the police radio ... It is Indio Gerónimo,

"I said that I don't want to see any cops in Canjilón! I got hostages. Over!"

Detective Facundo parks 200 yards below the home of José María in Canjilón. He stands off the road looking through his binoculars, watching the movements of the Aliancistas. He makes eye contact with Zara. Facundo lowers the binoculars and they stare each other down. Zara walks over to his wife and their baby and gives them a kiss, assuring them that they will be alright. Libertado and Martín make their way into the mountains with Terijú and Jerry Noll who is stuffing his pockets with tortillas and scurrying behind them. Zara follows.

Detective Facundo takes the bullhorn from the backseat and Romero takes the shotgun. They get behind a nearby wood pile. Facundo is looking through the binoculars, scanning the Alianza camp. He turns and looks down the road. Everyone is moving in slow motion. The New Mexico Mounted Police are closing in. State Police are working the perimeter. Detectives Facundo and Romero lie in wait some distance away. More officers show up, taking defensive positions. An americano sharpshooter settles next to Facundo and sets his sights on Indio Gerónimo as he slowly drives into the village.

Detective Facundo pushes the rifle down, "Don't be so crazy. Stand down."

The police observe the GTO approaching. The muddy road is slippery. Indio Gerónimo attempts to turn around and gets stuck just beyond the Fundamentalist Church. He gets out of the car, holding a pistol on Prado. Elder Aliancista Apodaca gets out of the car holding the long-barreled pistol to Calloway's neck. They walk backwards towards the church. Detective Facundo yells, "Let those men go!" They continue moving towards the church.

"Stay back!" Indio Gerónimo holds the pistol to Undersheriff Prado's jaw. "I will kill him if you come any closer!" He walks backwards towards the church. Apodaca is following behind with Calloway.

As they approach the entrance to the church Detective Facundo yells at Calloway, "Get away from him! Hit him!" Calloway elbows Apodaca in the ribs. Apodaca slips in the mud, bringing Calloway down with him. Detectives Romero and Facundo run up to them. Apodaca gets off five pistol shots in the direction of the police. A few slugs slap the mud near the Detectives. Facundo runs towards them, and slips, sliding into Apodaca and kicking the pistol away.

Apodaca attempts to recover his pistol. Romero grabs Apodaca and lifts him up, turns him around and handcuffs him. Other policemen go around to the other side of the church and close in on Indio Gerónimo.

Taking the Undersheriff with him, Indio Gerónimo goes through the front door of the chapel and out the back. The sun is now shining, blinding the police as Indio Gerónimo escapes and runs through the general store and out the back door, past La Villa de Cruces, a memorial on the hilltop at the edge of town. The police keep moving closer. They have their sights on Indio Gerónimo, and again Detective Facundo tells his men to stand down. The young García family is at the store buying milk and some other items. The teenage father gets into his worn out 56 Malibu.

Indio Gerónimo tells the boy, "Take me to the mountain!"

The young man says, "Tengo muy poquito gas." (I have very little gas.)

Indio Gerónimo tells his hostage Deputy Sheriff Jaramillo to get in the car.

The mother and kids climb into the back seat. Indio Gerónimo instructs the driver to head north into the mountains.

## Indio Gerónimo and his Mother Threaten the Police

Calixtra, Indio's mother, appears from nowhere, yelling. She is wearing a dress with small flowers, a full apron, and early century black carriage boots with a tapered heel and rounded toe.

"Correrá mi sangre antes que la sangre de mi hijo - desgraciados hijos de puta, ni piensen en matar a mi hijo." (My blood will run first before that of my son, you disgraceful sons of bitches. Don't you dare think of killing my son!)

She gets between the cops and the car, pointing her finger at the police, scolding them to back off, repeating what she said before.

Calixtra points her finger at the pólice, "Desgraciados marranos, están locos si creen que me van a matar a mi hijo. Van a tener que matarme a mí primero." (You no good pigs! You are crazy if you think you're going to kill my son. You're going to have to shoot me first.) She gets in the back seat of the car.

Indio Gerónimo orders, "Apúrate, llévanos a la sierra." (Hurry, take us up the mountain.)

Two police vehicles follow them through the hamlet village and up the gradual slope of Canjilón Mountain, past a cluster of ranchitos. Indio Gerónimo intently watches them following him—two State Police cars with officers in the front and back seats. Captain Vigil leads the chase. Other armed State Police follow behind. They turn down another forest road, shortly losing sight of the police. Indio Gerónimo orders the driver to stop. He gets out with Deputy Undersheriff Jaramillo and heads down to an arroyo. Prado falls in the sand. Indio Gerónimo leaves him behind and looks over his shoulder. Two shots are fired. The slugs plunge into the arroyo ridge near Prado. Prado puts his hands up in the air and runs towards the police officers. Indio Gerónimo continues up the arroyo and around a bend into a thicket of woods. He disappears into the mountainside.

Police storm the Alianza camp and the home of José María. The principal raiders manage to escape amidst families who are camping in a clump of trees and brush oak just past a meadow near the ranch house. The rain picks up into a steady drizzle. The people are rounded up, and the men are instructed by the police to hold their hands behind their heads. They are marched into a sheep pen and held as though they were corralled POW's in their native land. Soon the village is taken over by State Police, sheriffs, officers, and other law enforcement agents who have come to help in the search.

Calloway, regaining his wits, smokes a cigarette. He walks into the general store and calls the paper, dictating the hottest story he has ever had. The story will soon go international, second only to the six-day war in Israel.

Porfirio and Feliciano pull up, thank the driver, and go into the Hernández Alianza office. Valentina hugs Porfirio and excitedly asks what happened to him. She updates him on what has been going on with the upcoming conference, oblivious to what has been going on in TA and Canjilón. She goes over the rescheduled meeting and how it was moved to Canjilón.

"When did you get out?" asks Valentina.

"Esta mañana," replies Porfirio. "¿Qué está pasando?"

Valentina responds, "Cambiamos la conferencia para Canjilón."

Porfirio says, "Está bien, vamos p'allá."

They get in their car and head north to Canjilón. As they are approaching the turn-off they see that the police have a roadblock. A State policeman is at the checkpoint on the highway. The officer is pale, and his voice shows concern. Valentina asks what's going on.

The police officer replies, "You guys better turn around if you don't want to get arrested again."

Valentina asks, "Well, what's happening? Why can't we go through?"

Police respond, "Something happened at the courthouse. They found the judge on the roof and some people got shot. I'm telling you, Porfirio, if you and Feliciano don't want to go back to jail you had better turn around and go back where you came from." They turn around and head back. The car radio doesn't work. Valentina opens the glove box and takes out a transistor radio but can't get reception, the batteries are too weak. They drive back to Hernández without a clue as to what has happened.

The phone is ringing as they enter the office.

"Bueno?" Valentina answers the phone.

"Valentina, what's going on?" responds the voice on the phone.

Valentina says, "No sé, ¿y tú, no has oído nada?"

The voice on the telephone says, "It's all over the news, someone raided the courthouse, turn on the TV and radio."

Valentina asks, "What do you mean, someone raided the courthouse? We just came from Canjilón and they didn't tell us anything. Just lay low and let us find out what happened."

Meanwhile, Porfirio turns on the television and is fiddling with the rabbit ears trying to get a clear picture and sound. Feliciano turns on the radio.

A news bulletin: "Armed terrorists have raided the courthouse in Tierra Amarilla. We will keep you updated as we find out more information."

The State police speed past the Hernández office, headed north towards Canjilón. Pueblo and Pueblo police follow in hot pursuit.

The State Capital is in a frenzy. Lieutenant Governor Lee Francis is in a meeting with DA Sánchez and State Police Chief Black. Sánchez is claiming communist influence, and saying that he has evidence the

Alianza is planning a military takeover of Río Arriba County. He believes that the National Guard should be sent up there to squash the movement before the Cubans are parachuted in. After heated debate the Lieutenant Governor decides to mobilize the National Guard over Chief Black's objection. National Guardsmen headquartered in Santa Fé and Albuquerque prepare to head north.

In Canjión José María's wife is scolding him. The wife is angry, "You stupid!" She slaps her husband with her shoe on the shoulder. "¿Qué demonios estabas pensando? Mira lo que has hecho. ¿Qué piensas que va a hacer la policía contigo? Míralos, nos están apuntando rifles." (What were you thinking? Look at what you did. What do you think the police are going to do with you? Look at them, they are pointing rifles at us.)

Zara, Martín, Libertado, Terijú, and Jerry Noll escape into the mountains.

Libertado asks, "¿Para dónde vamos?" (Where are we going?)

Zara says, "Llévanos al rancho de Uvaldo, tiene la casita de su papá vacía, y está metida en la sierra, allí podemos escondernos hasta que figuremos qué es lo que vamos a hacer." (We can hide at Uvaldo's ranch. His father's house is empty, and it's hidden in the mountains. We can figure out what we will do next from there.)

Martín says, "Podemos ir por el camino antiguo que va por la Mesa de los Navajos." (We can take the old road by la Mesa de los Navajos.)

Libertado, "No tenemos que cruzar el río. Está la corriente muy fuerte. Es mejor si pasamos por la carretera." (We don't have to cross the river. The current of the river is too strong. It's better that we pass at the highway.)

In Canjilón, Captain Vigil orders patrolmen to start moving in. The principal raiders have escaped into the forest without being detected. As evening approaches the sun reflects on Truchas Peak. The sun shines through the clouds, illuminating the snow-capped mountain tops in violet red. Three crosses emerge from the rocky crevice. It is dusk. Aliancista women, men, and children are lined up in the sheep's corral. A slow, steady drizzle stops and starts. A solemn overcast looms over northern Nuevo México. The men are ordered again to keep their hands above their heads as Aliancistas are lined up against el jacal, a sort of log cabin but with the logs standing up rather than lying down and plastered in mud.

Indio Gerónimo sits on a sandstone mesa high above the village of his boyhood. A convoy of military vehicles on the highway heads north. The sun sinks below the horizon, casting a bloody violet color over the evening sky.

Indio Gerónimo builds a fire. He takes out a pouch of mountain tobacco, rolls a cigarette, and smokes, gazing into the fire as evening turns to night. He takes a transistor radio out of his pocket and fiddles with it. He gets a clear reception from a station in Juárez, México. "El Corrido del Caballo Blanco" by Mexican singer José Alfredo Jiménez is playing. Indio Gerónimo curls up and falls asleep next to the fire.

Zara, Terijú, Libertado, Martín and Jerry Noll make their way through the mountains. It's a starless, pitch dark night. They stumble upon a National Guard campsite and hear a guitar accompanied by singing and laughing. Cunning as foxes, the Aliancistas slip by ever so quietly, terrified, hearts thumping, breathing heavily. They can't see their hands in front of their faces. They reach a peñasco. (a rocky outcrop with gnarled pine roots wrapped around the rock.)

Libertado says, "This is a good place to stop and rest for the night."

They agree and huddle under the peñasco to stay out of the weather. Everyone is wet and cold. Zara offers words of encouragement: "Este día el mundo oyó el grito por la justicia. Es buena noche para ser hombres libres." (This day the world heard the cry for justice. It's a good night to be free men.)

The drizzling rain picks up. It's cold, with not a star in the night sky. Tired, thirsty, and hungry, they take refuge and comfort in each other, huddled together under the rock's ledge, doing their best to stay out of the rain. In the morning, the Aliancistas discover they are at the edge of a cliff. Had they gone a few more feet they would have gone over the mesa's edge.

A helicopter and single engine plane are heard in the distance. Jeeps and voices from military personnel echo in the canyon. The Aliancistas walk through the forest brush so as not to be detected by the aircraft above. The sun is out. It's hot and sticky, and they are thirsty — no one thought to bring water.

Jerry Noll falls behind, unable to keep up.

Army tanks rumble as they make their way through the mountains.

Detectives Facundo and his partner Romero are headed in the direction of Cañón de Los Navajos. They have received information that the Aliancistas had been seen in the area. They turn off the highway onto an old wagon trail from Canjilón to Coyote through Cebolla. Not far from the turnoff to Cañón de Los Navajos Detective Romero, on the passenger's side of the vehicle, sees someone running. Detective Facundo stops the car. Romero grabs his rifle as he gets out of the car and starts running. It is Jerry Noll, the judge, and King of the Indies.

Romero easily catches him hand cuff him and asks, "What are you doing here?"

Jerry Noll responds sarcastically, "I'm looking for rocks."

Detective Facundo goes through Jerry Noll's pockets and finds them full of tortillas. Detectives Romero and Facundo look at each other with a sneer. They handcuff him, put him in the car, and drive off.

The Aliancistas continue to make their way to Uvaldo's. They reach a high ridge overlooking the Chama River. From there they can see tanks and National Guardsmen closing in from the other side of the canyon. They start down a very steep hillside, slipping and sliding, eventually getting to Highway 84. No sooner do the Aliancistas cross the road than the police drive by.

Indio Gerónimo moves up a steep incline as the rumble of tanks and National Guardsmen's voices echo in the distance. Indio Gerónimo surreptitiously makes his way into a thicket of woods to keep from view. A plane circles the area. A pilot spots Indio Gerónimo and calls to the troops on the ground, "Air to ground, over."

He receives the response, "Ground to air, do you have something?" A lieutenant stands next to a jeep holding a phone.

The pilot informs the ground troops, "Yeah, I got one...He's headed up towards the canyon four clicks to the east of your position. Over."

Indio Gerónimo suddenly finds himself surrounded by National Guardsmen.

There are no helicopters in the area. The pilot of the plane continues his search, continuing to hear the National Guard over his radio. The plane zeroes in, circling the area. The pilot loses the Aliancista when Indio Gerónimo hides under some brush. There are occasional potshots from National Guardsmen, but Indio manages to escape.

It's nightfall. On the mountainside the lights of the village shine and dogs occasionally bark. These sounds carry into the distance. Indio Gerónimo makes his way down to Libertado's and his girlfriend's mother's house. Indio Gerónimo has known his girlfriend, Fátima, all his life. He knocks on the door.

Fátima opens the door, startled, "¡Ay qué milagro, Gerónimo! What are you doing here?"

Indio Gerónimo replies, "I just couldn't stay away from you, eres tan amada y bella...I love you so." They hug.

"Are you hungry?" she asks.

"Sí, pero antes dame agua por favor," answers Indio Gerónimo.

Fátima's mother puts wood in the stove and takes out tortillas, chile, and beans. She gets some potatoes, washes them and peels them.

Fátima hugs him, "Let me prepare you a bath." She goes out to the porch and gets a large round cajete (tin tub). Indio Gerónimo brings in water from the well and puts it on the stove. Fátima's mother puts more wood in the stove and stokes it, stirring the food. Fátima goes into the bedroom, takes towels out of a chest, and gets a bar of soap. Together Indio Gerónimo and Fátima carry water and pour it into the cajete. Indio sits down and eats while Fátima takes a ladle, dips it into the hot water from the stove and pours it into a large pitcher. She turns and walks over to the bath and breaks down in a whimper. She is frightened, yet relieved. Indio Gerónimo hears her. He walks and embraces her. "No te preocupes, todo va a salir bien." (Don't worry. Everything will be all right.)

Fátima says, "Is it? They are saying they got a reward on you, dead or alive. How are you going to get out of this? The tanks and soldiers are all over the place. Why don't you turn yourself in? They will find you. Turn yourself in. I'm so afraid, I don't want you to get hurt."

Indio Gerónimo answers, "Me siento tan contento de verte. Tenía que venir." (I'm so glad to see you. I just had to come.)

He kisses her, and she unbuttons his shirt. She tells him to get ready for his bath.

Indio Gerónimo, "Y tengo hambre," (Besides, I'm hungry). He starts to nibble her neck.

She playfully slaps him on the chest, pushing him away. "Desgraciado. Is that the only reason you came by?"

She shyly turns away, gives him a flirtatious look over her shoulder, and begins to walk out of the room. Indio Gerónimo gently takes her by the arm.

Indio Gerónimo, "Oh no, mi amor—I had to have some of your mamá's papitas con chile y tortillas frescas."

She pushes him away, "Y eso es todo lo que vas a agarrar, malcriado."

"And to see you, mi cariñosa." He holds her arm and pulls her to him, she gently resists, pushes him and walks away. She takes out some more towels and hands them to him. Then she turns to go back to the kitchen and hesitates, looking over her shoulder modestly as Gerónimo undresses. She closes the flowered cotton curtain that acts as a door and says, "Oh sí, éso es todo lo que quieres, ¿verdad? - Well, déjame ver qué tenemos, a ver qué tal está de picoso, tal vez no lo puedas aguantar." (Oh, really, that is all you want, right? – We'll see. It may be hotter than you can stand.)

It is early in the morning. A car is heard approaching the house. It's the police. Fátima's mother is in the kitchen putting wood in the stove when she looks out the window. She calls out, "¡Levántense! Viene la policía."

Indio Gerónimo is startled. He gets up, gets dressed, kisses his girl goodbye, and slips out the window while Fátima's mother waits to answer the door. Indio Gerónimo makes his way up the mountainside. He turns, looking down on the pueblo of Canjilón. He can hear the army tanks starting up and activity at the National Guard camp. He hides high on the mountainside. Tanks rumble through the forest roads. National Guardsmen with M-16's follow. Another tank pulls up to the gas station. A man climbs out of the turret and goes inside the general store. He buys a carton of milk and sweetbreads. General John Perishing Jolly, under a military canopy, discusses strategy with his lieutenants. A fresh platoon of soldiers is getting ready to head into the mountains.

# CHAPTER FOURTEEN

## THE STATE REACTS

A NEWS REPORTER ASKS, "Well, General, what can you tell us of the situation up here? How soon do you think we will see an end to all this?"

The general answers, "These boys that raided the courthouse know the terrain, but I'm certain we will get them, and soon. We have mustered 750 New Mexico National Guardsmen out here combing the mountains. It's only a matter of time before we get them."

On June 5, 1967, the day of the raid, Professor Dr. Knowlton gets a phone call from friends in northern New Mexico, "Hello, Knowlton, how are you doing down there? This is Porfirio."

Dr. Knowlton says, "Fine, Porfirio! What's going on? What are you doing?"

Porfirio says, "I called to tell you that some of the Aliancistas raided the courthouse today." Dr. Knowlton responds, "WHAT! They did WHAT?"

"Yeah, Zara, and the others attacked the courthouse about 3:00 this afternoon. And the Lt. Governor has called out the National Guard."

"They did what? - I can't believe it! The Lt. Governor called out the National Guard! That's madness."

"Yeah, it's all over the news. Turn on your radio."

"Okay, I'll call you later."

He hangs up the phone and turns on the radio in his office. Just then, his secretary peeps in and tells Knowlton that he has a call from the Governor's office in New Mexico.

Knowlton picks up the phone, "Hello."

"Knowlton?" This is Father García."

"Yes, Father, what's going on up there? I just got a call and they told me that all hell has broken loose in TA."

"You heard. You got to come up here and help me settle these people down" Father García tells him.

"They're ready to start a war!"

Dr. Knowlton, "Absolutely not! I tried to tell those State leaders that something like this was inevitable, and they ran me out of the state. No! Absolutely not! They created the problem, let them fix it."

"Knowlton, be reasonable. This is no time to take what happened to you personally. We both know that those people who got you out of here were only looking out for their self-interest and not taking responsibility to govern and protect the natives."

Dr. Knowlton, "Well there's nothing I can do. I tried to warn them, and I got paid by being run out of town."

"Knowlton, this isn't a time to be thin-skinned. If blood is shed it will be on your hands because you could have stopped it. Now I got the Governor's plane ready to pick you up. How soon can you be ready?"

"I guess I can cancel class. How soon can you get down here?"

"The plane can be down there in two hours."

"Okay, I can be at the El Paso airport this afternoon. Let's say 3:00 o'clock."

Meanwhile, Governor Cargo is at a meeting in Rapid City, Michigan, with Governor Gerald Ford. Ford's secretary knocks on the conference door, opens it, walks up to Governor Ford, and bends down whisper in his ear.

Governor Ford turns to Governor Cargo, "David, there has been an incident in New Mexico. You had better take this call."

David Cargo takes the phone next to him, "Hello?"

LT. Governor Lee Francis informs him, "Governor, it seems that we have a revolution on our hands down here. Yeah, Zara and his boys raided the courthouse this afternoon and we've got reports that the Cubans are behind this, so I called out the National Guard."

Governor Cargo, "You did what? I can't believe this! I'll get down there right away."

It's dusk. Indio Gerónimo makes his way down to a vacant house at the edge of the village where he takes refuge for the night. He finds an old jar of moldy jelly. He scrapes off the mold and eats it. He stays there for several nights and then decides to go to his Tía Lucia's house. He makes his way in the dark of night. Dogs are barking so he backs off. He soon realizes that the police are surrounding him again, but once again he escapes. The police dogs follow Indio Gerónimo's scent. National Guardsmen comb the area. Indio Gerónimo scrubs himself down with a stinky weed (yerba jedionda) and the dogs lose his scent. A chilly breeze comes up and Indio Gerónimo crouches up against a rock.

Although surrounded by police, he builds a campfire and falls asleep. The next morning, he awakens to silence. The National Guard is gone. They have disappeared as quickly as they came. The village of Canjilón is quiet. It seems as though it had all been a dream. The

National Guard and state law enforcement are all gone, they just disappeared. Indio Gerónimo stands on a high ridge overlooking the village, awed by the silence. He turns and continues up and over the mountain and walks to El Rito, a small village north west of Canjilón.

At State Police Headquarters, the phone rings, "I want to report that I spotted Zara and the other Aliancistas near Mesa Poleo."

The Detective asks, "Where?"

The voice replies, "Northwest of the mesa near Los Ranchos de Los Mascareñas."

Detective Facundo, "Who is this?"

Silence ... and then there is a click, the phone line goes dead.

Detective Facundo turns to his partner Romero, "Let's go to Mesa Poleo. Someone just sighted them up there." They leave the building and head north on Highway 84.

A police car approaches Mesa Poleo. The detectives turn off the main road and head up through some trees, coming out atop the Mesa. The Mesa stretches out into a long plateau giving way to a clump of trees high on a ridge with homes situated there.

The police stop and get out of the car.

Detective Facundo, binoculars in hand, says, "Let's see if we can see anything from here."

Detective Romero replies, "I can see some movement up over near the corrals."

Facundo sees someone resembling Zara but can't really tell if that's who it is. They get back in the car and head up to the ranch houses. A man stands staring them down as they stop and get out of the car.

Children run around.

The man asks, "¿En qué les puedo servir?" (What can I do for you?)

Detective Romero, "Oímos que se ha visto Zara por aquí. ¿No has visto a nadie?" (We heard that Zara was seen around here. Have you seen anybody?)

"No, no he visto nada fuera de orden." (No, I haven't seen anything out of the ordinary.)

"Podemos dar una pasada y ver nosotros mismos." (Could we look around ourselves?)

"Sí, sigan adelante." (Yes, go ahead.)

Detective Romero walks over to the corrals. Facundo goes to the house and talks with the wife and a young woman.

Detective Facundo, "You don't mind if I take a look inside, do you?"

The raiders are nowhere to be found. They walk out towards their car and tell the man working on his truck, "Thank you."

Detective Facundo asks Romero, "What do you think?"

"I don't know."

They get in their car and head down the plateau.

Then Detective Romero says, "Stop here."

Detective Facundo asks, "Why?" He pulls over and stops. "Let's have some target practice."

Detective Facundo takes a couple of sodas from an ice chest in the trunk of the car. Detective Romero gathers some cans and sets them out some distance away.

### THEY FIND WATER

The Aliancistas are on the run. They get to the top of a hill. On the other side is a steep decline to Highway 84. They make their descent, slipping and sliding. They cross the road and begin their second descent, over an even steeper decline, further down into the canyon. The police drive slowly by, looking right down on them. Somehow they remain unseen. They keep going, slowly stalking their prey. The

Aliancistas crunch down against the slope. The sun is out and it is very hot and humid. They have no water. It starts to rain. The Aliancistas take cover under a short bushy piñón surrounded by cedar brush. They get as far under a large piñón with a canopy as they can to attempt to get out of the rain and to keep from being spotted by a plane flying overhead.

Morale is low. They are crouched under the tree. The slow steady rain picks up, and they are sopping wet, trembling, cold and thirsty. Zara burrows back into the bushes. He lies back to rest with his hands folded behind his head and discovers a one-gallon canteen of water. At that moment a warm light envelops them. There is a sense of camaraderie which lifts their spirits. They drink and laugh. The sun breaks through the clouds, and a renewed sense of life fills the air. The rain stops momentarily. They all drink and settle in for the evening attempting to get some sleep, but they can't. They are still cold and wet. The summer breeze murmurs through the canyon. The sun is hidden behind the black clouds, and rays of light form a halo on the crest of the horizon casting beams over the land. Time passes. The summer rain picks up to a slow steady drizzle. In the starless night, a coyote walks up close to them and sniffs. He lowers his head and stares with deep green eyes at Libertado. Nobody moves or breathes. Libertado and coyote stare each other down.

The coyote slowly lifts his head, turns, and walks away.

At daybreak, an airplane flies overhead high in the air. This goes on all morning long, and no one can rest. Soon it's dusk and they make their way to the river.

The Río Chama is full. The river's current is fast, and Libertado and Martín don't know how to swim. They are petrified.

Libertado, terrified, tells his comrades, "No…noo…puedo cruzar aquí. Mejor voy más p'abajo y busco mejor lugar para cruzar." (No, I can't cross here. I'm going further downstream to find a better spot to cross.)

Zara, "No está tan profundo. Lo puedes hacer, ándale vámonos." (It's not that deep. You can do it. Come on, let's go.)

Libertado is so afraid that his knees shake. He goes into a panic as the water rises to his shoulders. He can't move. "No—No quiero cruzar" (No, I don't want to cross.)

Terijú helps Martín cross the torrential river, and Libertado follows.

He almost makes it, but the current is too strong and takes him downstream. Zara, on the other side, is sitting on the bank wringing out his shirt when he sees that Libertado is in trouble. He yells at Libertado, "¡Allá voy! ¡No te muevas!" (Here I come! Don't move!)

Zara jumps back into the water. It is cold and rushing fast. Their heads bob just above the water. Libertado is gasping, spitting water. Zara grabs him and they struggle across to the riverbank together. They gather their wits and continue their journey. They walk all night long until they can go no further and sleep in a small arroyo. The next day, Zara cuts off the tips of his shoes so his feet cool down. They continue to walk.

That night the Aliancistas again sleep up against an arroyo embankment just below a forest road. The jeeps throw up a lot of dust as they drive by. The helicopters hover overhead. The Aliancistas continue on their last leg towards the Velasques ranch. Zara can't go any further, he has a fever and coughs up a lot of mucus. Martín and Libertado go ahead to the Velasques ranch. They return with a horse to find their comrades resting bootless. Zara mounts the horse, and the others walk to a ranch house tucked away against a mountain under some trees. Uvaldo brings them clean clothes, food, newspapers, and a radio. The newspaper headlines read, "The New

Mexico National Guard searches for the raiders along with many other police from various agencies." "The raiders have still managed to elude authorities after seven days on the run." The only one who has been apprehended is Jerry Noll. General John Perishing Jolly says, "It's only a matter of time. It's unbelievable that these mountain boys have been able to remain on the loose for seven days!"

Zara lies on the couch, sick. The others mill around the house resting, bathing, warming food, making coffee, and playing checkers.

Zara says, "I think it may be better that I turn myself in. I mean, they are after me and surely, they will go easy on all of you. Look at the way they have our people corralled in the sheep pen." He looks at a newspaper. "I have a hearing coming up in a few days, and Santiago put his land as collateral for the bond. He will lose it if I don't show up."

Libertado turns to his cousin, "How are we going to turn ourselves in?"

Martín says, "We should talk to the Governor and see if he will give us clemency."

## FATHER GARCÍA PICKS UP DR. KNOWLTON

Dr. Knowlton arrives at the Santa Fé Airport. He sees some Mexicanos at work and approaches them. In his heavily flawed, broken Spanish he attempts to tell them that he would like to speak with Zara. He says, ""Me querer Zara hablar, ¿puedes decir él por favor?"." The airport attendants look at one another, confused, and then at Knowlton again.

One of them responds, "¿Qué dijiste?"

The other attendant replies, "No te entendemos, ¿qué quieres decir? Habla en Inglés, tell us in English so we can understand."

Knowlton recognizes Father García, Director of the Home and Livelihood Program, walking up to him. Joe Benítez of the Vista Program is with him.

Father García smiles and shakes his hand vigorously, "Knowlton, I'm so glad you're here. The governor's office is in a tither. This is Joe Benítez with the Vista Program. He will be going with you and Nabokov to meet Zara. Well, gentlemen, this constitutes the committee that will assess the situation for the governor."

They introduce themselves. Father García opens the trunk of the car, puts the luggage in, and they head to the hotel for the night. It's late in the afternoon when they sit down to dinner.

Now it is sunrise. Governor Cargo is in a private plane flying over the State Capitol. He observes the National Guard convoy on the highway headed north on I-25 through Santa Fé on the way to Española.

Meanwhile, Dr. Knowlton, Joe Benítez, and Father Garcia make their way to the Governor's office. The Capitol is buzzing with activity. They walk through the hallway of the Capitol. Photographs of past governors' loom over them as they make their way to the Governor's office. The three of them walk into the conference room. General John Perishing Jolly, Chief Black, Captain Vigil of the New México State Police, Captain Holder of the New Mexico Mounted Patrol, District Attorney Alfonso Sánchez, and other state officials are present. A large state map that outlines Río Arriba County and the areas in question hangs on the wall. There is nowhere to sit, so Father Garcia, Joe Benítez, and Dr. Knowlton stand.

Lt. Governor Lee Francis starts the meeting, "Good morning, everyone. The Governor should be arriving this morning, so for now we'll go over the progress of yesterday's discussions. I will ask District Attorney Alfonso Sánchez to give us a briefing. Al."

The Governor walks into the meeting, "Good morning." A chair is brought in, and Lee moves over to make room for him. "Go on, don't let me interrupt," says Governor Cargo.

D.A. Sánchez says, "Thank you, Lee. We have received information that leads us to believe that Fidel Castro and his Cuban cronies sent planes over here and have dropped heavy military equipment and experts in guerilla warfare. We also have information that assassination squads are being formed to go after anglos living in northern New Mexico."

Captain Tom King says in a thick Texas drawl, "Those goddamn Mexicans are craaazy if they think they gonna start a revolution heeere."

Dr. Knowlton interrupts, "That's preposterous. Zara just simply wouldn't do anything like that. I don't believe any of this. All this is ridiculous, it's absurd."

Governor Cargo calms them, "Now, now, gentlemen, let's be rational."

Dr. Knowlton tells them, "All of you are overreacting. It just doesn't make any sense. These ranchers would never do this. You are wrong."

Father García says, "Yes, I agree. We have to calm the situation down and allow everyone some time to look at this rationally. I implore you, Governor Cargo, to exploit this advisory committee to your advantage. You know that Dr. Knowlton knows Zara, and he will talk to him. I beseech you, before anyone else gets hurt."

Lt. Governor Lee Francis is frantic, "But we've got reports of Cubans training the Aliancistas in guerilla warfare."

DA Alfonso Sánchez agrees, "Governor! We have confiscated a map of how they are going to close off traffic on public roads in Río Arriba County."

Dr. Knowlton attempts to say something but is ignored.

Father Garcia blurts out, "You people are acting like you're in a war. You're all overreacting! May I remind you that these are native New Mexicans, American citizens, our people?"

Dr. Knowlton says, "I don't believe any of this. This situation should never have been permitted to develop and can be resolved without violence."

The newspaper headlines and TV news are consumed with the raid. Newspapers lie on the conference table.

Dr. Knowlton says, "These people are poor ranchers and nothing else. I know them. They would not wage war against the United States, nor are they capable."

Dr. Knowlton is livid and storms out of the meeting. Don Devereux, Poverty Program Consultant and a Vista supervisor follows Dr. Knowlton out the door.

Don Devereux implores Dr. Knowlton, "Wait, just wait a minute Knowlton, wait a minute. Listen Knowlton, let me see if I can get you to talk with Zara."

Dr. Knowlton stops and stares into Devereux eyes. "Can you? Can you do that?"

Devereux says, "Yes."

Dr. Knowlton says, "We need to calm these fools down. They are all overreacting. I don't need to repeat myself. If you can do this, it would be great."

Devereux gets in contact with Peter Nabokov, a reporter for *The Santa Fé New Mexican*.

## RENDEZVOUS WITH THE RAIDERS

Porfirio is on the phone talking with Peter Nabokov.

Nabokov says, "I'd like to tell the story from the Alianzas' point of view. Can you get me an interview with Zara?"

Porfirio responds, "We don't know where he could be, but let me see whether I can find him."

Porfirio makes some phone calls. The phone rings at the home of Uvaldo, he picks it up, "¿Bueno?"

The voice on the phone responds,"¿Qué tal? Uvaldo. Tenemos un recado para Zara. El periodista Nabokov quiere una entrevista con Zara, y quiere traer al Doctor Knowlton." (Hello, Uvaldo. We have a message for Zara. The journalist Nabokov wants an interview, and he wants to bring Dr. Knowlton.)

"Bueno, te hablo ahorita; déjame ir a hablar con él," responds Uvaldo.

Uvaldo walks to his father's ranch house. "¿Cómo están? Aquí tienen comida, y algunos periódicos."

Uvaldo turns to Zara, "Quieren venir el periodista Nabokov y Knowlton para hablar contigo." (The journalist, Nabokov, and Knowlton want to come and talk with you.)

"Sí, dils que está bien, que vengan por la noche," Zara responds. (Yes, it's okay. Have them come at night.)

Uvaldo walks back to his home and waits for a call from Porfirio. The phone rings.

Uvaldo answers, "Está bien, Porfirio. Diles que vengan por la noche."

Porfirio calls Nabokov, "Okay, we'll agree to have an interview, but under the condition that you to bring Dr. Knowlton with you." Nabokov says, "Okay, I'll get him and be in touch as soon as I talk with him." Nabokov hangs up and calls Devereux. Don Devereux is with

Knowlton, Father García, and Joe Benitez, a Vista Volunteer who acts as interpreter. Nabokov calls Porfirio and explains to him that he has formed a party of three. Porfirio agrees and tells Nabokov, "But only with this condition - you will be handcuffed and blindfolded. You also have to say in your story that you were kidnapped and taken to Zara. Is that understood? That way when the story breaks you will not be blamed or accused of, how do they say, colluding with the enemy."

Peter Nabokov answers, "Yes, okay."

Porfirio tells him, "You meet us at the parking lot of the elementary school at Agua Fría and San Francisco with your backs to the street."

Benítez, Nabokov, and Dr. Knowlton stand in the school parking lot as instructed, illuminated only by streetlights. A car pulls up behind them, and someone gets out. They are told to turn around. They are blindfolded, and two of them are put between the front and back seat on the car floor, kneeling in a fetal position.

The third man, Joe Benítez, lies across the seat face down.

On their way into the mountains, they drive cautiously. Nobody speaks. Valentina, the 17-year-old girlfriend of Porfirio, Feliciano Martínez, and Porfirio's niece Adelita, daughter to Zara, are all in the front seat of the car.

They stop at a general store in Cuba, New México. Porfirio and Feliciano go into the store to buy supplies and ask the storekeeper whether he has any boots. They get cigarettes and groceries as well. Valentina and Adelita are confused, not sure where they are. They are sitting in the car waiting for Porfirio when a big guy in his twenties with very broad shoulders comes out and talks with them. He is the store owner's son. A police car passes by. They are anxious, and watch the police slowly turn east toward Gallina.

The young man asks, "So, what's going on? You girls afraid?

The heat is really on the Alianza, que no?"

Valentina answers, "Afraid? Afraid of what?" They laugh.

Porfirio and Feliciano walk out with several grocery bags and newspapers and pass them to the girls. The young man steps back and watches them drive away as they back up and leave.

In the dark of night, they drive into a cemetery and wait. Uvaldo pulls up beside them and signals them to follow. They cautiously make their way towards the hideout, being especially careful as cars pass or follow too closely. The girls push their stowaways down so passersby won't see them.

They turn onto a mountain back road. A truck is waiting for them. The three men are transferred to a pickup bed face down, and they start up a steep grade with tree limbs hitting the side of the truck.

The truck stops. They are taken out of the truck, and their blindfolds are removed. The men rub their eyes and look around. It's dark. Dr. Knowlton is in a new suit and Florsheim shoes. They find themselves surrounded by several armed men. Knowlton recognizes them.

Libertado tells them, "Vénganse, síganme." They go through the mountains for quite some distance, through the brush and down a rugged mountain slope. Suddenly they come upon the Alianza hideout. The mountain cabin is built right up against a cliff face and is surrounded by pines and other coniferous trees. Porfirio and Feliciano meet Uvaldo at the door, Terijú and Martín stand sentry rifle in hand. Libertado asks Martín for a cigarette. Nabokov, Dr. Knowlton, and Benítez standing in the doorway. Knowlton recognizes all of them.

The three are patted down and told to step into the cabin. Zara is seated at a table. A kerosene lamp hangs over the table. Zara stands up and embraces his friend Dr. Knowlton, shaking his hand vigorously. "¿Cómo has estado, Doctor Knowlton?" relieved to see him.

Dr. Knowlton introduces Nabokov and Benítez. Zara invites Dr. Knowlton to sit down, and they talk. Zara is congested. He blows his nose.

Dr. Knowlton warns, "Zara, you need to be very cautious. The hysteria is such that you all run the risk of losing your lives if you turn yourselves in now."

Dr. Knowlton looks about, "Do you have any automatic weapons? Are you in collusion with the Cubans? Has Fidel Castro sent any mercenaries to help you take over the north?"

Zara looks around at his comrades. They look at one another and he laughs, asking in disbelief, "Where does that come from? This is our struggle, for our land. We are not communists. We are Americanos! Indo-Hispanos, Nuevomexicanos. That's crazy!"

His shiny black hair looks dark blue under the light, and his glaring green eyes pierce through everyone as he looks at each in turn.

Zara asks, "Collusion? What does that mean? What do the Cubans have to do with our fight? Why would they be interested in our fight?" los únicos Cubanos que conocemos son del tronco, aquí, de la carretera para Farmington aquí mismo. (the only Cubans I know are the ones at the crossroads, here on the highway to Farmington) Why would Fidel be interested in our fight?

Dr. Knowlton responds, "Okay, Zara, I had to ask. I'm telling you, don't come out of hiding. Stick it out until things settle down. Use this opportunity to tell the world of the injustice. Don't turn yourself in, not yet. Wait and see what happens. The Governor will be calling back the National Guard soon, I'm sure of that. Hold out and let's see how we can resolve this without any further violence. I'm going to turn you over to Peter Nabokov and Joe Benítez now. We'll talk more later."

Benítez walks up to the table, "¿Cómo está? Es un placer conocerlo, voy a servirle de intérprete, si es necesario Zara." (How are you? It's a pleasure meeting you. I will be your interpreter if necessary, Zara)

Peter Nabokov steps out of the darkness putting his hand out as well. Benítez interprets for Peter. Zara stands leaning over the table and looks towards his friend Dr. Knowlton. Dr. Knowlton looks over his shoulder. He makes eye contact with Zara, turns, and walks out the door. Dr. Knowlton recognizes Libertado, Martín, and Terijú. He looks at the rifles they possess for evidence of Cuban infiltration. He can see no evidence of any automatic weapons, only their hunting rifles. There is nothing whatsoever that would lead him to believe that these people are preparing for warfare.

Lanterns light up the cabin with a subdued, soft yellow luminous glow.

Zara tells Nabokov, "Está bien, siéntase" (It's OK. Sit down.)

Nabokov asks, "What happened that made you attack the courthouse, Zara?"

Benítez interprets, "¿Qué pasó que te hizo atacar a la casa de corte, Zara?"

Zara responds, "Ya, es que estábamos buscando a Alfonso Sánchez…" (I know. We were looking for Alfonso Sánchez…)

The interview goes on for some time before Zara concludes the meeting. Martín and Libertado are outside with Knowlton. He asks them about what happened and whether anyone coached them to raid the courthouse. Terijú is inside standing guard over his father.

Zara says, "Okay, is that all? I'm tired," he blows his nose, "it's going to be light soon. I think you should leave."

Zara stands up and shakes their hands. Libertado and Martín are standing next to the door. They blindfold their three visitors and escort them out. Terijú, Zara, and Libertado stand in the shadows while Martín, Porfirio, and Feliciano walk the men into the woods where their vehicle is waiting. They walk up the mountain through some thick brush to the truck and make their way out of the backcountry where they are transferred to the car. Porfirio and Feliciano put the trio in the back as they were before and drive away. They drop the women off in Hernández and go on into Santa Fé, leaving them where they had been picked up. The trio leaves together. Peter Nabokov drops them off at the hotel and leaves to write his story.

# CHAPTER FIFTEEN

## KNOWLTON TALKS WITH THE GOVERNOR

DR. KNOWLTON SAYS, "Governor, this is preposterous, calling in the National Guard and other law enforcement agencies. This will only serve to further complicate the situation and agitate the natives!"

The Governor says, "Well, Dr. Knowlton, you were right. I didn't think those folks were capable of getting the Cubans involved."

There is a knock at the door and the secretary steps in.

The secretary says, "Governor, we just got word that DA Alfonso is sending the police up here to arrest Dr. Knowlton."

Startled, the Governor tells Knowlton, "Leave through here." He opens a secret passageway. "Get out of town. We will finish our conversation later."

Dr. Knowlton makes his way through a long narrow corridor and down some stairs and out into the underground parking. Just then a reporter drives up and recognizes Dr. Knowlton. He pulls up alongside him, "Dr. Knowlton, what are you doing here? I heard that the police are out to get you."

"Get me out of here!" Dr. Knowlton opens the car door and gets in.

"Where are you staying?" asks the reporter.

"I'm at La Fonda. Can you get me to Albuquerque?"

"Sure, will you give me an interview?"

"While we're on the road."

They arrive at the Albuquerque airport. "Well, you go by the hotel and have them send my luggage to the University Department of Sociology. Here's ten dollars, it shouldn't be any more than that."

Dr. Knowlton gets on the plane and, on his arrival in El Paso, heaves a big sigh of relief. The next day, he tells his students all about what happened.

## The Raiders Turn Themselves In

A few days have passed. Zara is sick with a cold. The only resolution he can see to end the ordeal is to turn himself in, in spite of Dr. Knowlton's advice to hold out and maybe even exploit the debacle to his advantage.

"Muchachos, me voy a entregar. Al cabo yo soy él que quieren y si me entrego, va a ser más fácil para ustedes." (I am going to turn myself in. After all, it is me they are really after, and if I turn myself in I think they will go easier on you.)

Wrapped in a blanket, shivering, he wipes his nose with a handkerchief.

Zara, "Y tengo que estar en corte la semana que entra, si no me presento, la fianza que Santiago puso para mí, la pierde." (And I have to be in court next week, or if I don't present myself Santiago will lose the money he put up for my bail.)

Libertado, "Oh no...noo...no yo - yo...yo yo, no quiero entregarme. Me van a sentenciar por la muerte del chota." (I do not want to turn myself in. They are going to sentence me for killing the cop I shot).

Martín and the others remain silent. Zara instructs Martín and Libertado to go and get in touch with the Governor. Uvaldo drives them to Española, and they pull into the Safeway parking lot next to a phone booth. Martín calls the Governor.

He dials the operator, "I need to talk with the Governor. "Just a minute," she responds, and buzzes.

"Governor, I believe one of the raiders is on the phone."

Governor Cargo answers, "Well, how you boys doing?

"Governor, we're okay, we want to turn ourselves in, but we want clemency," responds Martín.

"Well, why don't you boys just turn yourselves in and we will talk about that," says the Governor.

"No! We want clemency. And Libertado is innocent. The cop went for his gun, that's why he shot him and that's what started the whole thing. We only wanted to make a citizen's arrest, we didn't mean for things to get out of hand. We are innocent," explains Martín.

"We'll see what I can do. You boys just turn yourselves in, and I'll do everything I can. I just need you to come before anyone else gets hurt. Now you boys just come on in and we'll take care of you," says the Governor.

"Okay, you make a statement in the news and then we'll see what happens," responds Martín.

Martín and Libertado return to Uvaldo's ranch and report to Zara. A few days later Nabokov's article comes out, and the governor is accused of empathizing with the raiders. They decide to turn themselves in. Uvaldo drives Libertado and Martín back to Española and they pull into the Safeway parking lot next to the phone booth again.

Libertado calls his wife. This is the first time she has heard from him since the morning of the foiled citizen's arrest. Martín stands beside the truck, lights up a cigarette, and smokes.

Libertado's wife asks, "¿Estás bien?" (Are you okay?)

Libertado answers, "Estoy pensando en ir a México o a Cuba, tengo miedo que me vayan a condenar a muerte por balear al chota." (I'm thinking of going to Mexico or Cuba, I'm afraid that I will be given the death sentence for shooting the cop.)

"¿Y qué vas a hacer en México o peor aún en Cuba? No conoces a nadien allá... Y ¿qué de nosotros? No nos puedes dejar." (And what are you going to do in Mexico, and let alone Cuba? You don't know anybody there, and what about us here? You can't leave us.)

"¿Qué más puedo hacer? Y los hijos, ¿cómo están? ¿La niña?" (What else can I do? And the children, how are they? And the baby girl?)

"Están bien todos, estamos bien. ¿Cuándo te vamos a ver?" (They're all right, we're all right. When are we going to see you?)

"No sé. Bueno, hablo contigo más al rato. Martín tiene que hablar con la Susana." (I don't know. Okay, I'll talk to you later. Martín has to call Susana.)

The telephone operator cuts in, "You have one minute left."

Libertado says to his wife, "Bueno, ya me tengo que ir, ya no tengo dinero, te hablo después, vieja." (Okay, I have to go, I don't have any more money. I will talk to you later, my old lady.)

Martín calls his wife, Susana. She lives in Española, and she is angry. The house is a mess and several kids are running around dirty while she holds a crying baby in her arms."

Martín's wife is frustrated, "What are you doing? I told you not to get involved with that man, that he was nothing but trouble. ¿Qué esperabas? Nunca quise a Zara, siempre me hacía sentirme incómoda." (What did you expect? I never liked Zara. He always made me feel uncomfortable.)

She goes on, "Where are you and what are you going to do? We are behind on the bills, and the landlord wants the rent."

Martín says, "We are talking about turning ourselves in. Do you have Pajarito's number?"

"You get it yourself. I got my hands full, me tengo que ir. His dad's name is Persiliano Manzanares. He should be in the phone book."

"Can you get the number for me?"

"I got my hands full ... you look it up---¿Qué vas a hacer?"

"No estoy seguro. Tal vez pedirle a Pajarito que me lleve a entregarme. ¿Búscame el número, ya sabes que no leo muy bien—ya lo sabes. ¿Por qué me maltratas, vieja?" in a loving tone. (I'm not sure. I am thinking about having Pajarito take me in. Look for the number. You know I don't read very well. Why do you mistreat me that way, my wife?)

Susana refuses, "Tú búscalo." She hangs up the phone. The kids are running around, and the baby is crying. She just can't take it anymore.

Libertado asks, "¿Qué te dijo?"

"No, nada, no dijo nada, que ya quieren la renta," responds Martín. "Vamos a ver a Pajarito." (No, nothing, she didn't say anything. They want the rent. Let's go see Pajarito)

"¿Sabes dónde mero vive?" Asks Uvaldo. (Do you know exactly where he lives?)

Libertado responds, "sí más o menos déjate ir por aquí, para el Duende."

Uvaldo follows directions to Pajarito's. He drops them off and heads back home. Martín and Libertado are in a 1952 Chevy Impala convertible. El Pajarito is a long, thin, funny-looking guy with long thin legs and a sharp nose and chin. Some say Pajarito looks and walks like a flamingo and that's why they call him "Pajarito," the Birdie. He drives them to Española. Libertado sits in the middle of the backseat, ruffled black hair waving in the wind under a felt Stetson cowboy hat. Martín is sitting on the front passenger's side of Pajarito's 1965 Impala. They pull into the parking lot, and Martín goes into the police station.

Martín asks, "¿Está el capitán Vigil aquí?" (Is Captain Vigil here?)

The officer responds, "He's not here."

Martín asks, "¿Cuándo viene?" (When will he be back?) The officer says, "He should be back in an hour." Martín leaves. The officer turns to another policeman walking in from the jail. "Did you see that guy? Wasn't that Martín, one of the raiders?" They both walk over to the window. "Yeah, it looks like him," answers the other officer.

Martín, Libertado, and El Pajarito drive off with nowhere to go. They cruise through town and stop for a hamburger and fries at the local drive-up, Dandy's Burgers. Then they go by the police station again. Martín gets out of the car and turns to Libertado in the back seat.

Martín says, "¿Que no vas a venir? (Aren't you coming?)

Libertado says, "No, me van a matar, Martín. Tengo miedo de que me vayan a matar - mejor ve tú." (No, they are going to kill me Martín. I am afraid that they're going to kill me - better you go.)

Martín looks at his uncle-brother, turns, and walks into the police station.

Martín asks the same officer as before, "¿Ha llegado Vigil?"

The officer says, "No, he's still not back." Not wanting him to leave, the officer tells him, "Why don't you take a seat? Do you want a Coke? He should be back any minute."

Martín says, "Ahora vengo, déjeme avisarle a los que me trajeron." (I'll be right back. Let me tell my ride to go.)

Martín walks back out. The police officer rushes around the counter and follows Martín who waves to his ride to leave. The police officer relaxes, goes over to the Coke machine and buys a soda.

Martín sits down and smokes a cigarette. The officer hands him the soda, while other police officers hang around in the front office.

Captain Vigil comes in and sees Martín. He walks over to the officer on duty, "What's going on?"

The officer says, "He just walked in and asked for you. I told him to wait, and I gave him a Coke."

Captain Vigil turns and walks over to Martín, "Me da gusto verte, Martín, está bien que te entregaste. ¿Dónde están los demás?" (I'm glad to see you. It's good that you turned yourself in. Where are the others?)

Martín says, "No sé, nos separamos hace una semana." (I don't know, we got separated last week.)

"¿Dónde has estado?" (Where have you been?)

"En la sierra. En la sierra nomás."

"Bueno, vamos a llevarte para que te bañes." (Well, let's get you showered.) He turns to the officer on duty, "¡Mauricio! Llévalo para que se bañe."

Mauricio steps up and comes around the counter, "Sí capitán - Martín, sígueme." Porque no te bañes primero Martín y mientras mandamos." (Take a shower. Meanwhile we'll get you something to eat). Martín is treated with admiration and folk hero the police know Martín all their lives.

## UVALDO TAKES ZARA TO ALBUQUERQUE ·

Leaving the ranch, Uvaldo Velásquez, Zara, and his son Terijú drive south. They are heading to Albuquerque, taking Highway 44 through Cuba, NM. They stop in San Isidro to gas up, and Zara gets out to drink water from the hose next to the gas pump. He has a cold and is dehydrated. A young man recognizes him, waits until they leave, goes to the phone booth, and dials the operator. The boy tells the operator, "I need to talk to the State Police."

The operator responds, "Just a minute."

A voice answers, "State police."

The boy says, "I just saw Zara at the gas station in San Isidro. He's headed to Albuquerque."

Terijú is driving, Uvaldo is sitting in front with him, and Zara is in the back. They are driving southeast toward Bernalillo. As they approach town they see the police in an unmarked car coming from the opposite direction. They pass each other, and the police go up and over a hill, turn around and follow them through town at some distance. Another unmarked police car passes them as they go through town. They make eye contact.

Terijú turns to Uvaldo, "Son narcos. Ya nos chingaron." (They are narcos, they got us.)

Zara is in the back seat, tired and feeling miserable. Just as they reach the outer limits of Bernalillo heading to Albuquerque, near Sandia Pueblo on the old highway, they approach a roadblock. Sandía Pueblo police appear from a side road.

Zara and Terijú are taken directly to the penitentiary. Zara feels miserably sick. He and his son are escorted by the State Police car onto the penitentiary grounds. Horns blast, and the inmates are put into lockdown. They wonder what is going on. Everything had seemed normal for the inmates to that point. Zara and his son, Terijú, are escorted through a long passageway. Zara anticipates a victorious entrance, but instead he finds the echoing silence of jailhouse doors opening and hollow voices in the corridors. Not an inmate can be seen.

Zara and Terijú are booked and taken upstairs where they hold prisoners on death row. They walk past the gas chamber and go up a flight of stairs. Zara lies down in a cell. Terijú is locked up in the cell next to him. Martín shuffles around in the cell next to Terijú wearing his flip flops. He asks who it is.

"Soy yo, Terijú," he responds.

"¿Qué te pasó? ¿Cómo te agarraron?" asks Martín.

Zara lies feverish on his cot and listens to them talk. Terijú tells Martín how they were captured.

## LIBERTADO TURNS HIMSELF IN

Libertado is on the phone with his wife at the home of Pajarito talking about what to do. "Quizás me voy a entregar."

His wife asks, "Por qué no te entregas con Fidel, es policía en Santa Fé. Como es sobrino, estamos seguros de que nada te va pasar. Yo le llamo".

Libertado tells her, "Si tú crees que así lo debo hacer, así lo hago. Es buen muchacho. El hijo de Ambrosio Mascareñas, los dos siempre han tratado a la gente bien. Dame su número de teléfono." (If you want, that's what I should do. He's a good kid. The son of Ambrosio Mascareñas, the two of them have always treated people well. Give me his phone number.) He gets the number, bids her goodbye and hangs up.

Libertado tells Pajarito, "Decidí entregarme en Santa Fé. ¿Me puedes llevar?" He asks Pajarito to take him.

Pajarito asks, "¿Cuándo vas a estar listo?" (When will you be ready?)

Libertado says, "Cuando me llamen." (When they call me.)

Libertado's wife calls back and instructs him to go to Santa Fé and meet him at the Lota Burger.

Pajarito drives Libertado to meet his nephew. He gets in the front seat of the police car and Mascareñas takes him directly to the penitentiary. Late at night Libertado is booked and led to cellblock 3, death row, downstairs in the temporary cells next to the gas chamber. Martín, Terijú, and Zara are all in the same cell block but on the second floor below the gas chamber. The mood is quiet. Zara coughs. Libertado realizes he isn't alone. Terijú and Martín are asleep.

### Indio Gerónimo Turns Himself In

Indio Gerónimo is still at-large, hiding in an abandoned house at the edge of Canjilón. It is dark when he makes his way into the house, so he takes a lighter from his pocket. He finds a jar of jelly. His stomach aches with hunger.

He takes his bowie knife from his hip and scrapes the mold off, devouring the jelly with his fingers. There is a little left at the bottom of the jar. His knife is too big, and it doesn't fit in the jar, so he looks around, finds a stick, breaks it, and scrapes the jar clean. He hides there for another day.

Late that evening Indio stealthily makes his way to his mother's house. Dogs bark and porch lights go on. He hides. He sees a police vehicle pass on a nearby road. He lies still for a while and he calms the dogs down by talking to them. "Cálmense, necesito que se calmen," he says in a quiet, soothing voice. (Calm down I need you to calm down.) He continues making his way to his mother's house.

Indio Gerónimo enters his mother's house. She is at the kitchen table sewing some tattered socks and praying. She can't believe her eyes. She gasps, and, stunned, sits frozen in her seat thinking that he is an illusion.

"¿Eres tú, m'ijo?" she asks in a trembling voice.

"Sí mamá, soy yo."

Her face brightens as she realizes he's not an illusion. She makes a fuss, embracing him, "¿Ay, m'ijo, qué vas hacer?" (Oh son, what are you going to do?) She stands and walks towards him and hugs and kisses him on the cheek.

His mother gets a cup and pours him coffee. The radio is on. The corrido "El Hijo Desobediente" is playing. She puts wood in the stove and sets beans and chile out to warm, setting tortillas on the stove. Indio walks over to the kitchen counter and scoops water from a bucket to drink. He stares into the distance as he looks out through the kitchen window over the sink. The stars twinkle in the night sky. The Big Dipper and North Star look so close that one could pluck them from the heavens.

Indio Gerónimo's mother tells him, "Te tienen una recompensa de quinientos dólares, tienes que tener mucho cuidado, m'ijo."

Indio Gerónimo turns facing his mother, "Sí mamá, quiero entregarme, pero ¿cómo pudiéramos agarrar la recompensa?" (Mama, I want to turn myself in. But how can we collect the reward?)

"Ay m'ijo, ¿cómo vas a hacer?" (Son, how are you going to do this?)

"No sé. ¿Qué te parece si tú me entregaras con Miguel, así estamos seguros que te den la recompensa a ti?" (I don't know. What do you think about you turning me in to Miguel? That way we are assured that they give you the reward money?)

Indio Gerónimo says, "Bueno, mamá, vamos a llamarlo y a ver qué dice."

Indio Gerónimo's mother dials the phone. It rings. On the other end a man in a police uniform is getting ready to leave for work. Indio Gerónimo's sister answers the phone.

Her mother says, "M'ija! Buenas tardes, ¿Cómo están mis nietos?" (Daughter, good afternoon. How are my grandchildren?)

Her daughter answers, "Bien, mamá, ¿Estás bien? ¿No has oído de mi hermano?"

"¡Sí! Déjame hablar con tu esposo."

The daughter calls her husband, "Miguel, mi mamá quiere hablar contigo."

He takes the phone, "Sí, suegra. ¿Qué pasa?"

### Indio Gerónimo goes to jail

A police vehicle pulls up to the Santa Fé jail. Officer Miguel and Indio Gerónimo walk in. A bulletin board is displayed with wanted posters. Indio's face is on one: MOST WANTED MAN BY THE FBI.

The booking officer asks, "How did you get him?"

Miguel turns and calls other officers, "Hey, vatos, miren a quién traigo aquí." The other officers come around and make a commotion.

Miguel tells them to calm down. "Okay you guys, okay, remember he's a prisoner not a hero."

"What do you mean? This vato attacked the courthouse and is the one that held out longer than anyone else, and he did it in defense of las Mercedes," responds one of the other police officers.

"Yeah, I know, let's book him," says Miguel.

Prisoners peer through the bars of their cells as Indio Gerónimo is taken to a holding cell at the city jail in Santa Fé. The people in the cells begin to chant, "¡Tierra y Justicia VIVA!... ¡Viva, Viva, Indio, viva Indio Gerónimo!"

Later Indio Gerónimo is taken to the penitentiary.

### The Lt. Governor Talks to the Warden

The Warden is on the phone talking to the Lt. Governor. "Yes, Lt. Governor, the floodlights arrived yesterday afternoon and will be functioning tonight."

Lt. Governor, "Now listen, Warden, I have told you of my concern about reports that are coming in of Cuban mercenaries in those mountains. General Pershing Jolly will be sending you a company to patrol the perimeter of the penitentiary."

Jeeps patrol the area, and National Guardsmen patrol the road leading to the penitentiary. Armed guardsmen are at the entrance.

Indio is brought into the penitentiary. The inmates are in lockdown. The corridors are empty, and not a soul can be seen except the guards. Indio Gerónimo is led to cellblock-3 and taken downstairs where Libertado rests in one of two small holding cells next to the gas chamber. The guard leads Indio by the arm, directing him into the cell across from Libertado.

The sun is setting on the horizon. Helicopters fly over the penitentiary, and huge military spotlights comb the night sky for intruding aircraft. Jeeps drive the perimeter while spotlights comb the llano. It's the Fourth of July and fireworks can be seen from Santa Fé.

### JOSÉ MARÍA HANGS OUT AT THE VICTORY BAR

José María walks into the Victory bar. The TV is on, though reception is poor, A special news bulletin comes up, "Beep, beep, beep." The news broadcaster speaks... This is a News Bulletin...

"The mother of the FBI's most wanted man in America has turned her son in. He is the last of the Spanish Americans that raided the Tierra Amarilla Courthouse. She will collect the $500 reward for her son's capture. Indio Gerónimo, was booked moments ago in Santa Fé and will be taken to the penitentiary to await trial. That is all the information we have, but we'll keep you posted..."

José María is riveted to the television set drinking with fellow ranchers. Everyone is talking about the raid on the courthouse. They are all laughing in loud guffaws at the news that Indio Gerónimo's mom tricked the state into giving her the reward money.

A friend of José María puts his hand on his shoulder, "Qué suerte tienes tú, José María. ¿Cómo fue que te soltaron tan pronto? Mira hasta salistes en el periódico, como eres famoso ahora, vamos a tener que dirijirnos a ti usted con muncho más respeto— Don José María," (How was it that they let you loose so quickly? Look you came out in the paper, you're famous now. We are going to have to address you with the dignity and respect of a Don José María). He steps back, adjusting himself in a dignified manner. He shows José María the newspaper. The photo shows José María with his hands on his head. Walking up a slope to the sheep corral in a single file, men women and children are following him.

"Qué suerte tienes, José María. ¿Cómo es que te soltaron tan pronto? Mira, hasta saliste en la prensa. Ahora estás muy famoso. ¿Cómo fue que no te agarraron antes con los demás revoltosos?" (What luck! José María, how did you get released so soon? Look, you even came out in the paper. You're very famous now. How come you weren't caught with the rest of the rebels.)

José María, "Yo sé, la pura suerte que me escapé, porque me estaban buscando y cuando ya mero me agarraron en Abiquiú di la vuelta, y entré al rancho de Uvaldo por el camino viejo de los Navajos donde pasé por el pueblito de San Joaquín. Todavía se puede pasar por el puente viejo, aunque ya no hay nadien allá, todavía se miran las casas cayéndose y el puente está a punto de caer. ¿Sabían que todavía hay huertas de manzana allí?"

(I know, it was pure luck. They were looking for me too, but I was in hiding. When they almost caught me in Abiquiu I turned around and entered Uvaldo's ranch from the old road of the Navajos and passed through the village of San Joaquin. You can pass thorough the old bridge about to collapse even though nobody lives there anymore and you can see the houses falling down. Did you know that there are still apple orchards there?)

"Pero anduvistes allí cuando atacaron la casa de cortes verdad," asks a Patrón at the bar. (You were there when they attacked the courthouse, right?)

José María, "Sí, sí entré a las cámaras del juez buscando a Sánchez pero no estaba." (I entered the judge's chambers, but he wasn't there.)

A friend says, "¿Viste el periódico? Los tienen como prisioneros de guerra. ¿Los vistes?" (Did you see the newspaper? They have them like prisoners of war? Did you see?)

José María looks at the paper, "Mira como nos traen como si fuéramos POW's, nomás que estamos en nuestro país. Todo lo que queremos es justicia y nuestras mercedes, las tierras que son nuestras." (Look at the way they have us like POW's only in our own country. All we want is justice and the lands that were taken from us.)

# CHAPTER SIXTEEN

## Cell Block 3

THE JAIL GUARDS OPEN the gate to the entrance of the main corridor. One guard passes through, while the other stays behind to ensure their safety.

The first guard says, "Okay, you guys! Somebody loves you ... you are getting out today. Indio Gerónimo, you're first on my list, and I will be back for you in a few minutes, Libertado."

The guard opens the cell door, and Indio Gerónimo, with what little possessions he has follows the guard

The first guard continues, "Yep, get your blankets and roll up your colchón (mattress); you know the routine."

Indio can't move fast enough; he is so excited. Libertado, white knuckling at the cell bar, "Hey, cabrón, vale más que me esperes." (Hey you goat! you better wait for me!)

Indio Gerónimo scrambles to roll up his mattress, "Aha, Libertado, you'll be right behind me ése, no te apenes...no te apenes, hermano."

The first guard changes his mind, "Ahaa, okay, get ready! I'll take both of you. I don't think you guys are going to give me any trouble."

The second guard, is younger and less experienced than the first, "Hey, that's against procedure, no se debe hacer eso."

Indio and Libertado shuffle down the long corridor in their flip-flops, passing through the gates. Indio steps on his blanket which is dragging on the floor and stumbles. He falls. Libertado laughs, "Ay que pendejo, ya no puedes ni caminar, te dejaron en la celda por mucho tiempo, porque estás batallando." (Ay, what an idiot! You can't even walk anymore! They left you in the cell for too long. Why are you having such a difficult time?)

As they step outside the penitentiary, they see José María, Fátima, and Libertado's wife Raquel waiting outside. They hug and kiss.

José María says, "Okay, you guys, let's get out of here. Your mothers have a meal for you."

Driving down the long dirt road they eventually meet the highway. They turn and head north, arriving at Canjilón and the home of Calixtra, Indio Gerónimo's mother. They pull up to the house where there are a lot of cars and people.

Indio Gerónimo says, "Hey, it looks like a party, Libertado! Let's crash it."

Libertado says, "¿Eh qué hacemos contigo?" slapping on the side of the head, "It's for us, tonto."

Fátima snuggles up to Indio Gerónimo. She takes his hand and kisses his cheek as they walk in.

People greet them.

Indio's cousin says, "¡Hey, primo! We thought we lost you, ése."

Primo grabs his lifelong friend, Indio Gerónimo, "You didn't think we were going to let you go out like that, did you?" Everybody laughs.

Indio Gerónimo says, "Hey, vato, it's going to take more than the National Guard to keep me away from you," pinching his cousin on the cheek. His primo pulls away, wiping his face and spitting, "¡Cochino!

Chingao, vato, what did they do to you in there, turn you into a ruca?" More laughter.

José María, "Mira lo que te prepararon, lo hicieron para ustedes. No lo hacen todos los días." (M'ijo, come and see what the women have cooked for both of you. They don't do this every day.)

Libertado is excited, "Fresh tortillas, all right!" More laughter.

## Alianza Fandango

At the Alianza headquarters in Albuquerque it is dusk, Zara talks with people, Martín and Libertado are among them. The Brown Berets are standing at the entrance frisking people for weapons. Indio Gerónimo basks in his new-found fame. People are praising him. He stands with Fátima. He is confident. Fátima is talking with Valentina and other girls. Indio walks over to Zara who is talking with others. Indio listens.

Zara talks to los Aliancistas, "We are all brothers fighting in the same struggle. We are all human and should fight together against tyranny, Black as well as Red and poor Whites." Zara ignores Indio Gerónimo's presence, rudely turning his back on him. Indio's ego is bruised. Indio repositions himself attempting to get in on the conversation, but Zara cuts him off.

Indio Gerónimo asks, "What do you know of tyranny? Look at the way you treat your family."

Zara is startled. Never has Indio been so forthcoming. Zara gets angry. The veins on his forehead puff out and his piercing green eyes stare through Indio Gerónimo. Indio stands firm.

Indio Gerónimo, "I protected you from harm and you snuck around dressed like a girl when we were running from the police."

"Why don't you shut up? You are a child that knows nothing. You know nothing of justice. I am the one that taught you everything you know. You are not worthy of my time," retorted Zara.

Indio Gerónimo, "No, that's not true. My tío, José María, has taught me what I know of the landgrants, of honor and justice, long before you ever came here."

"Desgraciado, eres un pedazo de mierda." (Ungrateful, you are a piece of shit.) Zara aggressively comes at Indio Gerónimo. Libertado gets between them, and José María rushes up to them from across the dance hall. Zara attempts to grab Indio Gerónimo, but José María keeps him away and tells him, "Cálmate, m'ijo, cálmate ahora, no es el tiempo para responder con coraje, tęn control de tus emociones antes de que digas algo de que te vas a arrepentir." (Calm down, son, calm down. Now is not the time to respond this way. Control your emotions before you say something you will regret.)

Indio Gerónimo is very upset, "Zara, you will never learn what it is to be a man of honor. I know you better than anyone, and I have seen how you care for no one but yourself."

Indio Gerónimo walks away to Fátima and tells her, "¡Vámonos!" Taking her by the hand, they leave the dance.

## The Story of Eulogio Salazar

The jailer Eulogio Salazar is back to work and is serving food to inmates. His jaw is scarred from the shot he took during the raid.

A co-worker asks, "¿Cuándo vas a dar tu testimonio? ¿Es verdad que fue Zara que te balaceó?" (When are you going to testify that Zara shot you?)

Eulogio answers, "Me quieren entrevistar el miércoles de la semana que entra, otra vez." (They want to interview me Wednesday of next week again.)

Eulogio passes a tray of food to the prisoners.

The inmate says, "Este pan está rancio, nos vamos a morir de hambre, o nos van a envenenar." (This bread is rancid. We're going to die of hunger, or they will poison us.)

Eulogio responds, "No llores tanto, tú por lo menos puedes abrir la boca pa' comer." (Don't cry. At least you can open your mouth to eat.)

They finish passing food to the four prisoners and Eulogio gets ready to leave.

Eulogio says, "Bueno, voy a llevar a mi esposa a un velorio, nos vemos mañana." (Okay, I'm going to take my wife to a rosary, I'll see you tomorrow.)

Eulogio puts on his coat, hat, and gloves, and goes out to warm up his car. He comes back inside to finish his cup of coffee while the car warms up:

"Hijo, cómo está frío, la nieve se está congelando." (Wow, how cold it is! The snow is freezing.)

The other Jailer asks, "¿Quién se murió?" (Who died?)

Eulogio tells him, "El tío de mi esposa, Primitivo de la Puente." (My wife's uncle, Primitivo de la Puente.)

The other jailer responds, "Vaya, yo no sabía nada, conozco a su hijo Esteban—dale a la familia el pésame de parte de mí y mi familia." (I didn't know anything, I know his son Esteban. Tell the family I send my condolences.)

Eulogio says, "Sí, yo les diré, ay cómo está frío." (Yes, I will give them the message, God it's cold.) He rubs his hands, picks up his cup of coffee, and warms his hands on it.

The other jailer says, "You should have taken more time off the job. I don't know why you were in such a hurry to come back to work."

Eulogio tells him, "I am not going to hide from anyone. I'm only going to tell the truth when I give my testimony next week. Zara was there when I got shot, and that is all I got to say, the truth. I don't know for sure who shot me, but he was standing just outside the door, and that's all I'm going to say."

"Okay, I don't know, Eulogio, do you want me to have a patrol car follow you home?"

"No, estoy bien, nomás voy pa' la casa a recoger a mi esposa y luego vamos al rosario." (No, I'm fine, I'm only going to the house to pick up my wife, and we'll go to the rosary.) He takes a sip of coffee, staring into oblivion out the window. "Vale más irme, el carro ya debe estar calientito. Nos vemos mañana." (I better be going. The car should be warmed up by now. We'll see you tomorrow.)

It's pitch dark outside the courthouse. Eulogio Salazar's face is grossly disfigured from the gunshot wound. As he drives off into a cold, snow-packed moonless night and slowly makes his way towards his home another car pulls around the corner and stealthily follows behind with its headlights turned off. Eulogio is oblivious to the automobile behind him. He turns down his private road, the other vehicle holds back. His wife notices her husband coming down the road, and she goes into the bedroom to change shoes and put on her coat. Eulogio pulls up to the gate and gets out of his car. He hears the snow crackle as a vehicle pulls up behind him. It's dark, and he can't see. The car doesn't have the motor on, and it rolls to a stop. Someone gets out of the vehicle. Eulogio hears footsteps in the snow. He turns around. All he can see is a shadow walking up to him. He is clubbed and thrown into the back seat of his automobile. Someone gets into the driver's seat and someone else gets into the back seat with Eulogio. The vehicle backs out of the private road. Eulogio's wife notices the car backing out and leaving. She is puzzled, but figures her husband forgot something, so she gets ready for bed. She tosses and turns all night. Eulogio never comes back. She is worried and doesn't sleep. Before daybreak she calls the jail.

The dispatcher says, "Aha, buenas, Señora Salazar. ¿Cómo están todos?" (Good morning, Señora Salazar. How are you all doing?)

Señora Salazar asks, "¿Puedo hablar con mi esposo?" (May I speak with my husband?)

The dispatcher answers, "No lo he visto, déjeme preguntar si está aquí." (I haven't seen him. Let me ask if he's here.)

She put her on hold and walks across the hall to ask the Jailer whether or not he has seen Eulogio.

The jailer says, "No, se fue anoche, ¿Que no llegó a casa?" (No, he left last night. What? Didn't he make it home?)

The dispatcher says, "Quizá no, ¿Lo están buscando?" (I guess not. Are they looking for him?)

She goes back to Señora Salazar, "No está, dijeron que se fue anoche, ¿Qué no llegó?" (He's not here. They said he left last night. Did he get home?)

"No, vi las luces del carro, pero dieron vuelta, pensé que regresó al trabajo." (No, I saw the lights of the car, but they turned around. I thought he had to go back to work.)

The despachar says, "Voy a llamar al cherife en su casa." (I am going to call the sheriff at his home.)

Eulogio's wife calls her sister. Sheriff Benny Naranjo gets a call. He leaves directly for Eulogio's home. On the road leading to the house, he finds blood-splattered snow and three sets of footprints.

Eulogio's sister answers the phone, "¿Qué pasa, hermanita? ¿Por qué llamas tan demañana? ¿Qué te pasó anoche? (What's wrong, sister? Why do you call so early? What happened last night?)

Eulogio's wife asks, "¿No está Eulogio allí contigo?" (Eulogio is not with you?)

The sister answers, "No, los estábamos esperando anoche. ¿Por qué no llegaron al rosario, que pasó?" (No, we were waiting for you last night. Why didn't you come to the rosary? What happened?)

Eulogio's wife says, "Nunca volvió Eulogio, pensaba que había quedado allí con ustedes, que tuvo problemas con su carro o algo. Ya llamé su a trabajo, dijeron que no estaba tampoco, que iba para la casa cuando salió. Vi las luces del carro en la entrada de la propiedad, pero dio vuelta." (Eulogio never made it back home. I thought he had stayed there with you, maybe because his car had broken down or the like. I called at his job and they told me he was not there either and that he was going home when he left. I saw his car's lights at the entrance to the property, but then I saw he turned back and left.)

"¿Pues qué pasaría hermanita?" (What could have happened, little sister?)

"Ahorita te llamo, llegó Benny." (I'll call you back. Benny is here.)

Eulogio's wife talks to Sheriff Benny Naranjo and tells her story. Sheriff Naranjo walks to the gate and finds the bloodstained snow. He puts out an all-points bulletin in search for Eulogio. The State police are on the alert and head to the area.

A rancher on the road to La Puente, a village a short distance from Tierra Amarilla, stops to look at a car near the high school off the embankment of the road. He finds a body in the back seat. He is turning to walk back to his car when a State Policeman pulls up. He tells the officer what he found, and the officer goes to the vehicle to see for himself. He finds Eulogio with his face beaten to a pulp. It is so disfigured that he is unrecognizable. The State Patrolman walks back up to the road. The snow is up to his knees. He calls on his police radio.

It's not long before reporters and TV news journalists arrive.

The Journalist interviewing Zara in Albuquerque asks, "What do you think of what happened in the brutal murder of the jailer? The way he was found bludgeoned to death this morning, Mr. Zara."

Zara is on TV, "I'm shocked, I'm shocked. I can't believe that anyone would do this to Eulogio. He was a friend ... I can't believe it."

"Do you think your organization had anything to do with it?"

"Of course not! We are not a violent organization. Eulogio was our friend. He is a landgrant heir and supported our cause. We would never think of doing any such thing."

News reporter, "Well, there you have it. The leader of the Alianza de Pueblos Libres claims that he knows nothing about the murder of jailer Eulogio Salazar, the star witness for the prosecution. He was scheduled to testify that it was Zara who shot him during the courthouse raid."

There is a flurry of activity from all levels of government and law enforcement. The news reporter is standing in front of the courthouse in Santa Fé. "The judge has revoked the bonds of those men responsible for the courthouse raid and who are suspects in the jailer's death." All the Aliancistas have sound alibis and have been acquitted of the murder of Eulogio Salazar. The case remains unsolved to this day.

# CHAPTER SEVENTEEN

## ZARA'S TRIAL BEGINS

THE JUDGE PRESIDES OVER the arraignment stemming from the courthouse raid. He releases all but three of the raiders who are being held on felony charges: Zara, Indio, and Libertado. The trial is moved from Santa Fé to Albuquerque to Judge Larrazolo's court. The raiders are faced with sixty-four charges stemming from the raid on the courthouse, and the Judge tries each of the Aliancistas separately. In the primary case the D.A., Alfonso Sánchez, is intent on imprisoning Zara.

Zara fires his attorneys and defends himself. He stands up and addresses the Judge, "May I speak?"

The Judge looks up over his glasses, "Go ahead Mr. Zara."

"Yes, Judge, I would like to inform you that I have fired my attorneys and will defend myself." People in the courtroom gasp.

The prosecuting attorney says, "Judge, I move that this trial proceed despite this impediment. This comes as a complete surprise. I beseech you not to allow this trial to drag on indefinitely."

The Judge answers, "Mr. Prosecutor, will you please stop already. Remember you are in my courtroom, and I… I alone will determine how this judgment will be carried out." He turns to Zara, noticeably upset, "I will go along with this, Mr. Zara, but you only have thirty minutes to prepare."

Attorney Beverly Axelrod says, "Your Honor, that is unfair. You must give us more time!"

"No, you have thirty minutes to get ready. I suggest you get busy." He picks up the gavel - bam!

"This court will reconvene in thirty minutes." He stands and retires to his chambers.

The defending attorneys huddle around Zara

Axelrod, "are you sure you want to go through with this?

Zara, "Yes, this is my time. Everything I've been fighting for all of my life has come to this moment. I feel like a raging bull is on the loose, and I have been put here at this moment in time to make my stand, and I am ready to challenge the injustice committed on my people. I feel like an angry bull ready to duel for justice. No, I'm going to do this. I have been put here by God to defend my people, and that is what I am going to do. All of you have been brought as my counsel. Let's get to work."

The trial begins with the selection of jurors. The *Albuquerque Journal's* defamatory campaign works in Zara's favor, proving bias or prejudice by potential jurors who believed Zara was involved in some way in the murder of jailer Eulogio Salazar. This leaves Judge Larrazolo little choice but to dismiss them.

Attorney Jack Love had successfully convicted Zara in the Echo Amphitheater case months earlier in Las Cruces but lost his bid for attorney general. Alfonso Sánchez has hired him to help with the courthouse raid case. Jack Love, a tall, scrawny, red-haired Texan in cowboy boots, and Alfonso Sánchez, neat and well-groomed in a silk, gold, and black tweed suit, face off with Zara.

The courtroom and hallway are filled with people. Los Comancheros de Río Arriba are outside protesting. The police take away their protest signs. The leader, Pedro Archuleta, storms into the courtroom demanding from the judge that they be returned. Judge Larrazolo calmly orders the police to give them back. The people have won a victory. Though small and meaningless, it is significant in that it shows the partiality of some law enforcement officers in setting the stage for what is to become the vindication of the injustice they have experienced. The courtroom cheers the judge's order. Some jurors rearrange themselves in their seats, noticeably uneasy. Others attempt to hide their approval. The Judge slams his gavel demanding order and declares that if anyone continues unruly behavior they will be removed from his courtroom.

Judge, "Call your witness Mr. Zara."

"I call State Police Officer Nick Sais as my first witness." Nick is in the hallway with his fellow officers. He is called into the courtroom, He is tall, dark skinned and handsome. He takes his seat and is sworn in. Zara stands up from behind his table and calmly paces the floor. He walks toward Officer Sais and stops, putting his hand on the railing and looking at Sais. "Mr. Sais, do you carry a gun, and if so, for what purpose do you carry a weapon?"

Nick Sais, "To protect ourselves and citizens."

"Do you know anything about the rights of the people to bear arms?"

"Well, I know it is a constitutional right."

"Good, do you know anything about civil rights law?" asks Zara.

"No."

"And who do you think is at fault, you, or your superiors for not teaching you about civil rights law?"

"Well, I suppose these issues should have been addressed when we were in training."

"How can you protect the rights of the people - the people of the United States – if you do not know their rights?"

Nick Sias hesitates. He suddenly realizes the logic of the questioning and reluctantly answers,

"Well, I guess I don't have any right, do I?"

Zara addresses the Judge, "I have no further questions, Your Honor. Thank you, Mr. Sais. I would like to ask Mr. Alfonso Sánchez to the witness stand."

Prosecuting Attorney Jack Love speaks up, "I object, Your Honor. Mr. Sánchez cannot testify against himself..."

Zara defends his request, "Your Honor, it is necessary for Mr. Sánchez to take the stand so I can show that law enforcement is incompetent to enforce the law if they do not even understand these fundamental constitutional rights."

Prosecuting Attorney Jack Love objects, "This is ludicrous. I move for a mistrial, Your Honor." This is completely out of line. The charge before this court is assault on a courthouse, not on civil rights." Zara declares, "I oppose this interruption. This argument has merit, your Honor. I am attempting to show the reasons for the assault, and I cannot do this without showing the reasons and events that led to the alleged assault."

The Judge is firm, "Mr. Zara, I will not allow you or anyone else to dictate to me what I am going to do in my courtroom and will not allow Mr. Sánchez to testify against himself. Do you wish to call another witness?"

"Yes, I would like to call Deputy Sheriff Dan Rivera." Zara questions Rivera on different themes. Rivera unravels the events that led to the meeting in Coyote being quashed, describing the various police agencies involved and his participation in the events that led to the raid. During his questioning Zara makes him admit that he did not know federal law and of the constitutional right to free assembly. Zara also asks him about Emiliano Naranjo's control of the county.

Deputy Sheriff Rivera is nervous, sweating profusely. Zara asks if he participated in the pre-courthouse raid hysteria and whether he felt the Forest Service harassed the Alianza. Deputy Sheriff Rivera says, "No." Zara asks, "Do you think District Attorney Alfonso Sánchez violated the Alianzas' Constitutional right to free assembly?"

The Judge intervenes, "Mr. Zara, will you please get to the point." Zara explains that he needs to establish the context of events that led to the raid. The Judge responds, "Okay, speed it up. I will not allow this case to drag on indefinitely."

Zara continues his questioning of Rivera, "Mr. Rivera, given all that you have shared with the court today, could you hold me responsible for what happened that fateful day? Could you hold anybody responsible for what happened that day when the wrath of God descended on the Chama Valley, the very soul of our people?"

"No, I do not blame you, Mr. Zara, for anything that happened that day," responds Rivera. Zara, "I have no further questions, Your Honor." The judge dismisses the witness.

Defending attorney Higgs, working with Zara, makes a motion that the court dismiss the charges. The Judge denies it.

Attorney Jack Love asks for a recess. The Judge denies the request.

Zara continues, "Judge, I would like to call Nick Sais back to the stand." "Go ahead." The Judge responds in grudgingly rolling his eyes impatiently.

State Policeman Nick Sais takes the stand. Zara asks him to tell his version of the story of what happened when he was shot. Sais tells how he was looking at the bulletin board when he felt someone approach him and he turned around finding himself surrounded. He tells how he reached for his pistol and of then being shot. He describes what he saw while lying on the foyer floor, bleeding.

"Mr. Sais, did you see me fire a gun?"

"No."

"Did you hear me give any orders?"

"No."

"Thank you, Mr. Sais, that will be all. No further questions."

Judge, "Mr. Love, do you have any questions?"

"No, Judge."

Zara continues, "Judge, I would like to call Sheriff Benny Naranjo to the stand."

Zara asks Naranjo, "What did you hear and see on the day in question?" "I heard a shot and got as far as the door to my office when I got my gun knocked out of my hand and slammed to the floor." "Did you see who did that to you?" "Yes, it was you." "I did that to you? I knocked the gun from your hand and knocked you to the floor? Mr. Naranjo, did you hear me give out any orders?" "No." "Did you see me fire my weapon?" "No."

Although somewhat limited in the English language, Zara had learned firsthand the value of rapid questioning, timing, and misdirected questioning, setting the witness up with a series of mundane questions and then suddenly delivering a series of relevant questions while nervously pacing the floor. He dismisses Naranjo and calls his next witness. His exhilarating delivery has left the courtroom stunned. Not a shuffle or a cough was heard.

Zara continues, "I would like to call Officer Quintana to the stand."

Officer Quintana is in the hall outside the courtroom with other officers. He is called in and takes a seat. Zara asks him, "Officer Quintana, tell the court what you were doing that fateful day leading up to the June 5th, incident." "Well, Officer Santisteban and I were coming from Chama back to the courthouse when I turned the corner to drive up to the courthouse and we were fired upon. I put the car in reverse but didn't make the turn, getting stuck in the embankment of the road. We got out of the car and ran across the street, down to the school, then back up the hill, and observed some men shooting up police vehicles and pillaging them."

There is a deliberate, long pause. The witness shifts in his seat and looks over to the jurors. Zara walks up to the railing separating the spectators from the court floor.

Zara continues questioning Officer Quintana, "Is it not true, Mr. Quintana, that you were following orders the State District Attorney gave to stop citizens from having a public meeting in Coyote on June 3, 1967?" "Yes—I and Officer Sais manned a roadblock. We were ordered to ask people their destination and to discourage anyone from attending the Alianza meeting in Coyote. "Did you arrest anyone on that day?" "No," answers Quintana. "Did you arrest anybody involved who was planning to attend or participate in the Alianza meeting?" "Yes, Officer Rodela called for backup a day before the raid," replies Quintana. "And who did you arrest?" "Oh, I believe it was Cruz Aguilar, at his ranch, where we were called to." "And what happened that day?" "We arrived there about 5:00 o'clock in the afternoon and, well, this young boy came out of the house with a rifle and backed us up into a pig pen." Laughter. The judge looks over to the jurors sternly. The jurors attempt to hold a subdued posture.

"We were able to calm the situation down and arrest Mr. Aguilar."

"Thank you, Officer Quintana, that will be all. You may step down."

The next witness, Uvaldo Velasques, testifies that he had been arrested for unlawful assembly and was present for his scheduled arraignment on June 5, the day of the raid. Like Cruz, he was never called back to judgment. When asked the purpose of the June 3rd meeting, he explained that it was to draft a letter to petition the President of the United States for help with the landgrants, but the police stopped the meeting.

The following day Professor Dr. Knowlton outlined a long history of land loss and the marginalization of Nativo Nuevomexicanos. Knowlton goes on to explain the complexity of resentments that contributed to the success of the Alianza. However, the jury was removed during this testimony at the request of the prosecution, and Judge Larrazolo reserved his decision on the admissibility of Knowlton's statement.

The prosecution attempted to introduce into evidence some of the picket signs from the protesters who were in front of the courthouse. The signs bore hand-lettered challenges to Alfonso Sánchez. During the brief debate over the admissibility of the pickets a young activist, Pedro Archuleta, steps up to the bench and admits he was responsible for them, and that if Alfonso had nothing to fear, he should take the witness stand. Alfonso, looking down at a note pad and doodling, lifts his head and looks up over his reading glasses. He gives a defiant, melancholy shrug and goes back to his doodling. Jeers in the courtroom. The judge bangs his gavel demanding order.

Gloria Acuña testifies that she heard the defendant say in Spanish, "'Acaba con ellos," (Do away with them.) "I took it as doing away with us all."

During cross-examination the expressions "Acabe con todos" and "acaben con todo esto," have different connotations. Zara points out the similarities between the two phrases and the difference in meaning. The jury was reminded of Pedro's testimony about hearing an unidentified voice saying, "acaben con esto," (Finish with this.) verses "acabe con todos" (Finish with these people). He concluded in a gentle voice ... "Weren't you surprised to find everyone in the conference room safely together?"

"Yes," replied Señora Acuña. She turns her head and looks out the window.

Although the formal charges included false imprisonment, kidnapping, and assault on a jail—not a courthouse—no statutes existed for assault on a jail. There were also no statutes in place for holding a demonstration. The law states that a victim who is taken from one place to another and held against their will constitutes kidnapping, and there was no evidence that the defendant, Zara, had participated in the holding of the courthouse employees. Señora Sifuentes' testimony corroborated this.

Deputy Sheriff Dan Rivera is called to the stand again. He is the state's key witness.

Zara asks him, "Where were you at the time in question?"

"I was in the courtroom of Judge Scarborough when I heard several shots and someone coming up the stairs, bursting inside the courtroom. Judge Scarborough and I were in his chambers when I heard shots fired. They sounded like they were coming from downstairs. I opened the door and started to go out to see what was going on, and I saw the intruders so I closed the door and locked it. More shots were fired through the door, and then a series of shots took out the lock. I attempted to hold the door closed while the judge escaped out the window. When I could no longer hold the door I was hit across the face with the butt of a gun. I was led downstairs to be held with the others in the conference room. Moments later I was pulled from the crowd of courthouse employees and told to go to the jail downstairs and release the prisoners. Someone followed me. I don't know who it was. I didn't turn around to get a look at them.

"Mr. Rivera, did you hear me give an order to release the prisoners?" "No." "Did you see me at any time during the alleged incident?" "No." "If you never saw the person who had a gun on you, then how did you know it was me?" "Sir, I am not blaming you for anything."

Attorney Higgs stands up and calls for immediate dismissal. "The State's key witness has exonerated the defendant, Judge. The defense moves for dismissal of all charges."

This time the motion is not denied but held under advisement by Judge Larrazolo.

## Closing Arguments

Zara outlines his defense, "The so-called courthouse 'raid' was the fault of the DA denying the Alianza the right to assemble publicly, and their constitutional right was denied to commit a citizen's arrest on DA Alfonso Sánchez because of his actions keeping the Alianza from having the conference. In addition, Nick Sais triggered the violence when he went for his gun. In summary, Judge, the prosecution has failed to establish that I had ordered anybody to be shot or that I shot anyone. Nor has the prosecution provided evidence that I was in charge. Sheriff Dan Rivera has testified, in this courtroom that he did not see me, therefore, exonerating me from any wrongdoing."

Waving his hands in the air, Zara breaks into a brimstone sermon comparing his battle with the status quo and his struggle for the landgrants to the battle between David and Goliath.

"Like David said to the Philistines, you come against me with sword and spear and javelin, but I come against you in the name of the Lord Almighty, the God of the armies of Israel whom you have defied. Today I will give the carcasses of the Philistine army to the birds of the air... and the whole world will know that there is a God in Israel. It is not by sword or spear that the Lord saves, for the battle is the Lord's, and he will give all of you into our hands. As Goliath moved in for the kill, David reached into his bag and slung one of his stones at Goliath's head. The stone sank into the giant's forehead, and he fell to the ground. David then took Goliath's sword, killed him, and cut off his head."

"Yes, ladies and gentlemen, we are guilty for claiming our land. Guilty of believing that the Treaty of Guadalupe Hidalgo is there to protect our rights. Guilty of demanding that we have an education that recognizes the history and contributions of our people made in the making of this country. But the guilt really lies with The State's District Attorney Alfonso Sánchez. It is he that should be brought to trial for violating our constitutional right to free assembly. It was his fault that led to the events of June 5, 1967, a day that will be held in infamy. Our cry was a scream of the eagle for justice, for the world to know of the injustice committed upon the people of New Mexico, the children of the Indio e Hispanohablante that has made for a new race, una Raza cósmica."

Everyone present is thunderstruck by Zara's closing statement. The prosecuting Attorney stands, pulls on his coat and clears his throat. He steps around his table and begins to pace the courtroom in front of the Judge. He walks up to the jury box and, in an undertone, begins his closing argument.

"The defendant is a known troublemaker and opportunist. Mr. Zara has come to New Mexico, misleading these poor New Mexicans to believe they could gain possession of landgrants lost long ago without due process of the law. Mr. Zara also failed to appear in court when ordered to prove whether their claims were valid or not. This talk of a citizen's arrest has only been an effort to divert a failed attempt of attacking a courthouse. The court's only concern is whether or not Mr. Zara is guilty of attacking the courthouse. This case has nothing to do with the landgrants and social justice. The defendant has demonstrated on a number of occasions his lust for publicity."

"The reason for the raid was to garner publicity for his cause. We have numerous witnesses who have testified that he was a principal of the raid and was armed. One witness testified that he maliciously beat a defendant, while another has said that he stood by while the man was beaten. As an accomplice, the defendant is guilty of a number of illegal acts."

"If Mr. Zara is so concerned for human rights, then what of the people he has terrorized? I appeal to you, the jurors, to consider what has happened here, with the attack on a courthouse, the beating of undersheriff Dan Rivera, and what of the harm committed to a state patrolman who was mortally wounded as a result of this heinous crime? And what of the deceased jailer, Eulogio Salazar, who gave a pretrial testimony accusing the defendant and asserting that it was Mr. Zara, who shot and wounded him while attempting to escape? We are now left to wonder just who brutally bludgeoned him, leaving his face so broken beyond recognition that his death still remains a mystery today. Yes, ladies and gentlemen of the jury, I beseech you to impose punishment to the fullest extent of the law and find Mr. Zara guilty on all three counts, including first degree kidnapping. It is your duty to hold him and him alone responsible for the attack on a United States Courthouse. Moreover, I recommend to the jury that he be given life imprisonment without consideration of parole. This Court must have jurisdiction over this man's life, for if let back into society he will incite the public to further disobedience."

Attorney Jack Love walks over to the defendant's table in a subdued posture. Confident, he bends over the defendant and looks him in the eye.

"He could have been such a great man had he only championed his cause, if only he had stayed within the boundaries of the American legal system. But No!" Turning around to face the jurors. "This man made a mindful choice to break the law, leading his followers into harm's way, and for that..." He slams his fist on the table in front of the defendant startling everyone. "He should be duly punished!" The attorney turns and faces the jury, pauses for some time, hands on the jury railing, looking the jurors sternly in the eyes. "Thank you. That is all I have to say." He turns his back to them and takes his seat.

Judge Larazolo takes his time shuffling through papers. He puts on his glasses and begins to read his instructions to the jurors in a purposeful voice. "The law states anyone who interferes with a lawful citizen's arrest does so at his own peril, and the arresting citizens are entitled under the law to use whatever force necessary to affect said arrest. They are thereby able to use whatever force is reasonably necessary to defend themselves in the process of making such an arrest."

"However, we must stay focused on the fact that the defendant is being tried on three counts: one, assault on a jail; two, false imprisonment; and three, kidnapping—not on an attempted citizen's arrest. Nor is this judgment about the landgrants. We are in court today on three charges and only those charges - assault on a jail, false imprisonment, and kidnapping. So, I ask the jury to review all that has occurred in this court with those three charges in mind, and only on those charges are the defendant to be tried. The jury is excused." The Judge slams the gavel, gathers his papers and files, stands, and leaves the courtroom. The jury is escorted out of the courtroom. People in the courtroom meander through the halls as they leave the courtroom. The attorneys talk to one another. Zara is escorted out.

Four hours later the jury returns. The defendant, Zara, is asked to stand. He leans forward, fists on the table, head lowered.

The Judge addresses the jury, "Jury foreman, will you please read the verdict?"

The jury foreman stands and clears his throat, "Judge, we, the jury, find the defendant Not Guilty on all three charges."

The air in the courtroom seems to be sucked out as everyone gasps, imploding from within. The defendant falls back into his chair slumped over, elbows on the table, hands wrapped around his head.

"He's free!" shouts a woman in the crowd.

Sánchez is dumbfounded but stoic. The defendant's family steps around the railing embracing Zara. "We won! We won!" His deep green eyes glossy with tears, he works his way through the crowd as reporters ask him how he feels.

Zara responds, "I feel incredible. I cannot find the words that express how I feel right now. I thank my God, my people."

The State Police stand against the marble wall of the courthouse hall. The New Mexico State Seal looms over the scene. It is a wood-carved mosaic depicting the imposing North American Bald Eagle coddling a miniaturized version of the Mexican Golden Eagle with a snake in its beak. The benevolent American Eagle is protecting its little people, Los Nuevomexicanos. It is a symbol of American supremacy. In reality the two eagles are close in size.

In the mosaic El Águila Mexicana is reduced in size proportionally to the Bald Eagle. The North American Bald Eagle is depicted as the protector of its people. The New Mexico State Seal shows the Bald Eagle protecting its citizens while showing the Mexican Eagle in a diminutive posture. Originally the New Mexico State Seal showed the eagles to be almost equal in size. But the symbolism has been transformed and now shows the Mexican Golden Eagle as a miniaturized version of the North American Bald Eagle. The Mexican eagle is now depicted as an immature eagle with its head white like an adult Bald Eagle. This is not only an inaccurate portrayal of the species but is also demeaning to Nuevomexicanos. The baby Bald Eagle does not, in fact, have a white head. It becomes white when the eagle matures. It is a not so subtle symbolic psychological diminutive of the status of Nativo Nuevomexicanos.

# CHAPTER EIGHTEEN

## THE BEGINNING OF THE END

IT IS SEVERAL WEEKS later. People are preparing for a hero's celebration at the Alianza headquarters. Mariachis are performing. Everyone is congratulating Zara. There's food aplenty. Children are playing, and there is merriment everywhere. Brown Berets are parking cars and checking people for weapons. Indio is helping. It's dusk and almost everyone has arrived. Lupita brings Indio a plate, and they sit in his 1955 Ford pickup listening to the radio. He finishes eating, leans back in the car seat, props his feet up on the open door, drinks a soda and smokes. Lupita is on the passenger's side curling her hair with her fingers.

"Ya hemos tenido una buena corrida con lo que hemos hecho este año, ¿verdad Lupita? Ahora todo el mundo sabe de nuestra historia," dice Indio. (We've had a good run with what we have done this year, haven't we Lupita? Now the whole world knows our history.)

"Sí, ¿ahora qué vas hacer? ¿A buscar trabajo?" asks Lupita. (Yes, now what are you going to do? Look for work?)

The sunset on the horizon behind the three volcanoes west of Albuquerque is colorful in shades of orange, violet, purple, and red.

Indio reaches over and gives Lupita a kiss. They become passionate. He opens her blouse and she suddenly gets aggressive. Indio panics and holds her off.

"What! What's the matter, don't you want me?" asks Lupita.

"Ahaa, yeah but you're coming at me like a wild woman. Have you done this before, what's wrong? Why are you so, I don't know, pushy? Where did you learn that? I mean, I've never known a girl to be so aggressive! Como si estuvieras enojada. Are you mad?"

"What do you mean? What's the matter? I thought you're supposed to act that way."

"Where did you hear that?"

"Well, I don't know. I just thought you're supposed to act like that."

"What do you mean you're supposed to act like that? You're acting like you ... you've done it before. Why do you act like that, like angry, like you want to force yourself on me? That's not right, that's just not right, Lupita. A man and women are not supposed to act that way. A man shouldn't even be like that to a woman. No somos animales." (We're not animals.)

Lupita, "Look, if you don't want to do it, just say so." Lupita buttons her blouse, fixes her hair and leaves gruff and humiliated.

Indio starts up the truck and heads to his cousin's house. He pulls up to the house at Guadalupe Trail and Morada Road. "¿Qué te pasa primo?" his primo asks. (What's up, cousin?)

"Lupita, like, she got really aggressive or something, vato. It was crazy. I don't know. She was like wild. I don't know. Tiene algo esa mujer, está loca." (There's something wrong with that woman. She's crazy!)

Crucita comes out to throw the trash and finds Lupita outside the kitchen door near the trash cans in a fetal position crying. The other women are inside cleaning. "¿Qué te pasa m'ija? ¿Por qué lloras, alguien te hizo algo, qué te pasa?" (¿What happened, my child? Why are you crying? Did someone do something to you? What happened?). Crucita kneels down and hugs her. "Llora y dime qué te pasó." Lupita sniffles and attempts to gather herself and talk. "Estaba con Gerónimo, y la estábamos llevando muy bien, me besó, y luego me acusó que era muy agresiva, que muchachas no deben de ser así. No hallo qué hacer." (I was with Gerónimo, and things were going nicely. He kissed me, and then he accused me of becoming too aggressive, that women are not supposed to be that way. I don't know what to do.) She covers her face and shakes it from side to side, whimpering.

Crucita holds her, "Está bien, m'ija, llora, todo va a estar bien, aunque no me gusta verte así, a veces nos hace bien llorar, no voy a dejar que nada te lastime, yo me quedo contigo. Cuando estés lista y si quieres, me puedes hablar. ¿Qué te pasa m'ija, por qué lloras? ¿Por qué te sientes tan lastimada? No tengas pena, te voy a proteger." (It's okay, little one. Cry. Everything will be OK. Although I do not want to see you like this, at times it does us good to cry. I will not let anyone hurt you. I will stay with you. When you are ready, if you wish you can talk to me. What happened my little one? Why are you crying? Why do you feel so hurt? Don't be ashamed, I will protect you.)

Lupita explains what happened with Gerónimo. Crucita probes, asking why she was so aggressive. "Mi apá, es que mi apá, mee, me..." She cries uncontrollably. "Me fuerza así, me dice que es la voluntad de Dios. Es que quiero a Gerónimo y pensé que así debería comportarse uno cuando quiere a uno como amante." (My father, does me like that. He forces himself on me, to have relations with him. He tells me that it is God's will. I like Gerónimo, and I thought that you were supposed to act like that when you want somebody as a lover.)

Crucita responds: "Oh m'ija, está bien, si deberías estar con él, se va a hacer. Llévala con calma, m'ijita, reconoce que el espíritu de Dios siempre está contigo y no hay nada malo que te pueda pasar porque el espíritu siempre es puro con amor y armonía." (Oh, little one, it's okay. If you are to be with him it will happen. Take it with ease my little one. Know that the spirit of God is always with you. He is pure love and harmony.)

Crucita helps Lupita stand up and walks with her into the kitchen. Calixtra recognizes that she is distraught, so she hands her a damp cloth to cool her face. The women surround her, consoling her and telling her that she will survive. Word of the conversation gets to Gerónimo.

Gerónimo is feeding the livestock when Libertado pulls up in his pick-up. Libertado gets out of the truck: "Hey, ¿cómo estás, hermano?" (How is it going, bro?)

"Bien, bien, muy bien, es que tengo que hablarte de lo que me dijeron. Lo que oí de Lupita. Es que Lupita le dijo a Crucita que Zara está molestándola." (Doing good, very good. I gotta tell you something though. It's about Lupita. She told Crucita que Zara has been molesting her.)

"¡Cómo! ¿Cómo molestándola? ¿A poco? ¡Oh no! ¿A poco? ¡Qué cochino! ¿Cómo puede uno ser tan asqueroso y tratar a su propia criatura como si fuera un animal? No, Libertado, ¿cómo puede ser?" (What?? Molesting her? Tell me it's not true! How can one be so gross and treat one's own child like an animal! No, Libertado, it can't be!!!) Gerónimo goes into the house and gets his pistol. His mother, Calixtra, follows him into his room. "¿Qué demonios piensas hacer?" she demands. (What the Hell is on your mind?) "Ese asqueroso no vale la pena, si lo matas, ¿qué te va a pasar a ti? Vas a la cárcel, y ¿por qué, m'ijo? ¿Por un hombre que no vale ni la pena? Piénsalo m'ijo." (That disgusting man is not worth it. If you kill him what will happen to you?

Why would you go to jail, son? All that for a man who's not worth it? Think about it, son.)

"Dame esa pistola, Gerónimo, dámela." Indio extends his hand and she takes the pistol.

José María walks in, "¿Qué pasa?"

José María hugs his nephew and sits him down on the bed: "Déjalo m'ijo, no vale la pena. Déjalo. Esa familia está muy enferma de la cabeza, no dejes que nos enfermen a nosotros, a nuestra familia. Si vas a matar a ese hombre, no nomás vas a desperdiciar tu vida, sino la de todos nosotros, toda tu familia que te aprecia. ¡No! Gerónimo, te vas a quedar aquí con tu familia, al cabo tenemos que reportarnos en la Morada el viernes y allí le pedimos reconciliación. Acuérdate, ser Hermano es caminar por esta vida en caridad." (Let it be, son. It's not worth it. That family is crazy! Do not let them drive us all crazy as well, all our family. If you kill that man you will not only ruin your life but the life of all of us, your family who loves you. No, Gerónimo. You will stay here with your family; we are to report to the Morada on Friday, and there we will ask for a reconciliation. Remember, being an Hermano is to walk in this life in charity and compassion.)

Indio Gerónimo replies, "Pero, ¿cómo, cómo puede uno dejarla vulnerable para que la siga engañando? También hay que proteger a los que no pueden protegerse a sí mismos." (But how can one leave her alone, vulnerable, and enable him to go on abusing her? One also has to protect those who cannot protect themselves.)

José María, "No, Hermanito, ahorita te tengo que proteger a ti y la reconciliación se va a ser en La Morada. Para que pienses bien las cosas y te cuides a ti mismo y a todos los que te quieren a ti. Así hallarás la paz y la fuerza para ser mejor hombre en lugar de rebajarte a ese nivel." (No, little brother. Now I have to protect you, and the reconciliation will take place in the Morada. You need to think straight and take care of yourself and all those who love you. And so you can find inner peace and the strength to become a better man instead of stooping to the same level.)

### BURNING OF THE FOREST SIGN

Zara's second wife burns the Forest Service sign. The State Police arrest her. Forest Rangers armed with weapons surround Zara and others.

Ranger Evans approaches Zara, "You are under arrest," and he grabs Zara by the belt of his pants. Zara attempts to pull away. Detective Gilliland is standing behind his car with his rifle over the hood aiming at Zara. He pulls the hammer back on his rifle. A young white boy is taking photographs of the scene, and he turns when he hears the click of the rifle. He suddenly realizes that he is directly in the line of fire. He backs out of the way, notices that he is out of film, and steps away to reload his camera.

Zara says, "You are the one under arrest."

Ranger Evans turns to Terijú, who is standing between the Ranger and Zara, "If you don't back away buddy, I will arrest you, too."

Zara breaks away from the Ranger.

"No! You are under arrest! I am going to arrest you for destroying National Forest property."

Zara turns away, walks towards his car, and reaches for his rifle.

Juan Roybal, an Apostle of La Mesa Cósmica, yells at Zara, "¡No! He goes over and tells him, Zara, ahorita no es el tiempo para esto." (Zara, now is not the time for this.) He takes the gun from Zara: "No, Zara, no hagas eso, mira nomás, quieren que hagas una tontería, déjalo." (No, Zara, don't do that! Look, they want you to do something stupid. Leave it alone.)

Detective Galliland has his sights on Zara. His elbow is resting on the hood of the car and his rifle is ready to fire.

Zara sets his rifle back in the car; both he and his wife are arrested.

Zara is standing before the judge. His wife is released of all charges, and Zara does 18 months in a federal penitentiary for burning Forest Service Property.

### Released from Jail

November 1967. The judge drops the charges, and both Indio and Libertado are freed. José María is driving. Fátima is sitting between Indio and José María. Libertado and his wife are in the back seat.

Indio has his arm around Fátima, "A hora somos libres, brother." Indio turns to Fátima and kisses her.

"Yeah, a hora sí, Hermano." Libertado and his wife give each other a kiss as well.

Indio Gerónimo says, "I can marry Fátima."

Fátima responds, "What? This is the first time I have heard of that!"

Indio answers her, "Ahhh, honey—you know you want to; I mean I asked my tío and he said it was OK."

"What does tío José María have to do with me marrying you?"

"Well, he knows you are my vieja, and you are his niece from another father."

"Did you just call me your old lady? Have some respect, I'm younger than you are." She takes his arm off her shoulder and they all laugh. "And besides, what do you mean another father."

"See tío, I told you she loves me," says Indio.

Fátima says, "Oh sí, repugnoso (stuck-up), I never told you that I love you."

"But you like me, ¿verdad?"

More laughter .... Fátima snuggles up to Indio and whispers, "I do love you." Indio hugs her.

Libertado, "I am free, and I can go back to my familia and work la floresta."

José Marí, "Yes, we have got the attention of the world about our situation. The world now knows that the land has been stolen by private businesses with the help of the government, y ahora que vamos a la corte tienen que oirnos decirles que las Mercedes están han sido robadas." (And now that we go to court they have to hear us tell them that the landgrants are stolen.) "We must keep our focus that this fight is for our survival, y tienen que ir a la Morada por una limpieza from this ordeal you have experienced, porque con una limpieza, you can go on with your lives with a clean spirit and a heart filled with a blessing that all this was for good intentions, as you both continue your lives' journey."

## LIMPIEZA

La limpia is a return to the cleansing waters of the ancient ritual of seeking spiritual and physical renewal and empowerment for the Hermano and acceptance of all that happens in life and for their immediate struggle for cultural survival.

It is late in the afternoon. Libertado and Indio Gerónimo knock on the door of La Morada. They step inside, crossing the threshold and leaving the ordinary world by entering the sanctity of the Morada. The Hermanos stand en escala (in order), "Santas y buenas noches Hermanos, esperamos que ustedes y sus familias estén bien." (Blessed and good night, Hermanos. We hope you and your families are in good health.)

The Hermanos respond: "Santas y buenas noches, Hermanos, esperamos que ustedes y sus familias estén en buena salud y que estén con la presencia de Dios." The Hermano Mayor adds: "ya íbamos a comenzar el rosario." (Blessed and goodnight, Hermanos. I am confident that you and your families are in good health and in the presence of God. We were about to get started with the rosary).

Responde, Indio Gerónimo and Libertado: "Muy bien, gracias."

The first Hermano asks: "¿Cuál alabado quieren cantar, Hermano?" (What alabado do you want to sing, Hermano?) "¿Y con cuál quieren terminar?" (And which one are we going to close with?)

The Hermanos talk among themselves and come to a consensus.

The Hermano Mayor says, "¿Bueno, Hermano Aguilar, tú y el Hermano Ángel van empezar el rosario, y tú Hermano la primera misterio, y tu Hermano López, la segunda...usted Hermano Miguel la tercer misterio y tú Hermano el cuatro, y usted Hermano la quinta? Hermanos Herman y Juan concluirán el rosario." (Okay, Hermano Aguilar, and Hermano Ángel will begin the rosary and you Hermano the first mystery and you Hermano López the second mystery...you Hermano Miguel the third mystery y tú Hermano the fourth, and you, why don't you do the fifth mystery Hermano. Hermanos Herman and Juan will conclude the rosary).

The scene looks chaotic but is actually deliberate. Some Hermanos talk amongst themselves while others ask questions. The lead Hermano starts to sing, and suddenly everyone falls into line and repeats the coro. Se ponen en escala y se preparan a caminar al oratorio (They line up in order and prepare to walk to the oratory). It is evening. People are entering and taking their seats. They take out their rosaries. The Hermanos sing an alabado as they make their way to the oratorio from the Morada. They are heard from a distance by the particulares (the ordinary people). Those unable to kneel stay seated on the bancos (benches or pews) along the wall to pray, while yet others stand and kneel as far as the entrance and outside. Others join the Hermanos as they enter the Morada and kneel. They begin the rosario.

The melancholy ancient cantos del sufrimiento de Jesús (chants of the suffering of Jesus Christ), the Gregorian melodic alabado, is sung as they enter. They stop at the altar. People in the oratorio sit in silence as the Hermanos conclude the alabado. The Hermanos kneel. José María takes the lead and starts the rosary in a soothing rhythm. The archaic prayers are recited as they have been since Christianity was introduced by the Spanish to the region centuries ago. Everyone present falls into a trance as the Hermanos devoutly pray.

The meditative trance takes each individual into a series of fast- and slow-moving flashbacks. As they pray, they are cast into a mystical mindset. Indio Gerónimo is hypnotized and slips into a trance. It unfolds like a silent movie reel flickering in black and white, then in color. The images sharpen of horsemen riding at night, tearing down barbed wire fencing and riding through a village. The scene comes into focus and then dissolves from the experiences of his ancestors into Indio's life experiences. The Hermanos come to the end of the rosary.

They stand up to sing la despedida as they walk backwards out of the oratorio and back to the Morada. Los particulares stay in the oratorio. The alabado fades into the midday sun as the silhouette of the Hermanos makes its way into the abyss. Though it's midday a full moon rests on the horizon of the Sangre de Cristo Mountains. The crest of the mountain range takes on the likeness of Jesus lying down as the sunset reflects scarlet colors and shadows. Some of the particulares leave, while others stay and continue to pray or just contemplate. At the Morada Hermanos relax, mingling and talking. At the back of la Morada is an outhouse nestled in scrub oak against a steep hill. The campo santo glitters with luminarias. Maderos (large crosses) are paired, leaning against one another in a line near the morada. Men drink coffee or rosario, rosemary tea. Hermanos mingle. Some are preparing for the evening vigil. Elders sit and talk.

The next day the Hermanos are preparing for the stations of the cross as Los particulares arrive to participate.

"Ave María Purísima," calls out the Hermano Mayor.

"Sea concebida sin pecado original," respond other Hermanos.

Each of the Hermanos is assigned a station of the cross. Los particulares come to join them, waiting outside the Morada. The stations of the cross conclude in the oratorio, and the Hermanos take requests for prayers for the living and the dead from the particulares.

The Hermano Mayor announces: "Hermanos, la casa está abierta la comida esta lista; vamos a comer." (Hermanos, the house is open and the food is ready. We can share our meal.)

The Hermanos mingle with their guests. Particulars go to the kitchen and prepare to serve the food.

The Hermanos take their places at the table. The Hermano Mayor blesses the table and those who have prepared the food and have come to pray with them.

The Hermanos are served, and they eat as two Hermanos perform an alabado. When they are through with the alabado two other Hermanos take their place, giving them a chance to eat. Once the Hermanos have completed their meal they give their blessings. People mingle and visit. The Hermanos make their way to the Morada after los particulares have left.

Inside the Morada, the Hermano Mayor calls out, "Ave María Purísima."

"Sea concebida sin pecado original," respond other Hermanos.

The Hermano Mayor continues, "Hermanos, la casa está abierta para discusión y tenemos al Hermano Hilario que nos quiere discutir el tema de qué es tener Fé." (Hermanos, the morada is open for discussion. Tonight, Hermano Hilario wants to instruct us about what it means to have faith).

"Santa y buenas noches Hermanos, que La Santa Madre, La Virgen Santísima siempre sea con nosotros," (Blessed and good night, Hermanos. May the Blessed Mother, Most Holy Virgin always be with us,) says Hermano Hilario. Los Hermanos respond, "Así sea Hermano." (So be it.)

"Muy buenas tardes, Hermanos. Hace tiempo que el Hermano Hermán nos hizo una pregunta, ¿Qué es tener Fé?" (Good evening, Hermanos. Some time ago Hermano Hermán asked us to ponder: what does it mean to have faith?)

"Bueno pues, me puse a pensar y estudiar el sentido profundo de la Fé. Cómo llega uno a tener Fé para llevar una vida plena. Quisiera saber si pudiéramos tener una discusión entre nosotros acerca de qué significan nuestros rezos y todo lo que hacemos aquí en la Morada, cómo llegamos a ese espacio para tener Fé. ¿Qué significan las catorce estaciones de la Pasión y cómo se reflejan en nuestras vidas? ¿Cómo nos ayudan los ejercicios para llegar a tener la Fé? ¿Comó nos ayudan en hacer nuestras vidas mejor? Y más que nada, cuando la vida nos la pone difícil, cuando nuestras vidas no salen como quisiéramos, o nos imaginábamos, ¿cómo llagamos al punto de aceptar lo que hay y escoger le bien en esos tiempos malos o difíciles? Son esos momentos cuando se invoca la Fé. Bueno, primeramente, quiero darles una definición de la Fé."

(So, I started to ponder and study the deep meaning of Faith. How does one acquire Faith to have a meaningful life? I would like to engage in a discussion about the meaning of our prayers and all we do here in the Morada especially during Lent. How do we reach that space to have Faith? What is the meaning of the fourteen stations of the Cross, of the Passion of Christ, and how is it reflected in our daily lives? How helpful are the exercises aimed at strengthening our Faith? Are they helping us to improve our lives? And most of all, when the going gets tough and life tests us, when things don't turn out the way we wanted or had planned, how do we reach acceptance and choose goodness in such difficult circumstances? It is in those times that we need Faith the most. Now first of all I would like to give you a definition of Faith.)

Hermano Herman says in English: "Faith is knowing that our intention, our heart's desire has been set in motion. Faith is the interaction of the conscious and subconscious mind. In accordance with one's faith it is done unto you as you set the law of cause and effect into motion.

What does that mean? To understand the hidden power of faith is to understand the hidden power of knowing. One needs to not only understand the thought process but to be conscious of what is manifested by those thoughts set in motion. This is what the law of cause and effect is. To be cognizant of the subconscious mind; to recognize how the law of cause and effect is set in motion. To understand faith is to become acquainted with these two functions of the mind, the conscious and subconscious.

The conscious mind is the mind of reason. What you choose to focus on is what is most likely to be. You make all decisions with your subconscious mind. You get up in the morning and get ready for the day. You go to work, and you tackle daily tasks or problems for your survival."

"Think of the subconscious mind as a garden and of yourself as the gardener, *you sow what you reap.* As the gardener you plant a seed without doubting that whatever you planted is what will grow. As long as you tend to it your subconscious mind will manifest what you are thinking. Every thought is a cause and every condition is an effect. When one begins to understand that our thoughts dictate our actions, and we realize how our thoughts are making us feel, then one is able to take control of those thoughts and steer them to manifest constructive actions in our lives. This is how one finds harmony and peace, and in this way one finds serenity and is able to walk through life in reverence, embracing all that life has to offer. Then one will recognize the power of the subconscious, the Holy Spirit, from within. When you are able to control your thoughts, especially when faced with a dilemma, and apply the power of the subconscious, you will consciously cooperate with the omnipotent law of cause and effect which governs all there is. Then matter will be manifested into form which will be if that is what you concentrate on. The world within—your feelings, thoughts, and imagery, make your reality. That is, everything that is in your world comes to be. It is an expression of your inner mind made conscious."

"Faith is the substance of our belief system, a mental process that is manifested through prayer. It is fashioned in the mind for a beloved outcome. Prayer is a profound expression of faith, communicated to God with the intention of creating the effect one wishes to set into motion."

"Bueno, Hermanos, con esto termino de lo que quería compartir con ustedes, y con eso les doy la sinceras gracias, y si les he enojado, agraviado, o escandalizado—perdónenme, Hermanos porque no le hice intencionalmente." (Well, Hermanos, with this I come to the conclusion of what I wanted to share with you. Thank you from the bottom of my heart, and may you forgive me if I angered, hurt or shocked you unintentionally.)

The Morada with three crosses sits at the edge of a mesa top. The sun is breaking on the horizon. Indio Gerónimo and other Hermanos are on their knees praying. Still others stand and pray. They all sing El Alba (the Dawn), an alabado that celebrates the renewal of life. The sun breaks over the horizon liberating all to a new day.

Libertado dice, "Qué bonito ese alabado, Hermano." (How pretty that alabado is, Brother.)

Responde José María, "sí, es lo que significa una limpieza. Durante tiempos de confusión, después de las experiencias horrorosas que hemos tenido en la lucha por nuestras Mercedes: el resumo de nuestro liderazgo, la toma de la casa de cortes, la persignación ansiosa, el escogernos por querer tener una asamblea parar defender nuestros derechos contusiónales, y todo lo demás que nos pasa en la vida incluyendo nuestras tragedias personales y las de nuestros queridos, la meditación rejuvenece nuestras almas y nuestros espíritus. Eso es él trabajó que se hace en la Morada, la limpieza de toda esa contaminación de la vida. Nuestros ritos curan las heridas de la vida y nos nutren para seguir luchando por la supervivencia." (Yes, this what a cleansing is. It is what we do here during times of confusion. Meditation rejuvenates our soul, our spirit, after the harrowing experiences we have had in the struggle for the landgrants—the rounding up of our leadership, the storming of the courthouse, the zealous pursuit all because we defended our constitutional right to free assembly. And these practices also help us with everything else that happens in our lives, personal tragedies and prayer for our love ones. That is the work that is done in the Morada, a cleansing of life from the contamination. That is what our rituals mean, to heal from the scars that we get in life. It is these practices that give us the nutrients, that give us the strength to go on with the fight for our survival.)

Indio Gerónimo and the other Hermanos contemplate what has been discussed.

## ZARA GOES TO WASHINGTON, D.C.

It is 1968. At the Alianza office in Albuquerque, the Albuquerque contingent earnestly works on Zara's itinerary for his speaking tour. He gets a call from Atlanta, Georgia.

Valentina Valdez answers, "Hello!"

"Yes, this is Rev. Abernathy, and I would like to talk to Mr. Zarfarano."

"Okay, just a minute, Zara, el teléfono," Valentina passes the phone to Zara.

Zara speaks, "Hello, this is Zara."

"Hello, Mr. Zara, this is Rev. Abernathy. I am calling you on behalf of the Southern Christian Leadership Conference, and I would like to invite you to come to Atlanta and meet with Dr. Martin Luther King and me. We are planning a Poor People's March to Washington and would like to invite you to participate."

"Yes, of course. When do you want me down there?"

"Well, we are thinking next month, let's say September eighth. The Southern Christian Leadership Conference will arrange for you to pick up an airline ticket at the airport. We will keep you updated and mail you an itinerary and schedule with the exact dates. We will be in touch. It is a pleasure, and we look forward to you joining us and the struggle of poor people. Together, we will change the world."

## SPEAKING ENGAGEMENT

It is April 4, 1968, and Zara is standing on a platform in the center of the Los Angeles stadium. People are cheering.

"¡Viva, viva, viva Zara!"

Zara emanates an electric energy caused by the ecstasy of the moment. He lunges into an explanation of La Raza Cósmica.

"What does the word 'Raza' mean? The original meaning of the word 'race' referred to breeds of animals. When the Spanish came to the New World, they referred to the indigenous people as 'esa raza', those animals. Yes, people, the Española's saw us as animals. But we took the term and made it ours. It is a term that empowered us, that made us strong and brought us together, uniting us as a new race of people. In time we mixed and became one. For those of us who are not white and who suffered much this way of thinking has changed, or should I say it is changing in some places and with some people, not so much in others. Attitudes of being better than people of color linger in many aspects of our culture, but so long as we understand this, we can make the world a better place. La Cultura Hispánica has given us much. It has given us a common language and a great literature tradition. It was the language that unified the Pueblos to challenge Spanish dominion over New Mexico. It has left us with Christianity, and we have made it our own without the interference of the Catholic Church. The Franciscanos taught us church doctrine with the alabado, poetics as a method of teaching us of the passion and its meaning. Initially Christianity was used to make us obedient to our ruler, but because we were so remote priests were unable to have a presence in many of our communities. And when the Spanish began to lose power over their colonies because they were overextended this left us Nuevomexicanos to fend for ourselves.

And this is what gave birth to this new race of people, La Raza Cósmica. Today, after many years of mixing, we are a people rich in culture. The Indo-Hispanohablante has contributed much to the settlement of this land. Yet, we have been treated as second-class citizens by americano de los estados unidos even though we are on our land by birthright. We are not a simple people, but a complicated people, Indo-Hispanohablante, a people given official citizenship by the colonial government on October 15, 1514. On that day indigenous peoples were officially recognized as human beings. This was the first human rights law of las Américas. Las Leyes de las Indias sanctioned mixed marriage. This act gave the people the right to own land under Spanish dominion and the right to equal citizenship. From that day forward, Indios y Mestizos could own businesses and hold political office, all the rights Criollos (European people born in the New World) y Españoles enjoyed, but it hasn't been that way in practice. We have been treated no better than dogs. In spite of having equality, even from the time when the conquistador roamed this land in search of the riches of Cíbola and the like, they pillaged in Mexico and in Peru. Los Españoles mistreated Nativos. This myth the gringo tells us of the grand Spanish conquest is a lie, puras mentiras, but the americano has even treated us worse, and they took the land that is ours by God-given right. We are of here; we are not foreigners but are treated as foreigners in our Native land. Gavachos are the foreigners, and they are the invaders."

"And since the gringo has taken possession of our homeland we have been denied the right to go into stores, restaurants, to get good jobs. The gringo tells us to go and fight in Vietnam for the United States and that this is our country too, and to defend the ideals of democracy stated in the constitution—a social contract that promises that we will be treated equally in the eyes of the government. Yet we are being forced off of our land. The legal system is not for us. The courts rule in favor of el capitalismo and do not protect the helpless and poor, people of color, La Raza Cósmica. Estos gringos think that Mercedes means it's free land for them. They come here, put up fences, make papers, and say they have the right to our land. Even though we have been here since the dawn of time, we have been working the land. Our cattle and sheep have grazed on this land for hundreds of years. We have alfalfa and orchards on these lands. It is time that La Raza Cósmica unite as one and claim what is ours."

"We never swam across an ocean. We have always been from here. Yet we are treated, como si fuéramos extranjeros. The gringo has forced themselves on our women, leaving bastard children to be cared for by our communities. Our Indian mothers are honored in our culture which is also mestizo, but even that has been destroyed by the gringo, making us feel dirty and unworthy by not recognizing our culture and the contributions it has made to mankind. Our adopted language that has brought us together has been Spanish, and even though the Spanish have mistreated indigenous people because of Las Leyes de Las Indias, we have been blessed by the union of Indios y Españoles, dos culturas that bridge Europa y las américas. We are a great people, a strong people. Yes, it is true that the Españoles were brutal when it came to treating Indios. But we have a legal precedent after the signing of Las Leyes de Las Indias, the first civil rights law en Las Ameríc as. We have a legal basis to demand equal rights. It is time to take control of our own destiny. It is time for La Raza Cósmica to take their homeland back...."

People go crazy and cheer him on.

"Los Españoles have a rich culture. We cannot deny the contributions they have made to the world. They have a rich literary history, architecture, el vaquero, el primer super héroe. Zorro was the first TV superhero, and we mustn't forget our very own hero, Elfego Baca. Walt Disney made the TV series The Seven Lives of Elfego Baca which illustrates his exploits defending our people. La música Mexicana has infiltrated all genres of music in the Americas. Yes, even the dollar symbol came about during the American Revolution. American bookkeepers came up with that symbol to disguise the financial assistance they were receiving from Spain, and then later the americano took our territories, the Southwest. Even though our story is filled with hardship, we need to embrace all of it. Yes, we have much to be proud of from our Indio e Hispano patrimonio (patrimony), and we have a duty to our community to know our history. Gracias.

He's led off the stage and whisked away in a 1940 black Cadillac.

At the home of Bert Corona, Zara is getting ready for the evening's festivities when they hear on the radio that Dr. Martin Luther King has been assassinated. Zara walks into the kitchen where Bert is sitting at the table drinking coffee. They just look at each other dumbfounded.

"¿Escuchastes eso?"

"Yes, I can't believe it"

Bert Corona and Zara are on a plane headed to Atlanta to attend Martín Luther King's funeral.

### DEFENSE FUND

Lupita is in the kitchen when Zara calls her to his side, "M'ija, ven para acá."

She drops what she is doing and goes to her father, wondering what he has to tell her. "Acabo de hablar con el chavo con que te vas a casar. Llegaron anoche y los voy a introducir formalmente en la comida mañana. Quiero que te arregles bien. Te voy a mandar con tu mamá pa' que te compre un vestido. Bueno, apúrate y prepárate para irte de compras. Eddy las va a llevar." (I have just spoken with the man you're gonna marry. They arrived yesterday, and I will formally introduce you tomorrow at lunch. I want you to look good. I'm gonna send you with your mom to buy a dress. Hurry and get ready to go shopping. Eddy will be driving.)

Zara goes over to Eddy who is his chauffeur and official door keeper of La Alianza.

The women are busy in the kitchen preparing for the fundraising dinner and dance. The men are bringing in tables and chairs, and they are sweeping the dance hall floor. The women bring paper table coverings and decorations to hang from the ceiling.

The young girls are giddy. The elder women are talking about the arranged marriage and the fundraiser while preparing the food. Lupita is finishing up at the beauty salon with her mother; she is nervous and anxious. "Mamá tengo miedo. Nunca he visto a este muchacho ¿qué pasa si no me gusta? Y no sé si quiero estar con un chavo ahora, mamá. No sé, tengo miedo." (Mom, I am afraid. I never met that man. What if I don't like him. I don't even know if I want to be with somebody yet, mom, I don't know. I'm afraid.)

"No, no, m'ija no te preocupes, todo te va a ir bien. Ándale, te miras muy bella. Vámonos, se nos está haciendo tarde." (Don't worry, daughter. Everything will be all right. Look at you, you look beautiful. Let's go, it's getting late.)

Lupita's mother gathers their coats and her purse and they meet Eddy who is outside in the car waiting.

### Fundraiser

Mariachis are playing while people are eating. Zara and his family are sitting together at a head table; Lupita and her husband-to-be are sitting beside one another.

Zara walks over to the stage and takes the microphone to make his announcement. "Atención, atención por favor escuchen." (May I have your attention please) People settle down. "Les quiero anunciar que mi hija Lupita, o sea Guadalupe María, se va a casar con este chavo de la capital de México. Su familia me ayudó mucho en México cuando estaba investigando la historia de cómo perdimos las Mercedes. Allí fue donde oí hablar por primera vez de las Mercedes en los archivos.

Esta familia me recibió. Sebastián Coriz. Vamos a darle un gran aplauso." (I want to announce that my daughter, Lupita, aka Guadalupe María, is going to marry this young man from Mexico City. His family helped me a lot when I was in Mexico to research the history of how the landgrants were lost. I was their guest. Please let's give Sebastián Coriz a big round of applause.)

It's late in the evening of the fundraiser. A local conjunto (a band) is playing Spanish music. All have had dinner, and the women have cleared the table. People are dancing and mingling. Lupita is dancing with her husband-to-be. She is frigid. He is clumsy. He asks her how she feels about getting married, and she responds, "okay... I guess..." They continue to dance...

Although the Aliancistas are talking about the assassination they stay focused on their work raising money for the defense fund of the raiders, announcing lottery tickets numbers and handing out items won by the public.

The next day Zara is in the Alianza office talking with his brothers. Indio and Libertado pull up to the Alianza. They walk in and approach Zara to talk to him about getting assistance for their defense. Porfirio asks, "What did we make at last night's dance?"

"Seven hundred and seventeen dollars."

Porfirio, "Okay, so how much do we have now in total?"

Eddy Chávez, the official treasurer, responds, "We have raised a total of eight thousand eight hundred seventy-six dollars and seventy-seven cents."

Zara extends his hand, "Está bien, dame lo que tienes allí y lo llevo al banco." (That's good. Give me what you have and I will take it to the bank.)

"Espérate, Zara, dice Indio Gerónimo, venimos a hablar contigo para ver si nos pueden ayudar con los costos para nuestra defensa."

(Wait, Zara, says Indio Gerónimo, we came to talk to you to see if we could get some help with the cost of our defense.)

Zara answers them, "Who do you think you are? There's no money for you. Every cent that is being raised is going to have to be used for my defense. I'm the one they are after. You guys are mice, rodents compared to me. You are on your own. The Alianza has to focus on keeping me out of jail. Without me there is no landgrant movement."

Indio Gerónimo asks Zara, "What do you mean? Our grandparents have been fighting for the landgrants long before you ever came. You are not the movement. The people are the movement! Leaders come and go, but the spirit of the movement is kept alive by the people, not by a man that demands to be set on a pedestal and idolatrized."

Both Indio and Libertado leave. Indio says to Libertado: "Ese desgraciado lo va a pagar, de un modo u otro lo va a pagar por el modo en que nos está tratando." (One way or another the rogue will pay for how he is treating us.)

Indio Gerónimo is sitting in front of a desk in the bank. The man he is speaking to is a loan officer.

Indio Gerónimo says, "Here you have the deed to my Mama's house."

The banker replies, "And here is a check for $5,200. I only hope that this will be enough to cover your attorney's fees and keep you out of jail."

He stands up, shakes Indio Gerónimo's hand and says with a grin, "I wish you the best of luck, and keep up with the loan payments. I don't want to have to take your mother's house from you."

Indio looks at the banker, "Muchas gracias." He turns and leaves thinking that he now has a debt he has to pay.

## GHOST RANCH DEAL

Zara sits at la Mesa Cósmica with his most loyal confidants, the Apostles. "Me parece que la iglesia Presbiteriana va a dar El Rancho de los Fantasmas a nuestros Herederos de La Merced de Piedra Lumbre, pero yo digo que tienen que darlo a la Alianza. Tenemos que estar unidos e insistir que nos dejen administrar los negocios de nuestra Merced. (It looks as though the Presbyterian Church wants to give Ghost Ranch back to our heirs. But it should come to the Alianza. We need to stay together and insist that they do not give it back to the Merced de Piedra Lumbre.)

Nobody is present to challenge him. The meeting is over, and the secretary, Valentina, completes the minutes and submits them to the Apostles. They send the letter to the Presbyterian Congress. The women get wind of the official position and warn other board members who are not present and who contest the Alianza's position.

Calixtra asks, "¿Y por qué? Las Mercedes nos pertenecen a nosotros los Herederos de la Merced de la Piedra Lumbre. ¿Porque tenemos que dar control a la Alianza? ¡Nos pertenecen a nosotros!" (Why? The landgrants belong to us, the heirs of La Merced de la Piedra Lumbre. Why do we have to give it to the Alianza? They belong to us!) The contesting side approaches Zara.

Gregorita speaks up, "¿Y por qué tenemos que darle nuestros terrenos? Las Mercedes son de los herederos, no son de la Alianza, son de los que las trabajan, de los que son indígenas, esos cuyos orígenes son de aquí. Tú ni eres de aquí." (And why should we have to give you our land? That land belongs to the descendants of the Merced, not to the Alianza. It's for those who work, those who are indigenous who are from here. You are not even from here.)

Zara replies, "Los estatutos de la Alianza dicen que la Alianza representa todas las Mercedes. Cuando uno se hace miembro, recuerda que la Alianza Federal de Pueblos Libres representa todas Las Mercedes porque con la fuerza unida pudimos forzar al gobierno a que nos devuelvan los ejidos. Estamos más fuertes juntos que separados." (The charter of La Alianza states that it is the representative of all Las Mercedes. When you became members we had agreed that the Alianza Federal de Pueblos Libres would represent all the Mercedes because with the united force we were able to force the government to give us back the Mercedes. We are stronger united than separated.)

José María says, "Eso no me parece bien. Las Mercedes pertenecen a nos otros, ni la Alianza ni ninguna otra persona debe entremeterse en los negocios de cada Merced." (That doesn't seem right to me. The Mercedes should belong to those who work them. Neither the Alianza nor anyone else should interfere in the business of the Mercedes.)

Zara replies, "¡No! La Alianza tiene que controlar los ejidos. Hemos dedicado siete años en este trabajo y yo, por mi parte, no voy a permitir que otras personas aprovechen ventaja de nuestro trabajo." (No! The Alianza has to have control of the land. We have dedicated seven years to this work, and I for my part am not going to allow others to take advantage of our work.)

José María objects, "¡No! Zara, las Mercedes no te pertenecen, son de los Herederos de esa Merced. Acuérdate que tú no eres de aquí, aunque nos has ayudado mucho para comprender cómo fue que nos robaron las tierras, no tienes nada que decir en cómo manejamos nuestras Mercedes. Las Mercedes son de los mercederos, los que establecieron y dieron sus vidas para establecer hogares en estos territorios." (No! Zara, las Mercedes do not belong to you. They belong to the heirs of that Merced. Remember that you are not from here. Even though you have helped us a lot to understand how they stole our lands, you have no right to tell us how to manage our landgrants.

The Mercedes belongs to the heirs, those who established them and gave their lives to establish homes on their lands.)

Zara responds angrily, "¡Lárguense! Retírense de aquí, nunca jamás serán recibidos en la Alianza." (Leave! Get out of here! You will never be welcomed in the Alianza.)

Gregorita Augilar asks, "¿Quién dijo que tú puedes corrernos de aquí?! La Alianza Federal de Pueblos Libres es una alianza entre las Mercedes, y tú no eres dueño de las Mercedes. Pertenecen a nosotros, a ti no, sino a nosotros los Nuevomexicanos que somos los mercederos." (Who said that you can throw us out of here? The Alianza Federal de Pueblos Libres is an alliance between the Mercedes, and you have no ownership over the landgrants. They belong to us, not you. The Nuevomexicanos are the landgrant heirs.)

Zara shouts at Gregorita, "¡Ya lárguense, lárguense de aquí! Tú ni perteneces a esta junta, eres mujer, no estás permitida en esta junta, lárgate de aquí." (Get out, get out of here! You don't even belong in this meeting. You are a woman. You are not allowed to be here in this meeting. Get out of here!)

Gregorita concedes, "Está bien, pero te voy a decir una cosa, me voy a llevar a mi esposo, a mi hermano, a mi familia, y estoy segura de que van a venir bastantes más personas conmigo también, porque sé que no estoy sola en cómo miramos y cómo se han de manejar las Mercedes." (That's fine. But I'll tell you one thing; I'm going to take my husband, my brother, my family, and I am sure that many other people will come with me because I know that I am not alone on how we understand the landgrants to be run.)

She turns and leaves, taking her husband and brother-in-law with her. Others follow. There are three apostles left from la Mesa Cósmica. They are Zara's brothers.

# CHAPTER NINETEEN

## Haciéndose una Vida Juntos

It is the day of Geronimo and Fátima's wedding which is being paid for from the reward money put up by Governor Cargo. In the dance hall the music comes to an end. Trumpets sound, and a drum roll announces the bride and groom's arrival with a marcha. The wedding party is in position, and the marcha begins. It weaves around the dance floor like a snake, forming a bridge with couples holding each other's hands, creating an arch for the rest of the people to dance under. As they come out the other end they form three concentric circles. The bride and groom dance in the center of the three circles. After their dance they move into the dollar dance.

Señora López comments to a friend, "I always knew they were going to be a couple."

"Yes, they are a fine couple."

Two young boys get in a scuffle over who is going to dance with Fátima first.

The first boy tells the other, "Hey, I'm going."

The second boy shoves the other taller, older boy. "Chale ese, I am going next, get behind me."

The first boy responds: "Órale, she doesn't want to dance with you, fly boy. Your head will land on her tits..." The second boy punches the first boy, knocking the air out of him.

José María sees them fighting and tells them: "Hey, hey...settle down! This is no place to be acting like that, esténse quietos." (Stay still and behave yourselves.)

Libertado says to José María, "Hacen buena pareja." (They make a good couple.)

"Sí me siento orgulloso por Indio, su papá siempre lo está cuidando desde el cielo." (Yes, I'm proud of Indio. His father is always watching over him from heaven.)

"Sí, era buen hombre también, lástima que no pudo volver de Corea." (Yes, he was a good man. If only he had made it back from Korea.)

The bride and groom take their seats at the table. Señoras bring plates of food to the wedding party.

Tranquilina says: "Me siento tan contenta de que sean pareja. Van a tener una buena vida con mucha familia." (I am so happy that they are a couple. I know that they are going to have a good life with many children.)

The Señoras coordinate the youth to help serve the wedding party and guests. None of Zara's family is present. Former Aliancistas recognize it but little talk is made of it. The women, however, are speaking amongst themselves. Indio Gerónimo has purposely not invited any of Zara's family as he is fuming, feeling betrayed by his leader. He still feels like retaliating for what Zara is doing to Lupita and over how he and other Aliancistas have been treated. He is doing everything he can to keep his anger in check.

The conjunto plays. People visit, laughing, and getting reacquainted with each other. The meal progresses into the dance.

After the second set the band takes a break. Calixtra spreads out an Indian blanket, two pillows, an Indian wedding vase, corn pollen, two candles, thirteen monedas (coins), and a lasso made of local flowers loosely woven, held together by a cross. José María stands up and claps to get people's attention. Standing at the center of the dance floor, José María clears his throat. Calixtra escorts the couple to the center of the dance floor as the bride and groom kneel on the pillows. José María begins to sing the entrega.

**La Entrega de los Novios**

| | |
|---|---|
| *En este día aventuroso*<br>*Les pido su atención*<br>*Para entregar a estos novios*<br>*En Buena disposición* | On this adventurous day<br>I ask for your attention<br>To present this couple<br>In good disposition |
| *Quisiera que mi Diós*<br>*Me diera en esta ocación*<br>*La pluma de San Agustín*<br>*Y el cincho de Salomón* | I would like my divine God<br>To give me this occasion<br>The feather of San Agustín<br>And the belt of Salomon |
| *Estando el mundo formado*<br>*Faltable un ser humano*<br>*Con el nombre Adán*<br>*Una imagen verdadera* | With the world being formed<br>One being was missing<br>With the name of Adam<br>A real image |
| *Adán con sabiduría*<br>*Y Diós con su poder*<br>*Le sacó una Costilla*<br>*Y de allí formó a su mujer* | Adam with knowledge<br>And God with his strength<br>He took a rib<br>And from there formed his wife |

*Se conocieron*
*Desde su niñez*
*Gerónimo, travieso*
*Fátima cariñosa*

*Se conocieron toda la vida*
*Y ahora son una pareja*
*Como un rosal blanco*
*Y una espina alva*

*Crece uno, crece otro*
*Los dos crecen juntos*
*Haciéndose una vida juntos*
*Y pariendo hijos*

Have known each other
Since childhood
Gerónimo mischievous
Fátima affectionate

They grew up together
And now they are a couple
Like a white rose
And a cactus

One grows, the other grows
The two grow together
Making a life together
And raising children

And la entrega goes on creating a vision for their lives. A montage of Indio Gerónimo and Fátima's lives are unveiled as la entrega tells their story. Calixtra puts the lasso around them symbolizing that they are one and lights the trementina (piñón sap) incense, smudging them with the smoke, using an eagle feather over their bodies.

Then she hands them the wedding vase filled with homemade vino de capulin (choke cherry wine). They both drink. She sprinkles them with corn pollen, the symbol of fertility, and gives Fátima the monedas, symbolizing that their union will always bear riches and everlasting growth.

They stand up to the sound of everyone clapping. The floor is cleared, and Indio and Fátima have their first dance as a couple. The padrinos form a line to dance with los novios. The dance goes until the wee hours of the morning. Fátima y Indio give hugs and kisses to loved ones and leave the salon. José María turns to the band, signaling them to begin another set of music.

## La Borreguera 1969

José María and Indio Gerónimo are on horseback in the mountains. A sheepdog is working to keep the flock from wandering. José María suddenly grabs his chest and falls off the horse. Indio Gerónimo sees his tío some distance away and rides his horse quickly to his tío yelling. "Tíioo!!! Tíoo!!..."

The horse is in a full gallop, but Indio Gerónimo pulls at the reins. The horse comes to an abrupt stop and he jumps off.

Indio Gerónimo: "Tío...Noo. ¡No no!... ¿por qué? ¡No te mueras! You can't leave me. Noo me dejes...No tío, don't leave me—ee!"

Indio Gerónimo holds his uncle in his lap crying, "¡No tío, nooo!"

## Sometime later

Indio and Libertado are in the Morada blessing the body with sage and corn pollen and praying. Hermanos are warming up, singing an Alabado, making sure they have la tonada. They wrap José María in a Pendleton blanket and stitch up the blanket, setting his body on a ladder made of latillas. Indio is in a trance. He hears and sees people, but it seems that he is standing still while everyone else is running about preparing for the velorio and to lay their Hermano pa que descanse en paz—to rest.

Months later, Indio Gerónimo and Fátima are in a 1955 Ford pickup. She is snuggled up against him and they are laughing, but it's a bittersweet laugh. They are talking about the beginning of a new life as they travel on the highway into Albuquerque.

Indio Gerónimo: "Let's see ... we get off at Lomas to get to Central and then to Wilfredo's house in Barelas. As soon as I get a job we'll get our own place."

Fátima replies, "Oh yes, we'll use the money from the wedding to rent us a place and I'll look for work, too."

Traffic is stopped on the freeway. They eventually get off and make their way to Central Avenue.

"Look, there's a parade," says Fátima.

The Black Berets walk along the side and in front. Young beret women and men are holding a banner that says, "No Vietnamese ever called me a Dirty Mexican." Indio pulls up behind the parade at the corner of Edith and Central but doesn't realize it until someone yells out at him: "Nice truck, vato! ¿Quiénes son? Los 'Beverly Hillbilly's?" His truck is loaded down with furniture and bedding. Someone else yells out: "Yeah, you should have decorated it." People laugh.

Fátima: "I don't think this is a parade. We are the parade." They see people lined up along the road blocking the side streets.

Indio Gerónimo says, "Yeah, I think you're right, I think it's a protest.

"Be nice. Wave like we're supposed to be here, and let's see where we end up," says Fátima, excited to begin a new life.

Waving, they end up near City Hall. The berets get up and lay out their demands that the police form a civilian investigation committee to stop police harassment and brutality. Indio parks a few blocks away and join the protest....

Y así me lo dijeron a mí.

# AGRADECIMIENTOS

There are few words that can express the deep gratitude I have for all those people who have journeyed with me on this project. I humbly apologize if I failed to mention anyone. Know that you are with me in espíritu. I recognize that I did not do this alone. I wish to thank Jenifer Hughes and Kathryn Galán for their laborious hours with me since I began this project and for the endless drafts they have painstakingly worked through. They have all been my angels in my time of need and have supported me through many personal hardship. Thanks also goes to Gabriel Melendez, who has been an Hermano and has stayed by my side, supporting me emotionally through the most difficult times in my life. His patience and *caridad* in looking after me and the endless hours he spent with me while I healed my wounded soul and looking at drafts of this manuscript are appreciated more than I can say. To Anselmo Arellano and Penny Pence, who also read and edited drafts of what resulted in my dissertation and helped me navigate the difficult road of acquiring my Ph.D., thank you. I am indebted to my mentor and a man I deeply respect, Dr. Ricardo Griego, beginning with the early days of my education, mentoring me when I arrived at the University of New Mexico. Thanks also go to Hiram Espinoza, Fitzgerald Lucero, and Nathalie Bleser, who focused on the Spanish text of the manuscript, and for the the time Ignacio Quiñones took to read over the manuscript. To Judy Kushner Bishow who has worked tirelessly editing and unwearyingly challenging me to refining my thoughts. The time she has spent with me, and her belief in me is immeasurable. I am forever beholden to her and all that have supported me throughout this jounery. Thank You.

To those generational ancestors and landgrant activists who persistently have come to object to the dispossession of their land base and the injustices they have endured, to those social progressives whose unyieldingly persistence in confronting the sociopolitical injustices in the world both in the past and currently, and to all those activists who have devoted their lives to addressing the social ills both locally and abroad that have put their lives on the line for the greater good of humanity—Gracias.

# ABOUT THE AUTHOR

FEDERICO READE, Ph.D., is an independent scholar and filmmaker. He has produced and directed a number of documentaries on New Mexico and other topics related to Chicano Studies, including the award-winning, *Una Lucha por mi Pueblo* and *Recuerdos de César Chávez.*

Given his particular background in the humanities, Federico Reade has developed an interdisciplinary approach to writing, leading him to develop a unique genre. Rather than a traditional literary novel approach, he has chosen to integrate a hybrid style using elements of screenwriting with short scenes that move graphically, a pattern common to the literary tradition of the corrido in which brief vignettes build climatic tension and give movement to the story while using expository embellishments to explain the complex colonial history that makes Nuevomexicanos who they are today.

He extends deep gratitude to Rodolfo Anaya. He has had an indelible impact on him. Dr. Reade had never read a book from cover to cover until his junior year in high school. He was unfulfilled with the way his community was depicted, it made him feel ashamed. It wasn't until he read Rudy's book, *Bless Me Ultima* and later the *Heart of Aztlan,* that he was taken on a literary journey that reflected his community. Justicia, was born in a writing seminar taught by Rodolfo Anaya. His inspiration and mentorship, along with that of his wife Patricia, were ever-present in support of my work. Rudy was reading Justicia weeks before he made his transition. Reade could only imagine what Rodolfo felt as he read *Justicia* and the opening scene—le ofrezco un sudario ha el y su esposa.

Dr. Reade is a fifth-generation Reade born in Deming, NM, and raised in Albuquerque. His ancestor and namesake came with the First California Column in 1860. His great-grandfather married a woman from Janos, Chihuahua, México. His grandfather was born in Albuquerque, grew up in Deming, and met the author's grandmother while at Camp Luna in Las Vegas, Nuevo México. She was born in San Gerónimo, Nuevo México, just south east of Las Vegas, and her father was among those who were indicted for being a Gorras Blanca. Her grandmother was a Navajo captive. Federico Reade's dad was born in Las Vegas, NM and raised in Deming, NM —de modo que el autor puede decir: "es puro Nuevomexicano."

# GLOSSARY OF SPECIFIC TERMS

**Acequia:** Irrigation ditch diversion from a main water source to areas where needed

**Alabado:** The alabado is a poetic scripture that is sung in a melodic tone and has monophonic features. It is sung acapella, and is a sacred prayer. It was brought to New Mexico during the colonial period. The alabado has become a principal factor in the influence of New Mexico spirituality and worldview and has been a major factor in community formation among early settlers migrating north from Mexico. It has greatly influenced the indigenous peoples of the Pueblo region as well as the mestizo farmers who populated New Spain's most northern remote frontier of the "New World."

**Aliancista:** Member of the Alliance

**Alianza:** In this context, the Alianza Federal de Pueblos Libres (Federal Alliance of Free Peoples) is an association of Hispanic heirs of the landgrants who got together to get their lands back.

**Apóstoles:** The Alianza Federal de Pueblos Libres leader referred to his confidants and official board members as Apostles.

**Carmelitas:** These ladies were commonplace in Northern New Mexico. They were a significant feature during velorios (wakes) when women would accompany the Hermanos and pray and wail during the wake.

**Cofradía:** This is the archaic term for fraternity. In the context of the story, it refers to the 14th century religious society of The Brotherhood of Jesus the Nazarene.

**Corridista:** Balladeer the composer and performer of ballads.

**Corrido:** A Ballad whose specific style and form are characterized by a formal introduction and farewell. Stanzas are octosyllable quatrains like the alabado texts in rhyme, schemes, and meter.

**Despedida:** Refers to the farewell or formal closing of the corrido.

**Ejido:** Land held in common specific to those heirs of the community landgrant.

**Herederos:** heirs to the community landgrant.

**Hermandad:** or Cofradía; The fraternity of Nuestro Señor Jesús Nazareno (Our Lord Jesus the Nazarene)

**Hermanos:** Members of the Cofradía de Nuestro Señor Jesús Nazareno

**Hijuelas:** land titles

**Madero:** The large wooden cross that is carried during a Penitente ceremony

**Memoria:** A memorial or homage to an individual

**Merced/Mercedes** A Community Landgrant

**Morada:** Last resting place. In the context of the Hermandad it refers to the gathering home of the Cofradía or brotherhood.

**Oratorio:** The room where the altar is kept.

**Sebastiana:** The patron Saint of death, the Northern New Mexican equivalent of the Mexican Catrina.

**Tinieblas:** Literally "deep darkness." Refers to a ceremony performed during the last day of Lent. It begins at dusk and symbolizes the moment Jesus died on the cross which causes the earth to tremble.

Made in the USA
Columbia, SC
06 January 2025